IRRESOLUTE CLAY

At a time of profound change and rethinking, this book provides insights into how environmental law in the UK has developed into its current form, and considers challenges it will face in the future. Irresolute Clay is not a legal history or textbook, nor a conventional set of legal memoirs. Instead it offers a personal account of the inside stories as experienced by one of the key architects of contemporary environmental law. Taking a thematic approach, it charts fundamental tenets of the subject (such as environmental sanctions, the European dimension, developing the academic discipline of environmental law, and environmental courts and tribunals), from the beginnings of the modern environmental law era in the 1970s to the present day.

Irresolute Clay

Shaping the Foundations
of Modern Environmental Law

Richard Macrory

·HART·
OXFORD · LONDON · NEW YORK · NEW DELHI · SYDNEY

HART PUBLISHING

Bloomsbury Publishing Plc

Kemp House, Chawley Park, Cumnor Hill, Oxford, OX2 9PH, UK

1385 Broadway, New York, NY 10018, USA

HART PUBLISHING, the Hart/Stag logo, BLOOMSBURY and the Diana logo are
trademarks of Bloomsbury Publishing Plc

First published in Great Britain 2020

A catalogue record for this book is available from the British Library.

Library of Congress Cataloging-in-Publication data

Names: Macrory, Richard, author.

Title: Irresolute clay : shaping the foundations of modern environmental law / Richard Macrory.

Description: Oxford ; New York : Hart, 2020. | Includes bibliographical references and index.

Identifiers: LCCN 2019053728 (print) | LCCN 2019053729 (ebook) |
ISBN 9781509928118 (hardcover) | ISBN 9781509928125 (Epub)

Subjects: LCSH: Environmental law—Great Britain—History. | Macrory, Richard. |
Environmental lawyers—Great Britain—Biography.

Classification: LCC KD3372 .M23 2020 (print) | LCC KD3372 (ebook) | DDC 344.4104/6—dc23

LC record available at https://lccn.loc.gov/2019053728

LC ebook record available at https://lccn.loc.gov/2019053729

ISBN: HB: 978-1-50992-811-8
       ePDF: 978-1-50992-813-2
       ePub: 978-1-50992-812-5

Typeset by Compuscript Ltd, Shannon

To find out more about our authors and books visit www.hartpublishing.co.uk.
Here you will find extracts, author information, details of forthcoming events
and the option to sign up for our newsletters.

To Tom and Ludwig

Long-standing environmental mentors and friends

> That hesitant figure, eddying away
> Like a winged seed loosened from its parent stem,
> Has something I never quite grasp to convey
> About nature's give-and-take – the small, the scorching
> Ordeals which fire one's irresolute clay.

C Day Lewis *Walking Away*

PREFACE

On 12 July 1990, Robert Carnwath, then a planning QC and now a member of the Supreme Court, gave a major lecture in London and concluded with the words that from now on, 'I for one will be proud to carry the banner of environmental lawyer'. This country, of course, has had a long history of laws concerning environmental issues, even if not termed as such but, in a little over a generation, the concepts of environmental law and environmental lawyers have become firmly entrenched in our legal system.

Profound shifts began to take place from the early 1970s – new ways of examining environmental challenges, a less insular approach, with a greater awareness of international dimensions and the development of environmental law and policy at EU level, together with the emergence of principles and rights such as public participation and access to environmental information. I had the great fortune to begin my legal career at the start of this process and have seen at first hand the enormous changes that have taken place over the years in this country – including the creation of new institutions such as the Environment Agency and a specialised environmental tribunal, the development of environmental law as a serious academic discipline in its own right and radical re-thinking on how we should best deal with breaches of environmental law.

This book is not intended to be an academic critique of environmental law nor a definitive book on legal and policy history. It is very much from the perspective of my own experiences; others will, no doubt, have different and maybe more profound views as to the causes of change. Although I start at the beginning of my work as a young environmental lawyer working for Friends of the Earth, I have deliberately avoided the structure and chronology of a more conventional set of memoirs, but instead explore a number of distinct themes of importance, many of which in reality – for me at any rate – crossed over in time.

Environmental law and policy are rarely static – the clay is never resolute – and in the past few years the implications of Brexit have demanded a re-evaluation of many aspects of our existing structures of environmental law and how they should best be developed for the future. At the time of writing, the Brexit story is by no means over but, whatever the eventual outcome, the next generation of environmental lawyers and policymakers will need to think creatively about the most effective role of law in meeting our existing environmental challenges and those yet to come. I hope that by providing my personal insights of how we have reached the present position this book will provide some pointers for the future.

Richard Macrory
December 2019

CONTENTS

1

Early Legal Environmental Activism

A bedroom in a Californian hotel. It's 1974 and Raquel Welch and film director James Ivory are having a blazing row on the set of *The Wild Party*. James complains that she is not putting real passion into a love scene with co-star Perry King, but Raquel reposts that she has been distracted by the bed which is squeaking too much. All eyes now turn to me. I am standing there with a toolbox and it is my job to sort out the problem. Only a few months before I had been at a formal ceremony in London wearing a gown and white bow tie with the Treasurer of Grays Inn declaring: 'I hereby call you to the Bar and publish you barrister.' As I gently oiled the springs and tested the bed while cast and crew waited expectantly for me to finish the repair work, I was asking myself what on earth I was doing there.

After qualifying as a barrister immediately on leaving university, I was not then convinced that a full-time career at the bar was yet for me. In any event, London in the early 1970s offered too many exciting possibilities for a 23-year-old. I had long been interested in film production and had the opportunity to work on several Merchant Ivory films. The American director James Ivory and the Indian producer Ismail Merchant had set up Merchant Ivory Productions in the 1960s and it was later to become one of the most long-lasting and successful independent film companies. These were still early days in the life of the company and I initially worked in a lowly capacity as a production assistant on *Autobiography of a Princess* filmed in London and starring James Mason and Madhur Jaffrey. On their next production, *The Wild Party*, I moved up the ladder a little and was assistant art director.[1] It was an eight-week shoot and I had never worked so hard or so intensely, returning to London physically exhausted but full of rich stories about the extraordinary world of film-making. Independent film production in the UK at the time was full of uncertainties and frustration and did not offer any real security. Law was still in my blood, so I kept my hand in, becoming a freelance legal columnist for an insurance magazine and the occasional law teacher, including a rather surreal period at the Lucy Clayton School of Fashion where I introduced bemused young women to the basics of divorce and planning law.

---

[1] I later became chairman of Merchant Ivory between 1988 and 2004, an unpaid position but one that allowed me to appear as an extra in several of their subsequent films.

The 1970s saw the emergence of many new single-issue pressure groups in the UK, a more focused development from the 1960s revolution and involving activists who wanted to engage in new approaches to policy change but from outside mainstream political parties. Friends of the Earth (FOE) had set up an office in the United Kingdom in 1971, two years after it had been founded in San Francisco and, at the time, was the only environmental organisation in the UK to employ an in-house staff lawyer. This was probably due to the group's US origins where law and the use of the courts was an inherent part of environmental campaigning. In contrast, British conservation bodies had tended to focus much more on policy and political engagement. In my last year at university I had already been impressed and attracted by FOE's new style of environmental campaigning, based on hard research that was combined with original and witty demonstrations. It was focused on core issues about the way we used resources rather than nature conservation and the protection of rural areas which had tended to dominate the concerns of many existing environmental organisations in this country. There was a small London office, as well as a growing number of semi-autonomous local groups. Dominic Sandbrook's social history of the early 1970s in Britain perfectly captures the impact of FOE as a new style of environmental group: 'Friends of the Earth succeeded because it was daring, irreverent, clever and often funny; crucially it was also highly decentralized, allowing local activists to set their own tone. It was a new kind of organization – assertive and dynamic rather than nostalgically conservationist, aiming not just to preserve what was left of nature, but to roll back the tide of industry and pollution.'[2] FOE had established itself as a limited company by guarantee which gave it the freedom to engage in political campaigning without the restraint of charity rules and almost as soon as it began operations in London, the opportunity arose for one of the most iconic environmental campaigns of that decade. Schweppes had announced it would no longer sell drinks in returnable bottles but was moving to disposable, non-returnable containers. FOE condemned the action as environmentally regressive and, in 1971, secured enormous publicity by organising the return of thousands of non-returnable Schweppes bottles to the doorsteps of their headquarters in London. I had spent much of my childhood in the 1950s collecting old bottles and doubling my pocket money by reclaiming the deposits and I found what FOE was doing inspiring and timely. My old university colleagues later told me that I was the only one in my particular group of friends reading serious books about the environment which were then being published. Max Nicholson's *The Environmental Revolution – A Guide to the New Masters of the Earth*, published in my second year as a law student, had struck many chords.[3] Nicholson was a distinguished British ornithologist, who had been director

---

[2] Dominic Sandbrook *State of Emergency: The Way We Were: Britain 1970–1974*, p 213 (London, Penguin Books, 1990).
[3] Max Nicholson *The Environmental Revolution – A Guide for the New Masters of the Earth* (London, Hodder and Stoughton, 1970).

general of the Nature Conservancy, set up by the government in 1949; he had been involved in many international governmental initiatives. The book traced the history of the conservation movements from the early twentieth century and was a lengthy, sober analysis of the environmental challenges facing both this country and the world. But despite their successes, Nicholson argued that the urgency of environmental pressures meant that we were on the threshold of a radical shift in thinking about the environment: 'It will no longer be sufficient to preach mainly to the converted and the readily convertible, since it is not they who are in the main responsible for the current widespread misuse and mismanagement of land and of natural resources, nor for the persistence of stubborn prejudices and inhibitions against adopting a more objective and scientifically defensible view of nature and man's place in it.' The book contained a great deal of practical advice on changing the underling politics and had a rational and optimist tone which I found compelling.

I was still wondering whether I should now commit myself to the life of a practising barrister when there was a chance meeting which, in retrospect, was the critical turning point in my subsequent career. In 1975, at a party in south London, I happened to meet a woman whom I had known at university. She was now working as a researcher for FOE on packaging issues and I said that I always meant to use my legal skills to assist them. She told me they already had a full-time staff lawyer and there the matter seemed to end. But the next day she rang to say their lawyer had suddenly decided to leave, she had mentioned my name to the director and he said I should come in as soon as possible. FOE was then located in 9 Poland Street in the heart of Soho. It was a building owned by the Rowntree Trust who had imaginatively decided to help kick start new pressure groups, not with financial grants, but by providing rent-free offices with common facilities such as meeting rooms and photocopiers. I had never visited a pressure group before and rather nervously climbed three floors passing the offices of groups such as Gingerbread (a charity for single parents) and Social Audit (conducting research on freedom of information) until I reached FOE. It then had about ten full-time staff, occupying two crowded rooms crammed with papers, people constantly on the telephone and the haze of cigarette smoke (this being the 1970s). It felt like the offices of a busy newspaper and, in a small back office, sat its new director, Tom Burke. Tom had studied philosophy and physics at Liverpool University – he would later say that philosophy taught him how to think and physics how to count – and had been involved in the local FOE group in Liverpool before moving to London. I explained my background and Tom told me to go and talk to the campaigners to explain what I had to offer. The next day they had a staff meeting and decided to invite me to join as the staff lawyer, an offer I readily accepted. The next three years proved to one of immense excitement and experimentation – and making long-lasting friendships with a group of highly intelligent and motivated individuals. The way that FOE analysed some of the major environmental challenges of the day such as transport, energy and agriculture was often well ahead of its time and the fundamentals continue to resonate today.

FOE at that time avoided taking judicial reviews in the courts – the judiciary were then less sympathetic to environmental claims and the prohibitive costs and inherent risk of litigation to a small organisation was simply not worth the gains that might be made. However, the legal perspective and expertise that FOE could bring to its campaigning gave it a distinct edge. Environmental law itself was beginning to change in this country and the Control of Pollution Act 1974 had recently been passed, the first piece of environmental legislation trying to address all the key areas of pollution (waste, water, noise and air), though not yet in a fully integrated way. The Act built upon laws which had existed for many years, but for the first time incorporated principles of public access to environmental information and public participation which had been largely lacking in previous laws and almost 20 years before the United Nations 1998 Aarhus Convention on the subject.[4] We decided it would be helpful to publish a citizen's guide to the new law and the opportunities it could provide for members of the public and local environmental groups. *Polluters Pay – The Control of Pollution Act Explained* was written by myself and Bogus Zaba, a scientist involved in one of the local FOE groups in Wales. It was a challenge producing a succinct book which was legally authoritative but accessible to non-lawyers and I took some delight in turning the intricacies of complex statutory text into readable flow diagrams. It was also the first time that I had come across the peculiarity of UK legislation under which an Act could be passed into law, but the Secretary of State was then allowed to bring its provisions into force by commencement orders at dates of his or her choosing. Without the internet, it was not easy to keep track of these orders which appeared in dribs and drabs several years after the Act was passed, sometimes just applying to the odd section or subsection and I had to spend many hours visiting Her Majesty's Stationery Office in Holborn to obtain the latest information. The need for a delay between the period when an Act is passed and actually comes into effect is understandable as institutional arrangements have often to be adjusted. However, the amount of discretion given to government in the power to make commencement orders makes for complexity and is open to abuse. In countries such as the United States, legislation normally comes into force on a set date and if government wishes to delay it must come back to Congress to justify itself. Most members of the public are unaware of these processes and they are even more obscure to anyone outside the UK. European Union legislation often requires Member States to send to the European Commission the texts of national legislation implementing the law in question. Certainly in the environmental field, there were times when the UK government informed the Commission of national laws but deliberately failed to explain that, although they had received Royal Assent, they had no legal effect since commencement orders had not yet been issued. It took several years before the Commission cottoned on to the deception.

---

[4] Convention on Access to Information, Participation in Decision-Making and Access to Justice in Environmental Matters, 25 June 1998.

FOE local groups appreciated *Polluters Pay* and it even received positive reviews in the trade press which helped to boost FOE's reputation as a serious organisation rather than a group of bohemian eccentrics:

'The book is sound and appears to be faultless' (*Waste*).

'In using the law as a weapon against pollution, its authors aim to increase the confidence and effectiveness of anyone who is concerned with environmental issues, while avoiding the emotional arguments which have been the downfall of many environmental groups in the UK' (*Materials Reclamation Weekly*).

Air pollution is now one of the dominant environmental issues in this country. Re-reading *Polluter Pays* today, it is striking that while the new legislation was fairly comprehensive on waste, water and noise, the provisions on air pollution were almost negligible. One of the reasons was that, at the time, there was a degree of complacency in government on the issue. Smog and smoke, largely from domestic sources, had been a major problem in the UK since the nineteenth century and the Clean Air legislation of the 1950s and 1960s had been a significant factor in bringing apparently unpolluted air to London and other urban areas. Many of the senior civil servants I met at the time had vivid memories of urban smog episodes in their youth and often referred to their success in dealing with the problem. Less visible forms of pollutants such as NOx from road traffic were simply not high on the agenda but, in retrospect, if the Control of Pollution Act had dealt with the issue far more comprehensively, some of the contemporary problems of air pollution facing this country might have been avoided.

Polluters Pay was focused on pollution control law but, at the time, FOE deliberately did not run mainstream campaigns on pollution as such. Instead, it was concerned with core issues which ultimately gave rise to environmental pollution and degradation – with campaigns on Energy, Transport, Resource Use, Agriculture and Wildlife Protection. The most visible feature of the Wildlife campaign, which attracted wide public support from all ages, was 'Save the Whale'. FOE challenged the prevailing science used by the International Whaling Commission (IWC) in the way it set quotas for killing different species of whales. Demonstrations were organised when the IWC held meetings in London and one of the campaigners told me one morning they were planning to demonstrate outside the Japanese embassy dressed as Japanese warriors who were committing hari-kari with a mass of fake blood. I advised that the police would probably not find this acceptable. The Wildlife campaign had also been particularly influential in the development of the Endangered Species Act 1976, which introduced new licensing controls for the import of endangered species and products made from them. My predecessor at FOE, David Pedley, was a solicitor particularly skilled in the technical drafting of statutory provisions; FOE had helped to secure many effective and detailed amendments to the legislation as it went through parliament. But it also provided a striking example of how a law, when passed, is not necessarily effective unless adequate enforcement mechanisms are in place. A year or so after the law came into force, FOE's wildlife campaigner saw a fashion shop in

Soho selling a new coat made from fur from an endangered species and pretended she was interested in buying it. She knew no import licences had been issued by government and, feigning innocence, asked the shop owner how they were selling the item as she thought there were new laws in place prohibiting this. The owner hinted that it was an illegal import. She then immediately rang Customs and Excise who said they had no jurisdiction beyond the ports and that illegal selling in shops was a matter for the police. When she reported the matter, the local police replied they had no knowledge of the new legislation saying, rather patronisingly, that they were more interested in live criminals than dead animals. She consulted me and we decided to mount a private prosecution, the first of its kind under the Endangered Species Act. It is a peculiarity of English law that generally, unless there are particular statutory restrictions, anyone may initiate a private prosecution for a criminal offence – no legal interest in the matter is needed and the costs involved are negligible. I was a little apprehensive that the magistrate might consider our campaigner's initial discussion with the shop was some form of illegal entrapment. Far from it. The shop owner pleaded guilty and was fined, the magistrate praised FOE for its initiative and publicly condemned the police for not bringing the prosecution. The case received considerable publicity in the trade press where many in the industry were still unaware of the new controls. A few days later, the Metropolitan Police rang our campaigner and asked whether she would help to produce a guide on the legislation for their officers. It was a good example of engaging in litigation which had positive results all round.

As part of its concern with transport issues, FOE ran a dedicated cycle campaign designed to encourage more people to use bicycles as a means of transport. Compared to the 1950s, cycle use was in decline in this country due to increased traffic on the roads, and the proper provision of attractive and safe road space for bicycles was still in its infancy – well behind countries such as the Netherlands and Germany. The cycle campaigner, Mike Hudson, brought together leading lights in the design of cycle routes and other facilities to promote best practice. We campaigned for the building of separate cycleways but found to our surprise that the main opposition came, not from groups such as taxi drivers or road hauliers, but from the Cyclists Touring Club (CTC), founded in 1883 and the oldest cycling association in the United Kingdom. In the 1930s the then Ministry of Transport had experimented with the provision of separate cycle paths, but the CTC had mounted strong opposition as they refused to be seen as second-class road users. This long-standing aversion was still in their blood when FOE launched its campaign and we struggled in vain to persuade them that while the insistence on sharing road space with cars was understandable when there were far fewer road vehicles, it was no longer appropriate for today's traffic levels.[5] I worked closely with Mike Hudson because it turned out that the law concerning cycles and

---

[5] Their approach did not change for some 20 years until, in 1996, the Cyclists Touring Club published joint guidance with the Institute of Highways and Transportation for the design and planning of cycle-friendly infrastructures.

the provision of cycleways was often complex, obscure and ill-suited to modern requirements. It became an engrossing area of research and my first legal article, published in the *New Law Journal* in 1979, reviewed some of the conundrums. I found there were few other lawyers fully engaged in the subject apart from one elderly solicitor in the Department of Transport. As the campaign team would discuss policy issues with the civil servants, the solicitor and I would huddle in a corner discussing obscure provisions in the Highways Act and whether, in law, it was possible to convert parts of pavements into cycleways.

We wanted local authorities to provide more cycle racks in the streets, but many were reluctant to do so. In law, a pavement is part of the highway. The installation of any street furniture on pavements is, strictly speaking, an illegal obstruction of the highway unless there is express statutory authority. Trawling through the legislation, I could find legal provisions authorising such items as street lamps, bus shelters, benches and even troughs for watering horses and cattle, but there was nothing about cycle racks. Some authorities were unconcerned, but others were advised by their lawyers that if, say, a blind person walking on a pavement bumped into a cycle rack, the authority could be faced with a legal claim for damages because, in law, it was an illegal obstruction. I persuaded my friendly solicitor in the Department of Transport that a change in the law was needed and was delighted to see provisions included in the Transport Act 1978 which finally authorised the provision of cycle racks.[6] Striking and original demonstrations had long been part of FOE's campaigning style and Mike Hudson organised a cycle ride through the streets of Windsor to Windsor Castle to meet Prince Philip. Everyone was asked to dress up as different professions to demonstrate the versatility of the bicycle and the streets were soon filled with FOE members cycling along dressed as painters, decorators, policemen, window cleaners, butchers and teachers. I decided to wear my barrister's wig and gown and found myself cycling next to someone dressed as a priest. I explained a little smugly that I was, in fact, a barrister in real life, only to receive the reply that he really was a clergyman! But in many ways, the cycling campaign was ahead of its time and almost 20 years later when the Royal Commission on Environmental Pollution looked at cycling in the context of the 1996 Transport report,[7] it was depressing how little real progress had been made. Even today I still find myself frustrated when I see local authorities constructing short, unconnected sections of cycle way or finding myself having to share bus lanes – all apparently designed by road engineers who have never actually cycled in urban areas. Riding in cities such as Amsterdam is a wholly different experience; families and young children are content to ride without helmets because they are completely segregated from road traffic. It is all too easy to assume that cycling is somehow inherent in the Dutch psyche, but this is not true: photographs of cities

---

[6] Transport Act 1978, s 12: 'The powers of any authority under the Road Traffic Regulation Act 1967 to provide parking places shall extend to providing, in roads and elsewhere, stands and racks for bicycles.'

[7] See ch 9.

such as Amsterdam in the 1950s show it to be as congested with road traffic as London is now. It was a conscious political decision by government to invest in proper and widespread cycle infrastructure. There are now some signs of a change in attitude in major cities, but I am convinced much more could be done to make cycling an attractive and safe experience.

The most memorable event of the cycle campaign was a public meeting FOE organised in Trafalgar Square involving thousands of cyclists and keynote speakers. We thought it would be a wonderful end to the day to have all the cyclists riding down Whitehall past 10 Downing Street and into Parliament Square. As the lawyer, I was normally chosen to negotiate with the police about our demonstrations, dealing with the highly professional Processions Office of the Metropolitan Police who would give immensely helpful practical advice and knew to the last minute how long a march from Hyde Park to Trafalgar Square would take. I reckoned that if I proposed everyone exiting down Whitehall it would be probably be rejected, so gently hinted I was concerned how we would get so many cyclists to disperse quickly after the event to avoid traffic congestion. 'Why not close Whitehall for half an hour?' was the response and, of course, I readily agreed to their solution. Standing on the plinth of Nelson's Column and seeing a completely empty Whitehall gradually fill up its whole width with an advancing block of cyclists – there were so many that at one point the whole length from Trafalgar Square to Big Ben was one solid mass of bicycles – was one of the most uplifting sights I have seen.

My role as an in-house lawyer was not always concerned with the mainstream campaigning issues. The local FOE groups were now expanding rapidly from just 8 in 1971 to140 by 1976. FOE had always given its groups a large degree of autonomy in developing local campaigns and one of my tasks was to construct an agreement authorising the use of the Friends of the Earth name and containing appropriate protections which still allowed a large degree of independence. In practice, many of the local groups considered themselves far more radical than the London office staff whom they saw as engaging in establishment politics and prepared to wear suits and ties to meet government ministers and politicians. It was a somewhat unfair perception but provided a useful tension. The small London staff were then all paid the same low wage; as for suits, we could not afford them and for a time there was a single shared suit hanging in the lavatory for the male campaigners to wear for important meetings. My drafting skills were also needed when the Food campaign initiated a scheme to bring together retired homeowners who had unused gardens with FOE supporters who wished to grow vegetables. A simple licence agreement was needed, clarifying the status of the visitors and the ownership of any crops. Other legal issues often came into play. One day we saw a large advertisement in a national newspaper taken out by Citroën promoting their small 2CV car as a 'Friend of the Earth'. Initially we were rather flattered that our name had now caught the wider imagination of copywriters, but then felt that readers would think FOE had endorsed the car. I expect that Citroën had not realised that Friends of the Earth was a registered company name or perhaps thought we were a rather 'head in the clouds' group who would neither notice nor care. I consulted some practising solicitors I had got to know through my membership of the Lawyers Ecology Group,[8] sent off a letter threatening a passing-off action and reported the matter the Advertising Standards Authority. After some exchange of letters, Citroën backed off and the advertisements were withdrawn.

Despite all the visibility of the campaigns, it was never easy to judge just how powerful we were in political terms and the 'brown bread and lentils' image then associated with environmentalists and promoted by the popular press remained something of a curse – as I was to find later when I eventually did my barrister's pupillage. The Schweppes non-returnable bottle campaign may have scored in terms of publicity but little was happening substantially on the issue and non-returnable bottles rapidly spread through the industry. From a legal perspective, FOE promoted the example of the Oregon Beverage Container Act passed in 1971 which required most glass, plastic and metal beverage containers to be returnable with a minimum refund value. Shortly after I arrived, FOE received an invitation from the Department of the Environment to join a new body, the Packaging Council, that they were setting up to look at the issue of non-returnables and involving government and industry. We held a long and heated debate in the office as to whether we should accept the invitation. Some thought it would be a waste of time and dissipate our more forceful campaigning stance. Personally, I was rather wary – I had been involved in some student campaigns at university and knew from experience that the setting up of a committee could often mean the death of any real progress. But our director, Tom Burke, argued forcefully that this was the first time that the government had treated FOE as a serious body, FOE had always believed in the power of rational argument and that it would be irresponsible if we declined the opportunity to engage. It was a powerful argument which won the day and FOE joined the committee. However, it sat for many years with little to show for the exercise. Almost 40 years later I met a recently retired DEFRA civil servant and we discussed our early involvement in environmental issues. It turned out that he had been a young civil servant when the invitation to join the new committee had been sent to FOE. He said it was then often common practice to set up such a group to diffuse the issue or put it into the long grass, but we clearly had not appreciated just how powerful FOE had become. If we had refused the invitation, he told me that the government's next response woud have been to promote legislation along the lines of the Oregon Act and a draft of the law had already been prepared. I have no idea whether this really was the case, but it illustrated the challenges of bargaining and negotiating with government when it is often near impossible to judge one's own strength in the process. I now have a certain wry satisfaction when I read policy documents published by the Department of Environment Food and Rural Affairs (DEFRA) in July 2018 announcing that it

[8] See ch 3.

intended to introduce a deposit return scheme for bottles and drink containers and would seek the necessary legal powers in new legislation.

During this period, FOE was rarely engaged in legal action before the courts. Far more productive were public inquiries, an official hearing normally held by an independent inspector appointed by government. Public inquiries were a device established in the nineteenth century and have been used in many areas of decision-making and regulation. They are especially prevalent in the planning field where significant planning applications have been proposed and developers wish to appeal against the decisions of local planning authorities. Their attraction to FOE was that it was free to appear at such an inquiry and, unless one behaved disgracefully, there was no risks of being made to pay costs even if one did not win the argument – unlike litigation in the courts where the losing party normally has to pay the other side's legal costs. More importantly, the precise terms of reference of these inquiries were generally fairly broad or sometimes barely stated and provided a unique, official public forum where FOE would articulate new arguments about how we should handle environmental issues. A good example was an inquiry concerning proposals for a new water reservoir where the planning issues were focused on the least-damaging location for the project. But the FOE local group submitted that if every home in the area had a brick in the lavatory, a reservoir would not be needed in the first place – an approach that was quite novel at the time and one which the planning inspector later told me was logical and compelling but he was unsure how to incorporate it in his recommendations. There were few other such opportunities for exploring issues in this way and specialist parliamentary select committees holding investigations were still a few years off.[9]

Another striking example of how a public inquiry offered the chance to articulate fresh perspectives concerned allotments. A London local authority was trying to close an allotment, and this involved a one-day public inquiry held in front of a government inspector under the Small Holdings and Allotments Act 1906. Our Food campaigner said he wanted to appear as a witness with myself representing FOE as an objector. But his argument was not going to be about the local recreational value of the allotment in question – rather that, against the long-term global demand for food, allotments represented a scare soil resource that should be preserved and that even this individual allotment could have its part of play in the future. I was hesitant about presenting such a case which as far as I knew had never been made before at an allotments' inquiry and thought we might be laughed out of the proceedings. But we did so, the inspector listened carefully and, in his report, found against the local authority (a rare occurrence then), arguing that allotments were indeed a potentially vital resource for future global food production, and in this context even this small one should be saved.

---

[9] Select committees in the House of Commons tracking each government department came into being in 1979 following a report of a Procedure select committee the year before. See ch 6.

Out-of-town shopping precincts were starting to emerge in this country and FOE appeared at many public inquiries arguing that they would damage town centres and increase traffic. Public inquiries held into proposed sections of motorway also provided another important public forum where FOE was able to challenge the prevailing approach of the Department of Transport to accommodate future traffic growth, characterised then as 'predict and provide'. The justification for new road schemes was based on complex, mathematical predictions of traffic growth produced by the government (known as the 'Red Book') and presented at the inquiry by expert government witnesses. They provided a critical building block to justify the new scheme, but were hardly intelligible to the layperson and, when the subject was occasionally raised in parliament, it was clear that politicians, including government ministers, were unable to engage in the detail. Largely through the expertise of John Adams, an academic from University Campaign and Mick Hamer, the Transport Campaigner, FOE was able unravel the presumptions behind the figures. We were permitted to cross-examine government witnesses on the issue and could show that the mathematics often disguised assumptions about matters such the future price of petrol which were neither factual certainties nor inevitabilities but fungible factors that could be changed by government policy, leading to quite different forecasts. We did not expect to win any particular inquiry, but the importance of the system was that it allowed these issues to be aired in public and to gradually infiltrate the thinking within government. It was almost 20 years later, following the Royal Commission on Environmental Pollution's seminal report on Transport and the Environment, that a government minister acknowledged on television for the first time that building more roads simply created more traffic.

One of the reasons that FOE and other groups were given such leeway at these road inquiries was that, as with many such public inquiries at the time, the precise scope of the inquiry was ill-defined and the issue had not yet been fully tested in court. But there was then a 100-day road inquiry concerning proposed sections of the M42 and M40 through rural areas near Birmingham. FOE was not involved, but the inspector conducting the inquiry had decided to refuse to let local objectors cross-examine government witnesses on the reliability and statistical validity of the traffic forecasts on the grounds they were really issues of national policy inappropriate for a local inquiry. He allowed them to make representations on the subject but not cross-examine. One of the objectors involved in the inquiry visited me in Poland Street to say they were planning to challenge the decision before the courts on the grounds that the inspector's decision was a breach of natural justice and wanted FOE to join them in the case. I advised against any legal action because I was concerned that the courts might impose much stricter boundaries on rights of cross-examination and that it was preferable for the environmental community that the position remained legally ambiguous. My perspective, though, was from that of a group campaigning on transport generally, while the local resident was quite reasonably concerned with using every avenue to protect his own home and the local environment. He said they would still go to court and my visitor turned out to be Mr Bushell. The seminal case of *Bushell v the Secretary of State for the Environment* eventually reached the highest court in the country, the House of Lords, in 1980[10] and, as I had feared, the judges did indeed place future curbs on cross-examining government witnesses on these issues.

The passions raised at many of these inquiries resulted in many troublesome scenes of disruption and protest where largely hapless Inspectors, often retired military men, found it difficult to keep control of the situation. In 1974, John Tyme, an academic from Sheffield whose wife had been killed in a motorway accident, began leading systematic protests at motorway inquiries to prevent them from opening. As he later said: 'I realised that the whole public inquiry thing was a complete farce, so I started the business of making sure that the inquiries simply didn't go on.' Friends of the Earth then had a policy of never breaking the law and as someone who still, perhaps naively, believed in the power of rational argument, I found the scenes distinctly uncomfortable and would usually slip out quietly before the police inevitably arrived. One of the core reasons why so many felt that these inquiries were fundamentally defective was because it was the Department of Transport which had proposed the motorway scheme and then appointed an inspector to inquire into its own proposal.[11] The first legislation that gave powers to central government to construct and compulsorily purchase land for main roads was the Trunks Road Act 1936. Others looking at the history of the transport law had noted that it was strange that such a significant transfer of powers from local authorities to central government received so little Parliamentary attention at the time. In 1928, the Lord Chief Justice had published *The New Despotism*, a powerful diatribe which gave rise to enormous publicity at the time. He described this despotism as government's wish 'to subordinate Parliament, to evade the courts and to render the will, or the caprice, of the Executive unfettered and supreme'. The Trunks Roads Act epitomised this tendency, but was surprisingly passed by Parliament with not a word of objection. Rather bizarrely, the reason for this only became apparent some 30 years later when, in 1979, a distinguished former Parliamentary draftsman published his autobiography entitled *In On The Act*. As a young draftsman in the 1930s, Harold Kent was asked to draft the schedules to the new legislation. As he recollected:

> 'Perhaps the most awkward feature of the Bill, politically speaking, was that for the first time a Government Minister, as distinct from a local authority, was taking powers to acquire land compulsorily. Such powers, when exercised by a local authority, were subject to confirmation by the Minister who would hold a public inquiry and hear the views of the authority and objectors and might refuse his confirmation. But now there was nobody to say nay to the Minister. He would still be required to hold an

---

[10] *Bushell v Secretary of State for the Environment* [1981] AC 75. The decision is further discussed in ch 4.

[11] It was only some years later that the decision was taken to have inspectors appointed by a different department.

inquiry but he would judge in his own cause. Then, as now, there was a powerful back-bench lobby against Ministerial powers and bureaucratic tyranny and, much talk of natural justice and its denial.'

The reason that Parliament never objected to the new powers became apparent: 'I got around this awkward point by perpetrating a piece of legislation by reference[12] which still makes me blush. Paragraph 6(b) of Schedule 4 of the Trunk Road Act 1936 applies the compulsory code of local authorities under the Local Government Act 1933 to the Minister of Transport with modifications of such repellent aspect than even the back-bench lobby passed them in bemused silence.'[13] Harold Kent's book still remains a compelling account of the challenges faced by parliamentary draftsmen, but I think he little realised when he published his life story just how relevant his early experience was to the upheavals and protests at motorway inquiries that were taking place at the time. But at least it explained how easily government had acquired the powers and the importance of always examining closely the technical schedules to proposed new legislation.

Nuclear power was the focus of one of FOE's most visible campaigns. Its concerns were not so much with the health effects of radiation discharges, but with the economics of the technology. Renewable energy technology such as tidal and wind power were then being developed, but the research investment was miniscule compared to the enormous sums of money being devoted by government to nuclear power. FOE raised security aspects, arguing that plutonium used to fuel nuclear reactors could be stolen and made into bombs by terrorist groups. The ideal was ridiculed by the nuclear establishment but one morning Tom Burke called me down for a private meeting in the basement office at 9 Poland Street. He told me in strictest confidence that FOE was designing a small nuclear bomb to prove its case. My legal mind naturally began racing and I immediately asked whether it was for real but was slightly reassured to hear that it was simply a paper exercise to show that it was possible. Two research students at Cambridge University had nearly completed the detailed designs which would then be shown to the Swedish Academy of Scientists to check their validity. *The Guardian* planned to run a major story and Tom and I met the two researchers with its then editor, Peter Preston. I never knew their names and did not want to but they were clearly extremely nervous about what they were doing. A few days later a thick brown

[12] 'Drafting by reference' is a drafting technique by which a statute is amended by incorporating detailed changes referred to in a later statute but without reproducing the full text of the amended legislation. It is, to my mind, one of the curses of British Parliamentary drafting style and makes it near impossible for a layperson or Parliamentarian to understand what is being proposed. One of the provisions in Harold Kent's Schedule to the Trunk Roads Act, which made it so difficult for parliamentarians to realise the legal changes taking place, read: 'In sections one hundred and sixty one and one hundred and sixty-two of the Local Government Act 1933 as applied by the said section thirteen, for references to a local authority there shall be substituted references to the Minister.'
[13] Harold Kent, *In On The Act*, p 77 (London, Macmillan, 1979).

envelope arrived with the full plans and I was asked to keep it safe overnight. I had no desire to look inside and felt extremely distinctly uncomfortable carrying the package on the tube back to my home in South London. It was a time of IRA activity in London and I reckoned any terrorist would find the contents of immense interest. The envelope remained under my pillow during a sleepless night. When the Swedish Academy checked through the designs, it concluded there was a good chance it would be viable. When I later moved on to Imperial College, I discussed the idea of home-made nuclear bombs with the then Rector, Lord Flowers, a distinguished nuclear physicist. He doubted whether a workable nuclear bomb could be constructed in someone's back yard, but thought it was perfectly possible at Imperial College's small 100 Kw nuclear research reactor at Silwood Park. FOE continued its campaign on nuclear power and soon became involved in the largest public inquiry to date on the subject, an issue that was to dominate my last year of work with the organisation.

2

The Windscale Inquiry

For the lawyer the public local inquiry is the central institution in the planning process. Amid the strange and murky world of jargon, the inquiry is the light that shines out and gives off a familiar glow.

Patrick McAuslan *The Ideologies of Planning Law* (1980)

The 1977 Windscale inquiry into a proposed nuclear reprocessing facility was, at the time, the most significant public inquiry on environmental issues ever held in this country. It did not come about by chance. I was still the in-house lawyer for Friends of the Earth (FOE) when, one morning, the energy campaigner, Czech Conroy, asked to meet me and FOE's director, Tom Burke, for a coffee in a Soho café. I could not keep up with all the activities taking place in campaigns and one of my roles as staff lawyer was to try to sensitise campaigners to a lawyer's way of thinking and when it might be helpful for them to seek my legal perspective on what they were doing. Czech was a man for detail and persistent research and completely understood the value of legal advice. The year before there had been public concerns about some leaks at nuclear plants and the then Secretary of State for Energy, Tony Benn, invited the public to send any questions on nuclear issues to the Nuclear Installations Inspectorate. The Inspectorate was the core regulator for nuclear facilities but a body then with little public profile. Czech sensibly first sought my input saying that before drafting any questions he needed to know the precise legal powers of the Inspectorate. I did some research, and found that the body was mainly concerned with safety, and really had no remit over the issues that were of core concern to FOE – nuclear proliferation, the economics and the need for nuclear power. As a result, FOE's set of questions to the inspectorate was the only submission to be accompanied by a legal commentary on the limited remit of the Inspectorate's jurisdiction.

Over our coffee, Czech explained there were two major developments in the nuclear field taking place in this country – a possible new fast breeder reactor programme and a proposed reprocessing plant for nuclear waste at Windscale in Cumbria. Both had enormous implications, but he could only work on one and wanted my legal perspective. I asked what stage both the developments had reached. Czech said the fast breeder programme was still at an early policy-level development, but that he had heard a planning application was about to made to the local planning authority by British Nuclear Fuels for the new reprocessing plant. I immediately advised focusing on Windscale. Once a planning application has been granted, it would be extremely difficult to revoke it because the applicant would then be entitled to compensation and we knew that planning procedures provided opportunities for public inquiries and public participation where FOE's arguments could be thoroughly aired.

The formal planning application was submitted to Copeland District Council in June 1976 who referred it to Cumbria County Council. Under the Town and Country Planning Act 1971, the Secretary of State had the power to 'call-in' any planning application for his or her own decision rather than the local planning authority. Call-ins generally involved a public inquiry, but the number of such call-ins were extremely small (around 20 a year out of around 4,000,000 planning applications) and were reserved for applications raising issues of national importance or new technology and similar criteria. The BNFL application seemed to perfectly fit the bill and initially FOE focused its attention on persuading the Secretary of State to exercise his powers before the local authority decided the application. We contacted other groups such as the Town and Country Planning Association, the National Council for Civil Liberties and the Council for the Protection of Rural England to lend their support. I was then attending meetings of the Lawyers' Ecology Group, a small body of practising lawyers interested in the environment.[1] I was particularly pleased to persuade the group to send in their own letter to government arguing for a call-in since they were approaching the issue purely from the perspective of experienced lawyers and had no particular axe to grind on the issue of nuclear power. Meanwhile Cumbria County Council had recognised the public interest in the application and had held local public meetings on the issue. They were uncomfortable in asking the Secretary of State to call-in the application as this might appear to be a derogation of their own responsibilities as a planning authority, but then cleverly invoked a little-known procedure by declaring that the application appeared to fundamentally depart from their own development plan for the area. Under the planning law at the time, this triggered a 21-day period for the Secretary of State, Peter Shore, to decide whether take over the application. Tom Huggon, one of the founders of the Lawyers' Ecology Group, has recently told me that he rang the Secretary of State's office on 24 March 1977, the last day on which he could make his decision, to find out what was happening. He spoke to the Permanent Secretary who told him he had just come off the phone with the Archbishop of York who was asking the same question. He told Tom that there would be a press announcement at tea-time and, a few hours later, Peter Shore, the Secretary of State for the Environment, declared he was indeed calling-in the application and that a public inquiry would be held starting on 14 June 1977.

FOE had achieved its initial objective, but there was now less than four months before the inquiry commenced. One of the reasons for the short period was that the BNFL was in the final stages of negotiating with the Japanese government a contract for reprocessing nuclear waste from Japan, a vital element in the economic

---

[1] See further ch 3.

viability of the plant. The contract might well be lost if there was undue delay. My advice was that we would need to use a senior professional barrister skilled in cross-examination to represent FOE since it was a task well beyond my experience and skills. Once again, my contact with the Lawyers' Ecology Group proved fruitful. One of its members was Geoffrey Searle, an experienced planning solicitor with the London firm of Denton Hall. He agreed they would assist us for a reduced fee. The terms of reference for the inquiry were published and Geoffrey said he had never seen such broad terms for a planning inquiry. A further precedent was made when it was announced that a High Court judge, Sir Roger Parker, rather than an ordinary planning inspector, would chair the inquiry, assisted by two distinguished technical assessors.

Oliver Thorold, who had previously given legal advice to FOE and was now a young practising barrister, agreed to help represent us. We were then faced with the choice of the lead barrister. These days there are published directories of barristers with rankings in different areas of law and succinct descriptions of their experience and qualities, but nothing of the sort existed then, so it was a question of asking around. We realised that the sorts of arguments we would be raising were not conventional planning issues and that we would should probably go outside the planning bar. The name of Raymond Kidwell QC kept cropping up. He had appeared at the Flixborough Inquiry following an explosion at chemical works in 1974 which had killed 18 people and had engaged in forceful cross-examination of highly technical issues. Through Denton Hall we arranged a conference at his chambers in 2 Crown Row in the Temple and six of us turned up, crowding out Kidwell's small room to explain our case and why the inquiry was so important. I do not think he had ever met representatives from an environmental group and initially listened in bemused silence as he chain smoked Benson and Hedges. The turning point was when one of our energy specialists, Walt Patterson, mentioned he had just come from a meeting with the Secretary of State for Energy. Kidwell immediately appreciated that, despite the majority of us being bearded and looking rather dishevelled, this was not some ramshackle organisation and that the inquiry would be one of the most important ever held in this country. He now wanted to be part of the action and agreed to represent FOE.

Denton Hall negotiated a fixed fee but we then had to launch a rapid fundraising campaign to raise the minimum of £25,000 needed to cover the legal and other associated costs. Under the deliberately ambiguous title 'Windscale – It's Cost the Earth' local FOE groups rallied to the cause. The millionaire James Goldsmith contributed and Tom Burke, FOE's director, even went on a sponsored diet – as he quipped later, the only time he has given his own flesh to the legal profession. Intense preparation for the case began and another conference with Ray Kidwell was arranged. At that point, Tom asked me why we all had to go to Kidwell's chambers when it would be far more convenient if he came to our Soho offices. Barristers these days will often visit clients, but at that time it was never done; conferences were always held in chambers. I explained this to Tom, but he said as we were paying the fees, we should still at least ask. It was typical of FOE's tendency at the time to question precedent if it did not seem sensible. The majority of the staff were in their twenties or early thirties – Walt Patterson, all of 40, seemed like a wise old man to the rest of us – and we were reluctant to follow established ways of doing things for the sake of it. I broached the issue to Geoffrey Searle who was also a little aghast, but I insisted he at least make the request. To my surprise Kidwell readily agreed, perhaps the first time a barrister of his seniority had done this. Although a highly distinguished member of the Bar, he was an unusual character – the son of schoolteachers, brought up in North Devon, passionately interested in both the sea and science, a designer and builder of elaborate water fountains and a poet.[2] He was, I think, someone who enjoyed the thought of slightly shocking his more conventional colleagues and relished the idea of regular meetings in Soho. These proved enormously valuable in preparation for the inquiry. Kidwell would test ruthlessly the arguments being prepared by the campaigners, questioned the suitability of the large number of witnesses we were proposing and refined FOE's case down to its core essentials.

Sir Roger Parker, the planning inspector, held a pre-inquiry meeting in May and noted that although this was technically a planning inquiry, it would be dealing with issues 'that may affect not only those already alive and residing in the immediate neighbourhood but also those who live far away and who will not be born for many years ahead'. The inquiry proper opened in Whitehaven Civic Hall two weeks later and lasted over 100 days. In the build-up, we had tried to persuade other environmental groups to focus on fund raising and allow FOE to lead the case since it had the greater technical expertise. But the world of environmental groups is highly competitive and, not surprisingly, others wanted to be separately represented and secure their own profile rather than allow FOE the exclusive spotlight. Apart from a number of individual objectors, other organisations appearing included the Town and Country Planning Association, the Oxford Political Ecology Group, the Isle of Man Government (mainly concerned with low level release of radioactive waste into the Irish sea) and a coalition of various groups under the soubriquet of the Windscale Alliance. At times, during the inquiry, this proved frustrating for FOE as we had developed highly focused arguments; in particular, we were deliberately not objecting outright to the proposal but instead arguing that it could be delayed for ten years without jeopardising the development of nuclear power. Alternative techniques for handling nuclear waste were beginning to be developed which did not involve the separation of plutonium and the vitrification of the remaining waste as proposed by BNFL and these appeared environmentally far more attractive. As Ray Kidwell noted in his closing speech, a decision to say 'not yet' required 'more courage than the ostensibly more forthright and outright pronouncement of a decision for and against the plant'. But this more

---

[2] He died in 2007. A posthumous collection of his poetry, *A Murmur of Surf*, was published in 2010.

subtle approach was rather overwhelmed by the blanket opposition presented by other objectors and was never fully reflected in Sir Roger Parker's final report.

This is not the place for a full examination of the inquiry[3] but some impressions particularly struck me. As we developed our case before the start of the inquiry, we rather imagined that BNFL witnesses would simply collapse under the strength and logic of our arguments and the questioning of our heavyweight QC. This did not happen and Raymond Kidwell noted their professionalism and expertise. He pointed out to me that the managing director was deliberately answering his questions by addressing him constantly as 'Mr Kidwell', a technique designed to personalise the barrister and soften the confrontation. Again, before the inquiry, we had imagined that BNFL would be seen as the hard, aggressive party compared to the more personable face of FOE. In terms of barristers, if anything it was the opposite. BNFL's leading counsel, Lord Silsoe, was charming, calm and ever accommodating, whilst Kidwell adopted a more forceful and hard-nosed approach. For its accommodation, the FOE team rented a former railway station on the Cumbrian coast about five miles from Whitehaven where the inquiry was being held – Raymond Kidwell had sensibly decided to remain a little detached, renting a rather more luxurious cottage on the other side of the Pennines. Lengthy evenings were spent analysing day's proceedings and sharpening up the evidence – though every so often we had to pause when the house began shaking as long goods trains carrying radioactive waste to Windscale trundled past. Perhaps not surprisingly the rather surreal and intense experience of being closeted so many days in Whitehaven Civic Hall with the BNFL team led to a degree of friendly respect and, fairly soon, weekly football matches between objectors and proponents became the order of the day.

Some flavour of the inquiry and, in my view, the value of the art of cross-examination in teasing out complex technical issues can be found in an extract from Raymond Kidwell's questioning of Dr Clelland, the lead BNFL witness in charge of the reprocessing operation.

BNFL's reprocessing proposals involved using various chemical processes to extract plutonium and uranium from the spent fuel pellets and then encapsulating the remaining highly radioactive liquid waste into glass blocks for ultimate disposal, a technique known as 'vitrification'. Kidwell was trying to explore FOE's arguments that, from the perspective of waste management, it was both preferable and possible to store the spent fuel for at least ten years rather than immediately engage in reprocessing. Research on long-term storage was still in its infancy, but a delay of ten years would allow scientists to acquire far greater knowledge of the comparative advantages of the two approaches and a more informed decision on the best option could then be taken. However, it became clear during the

---

[3] For an excellent account produced soon after the final decision see Ian Breach, *Windscale Fallout* (London, Penguin Books, 1978).

cross-examination that FOE's perspective was challenging for an industry which had already committed itself to the reprocessing route and Kidwell and Dr Clelland were often arguing at cross-purposes.

> KIDWELL: So if you glassify you are committed virtually either to that solid or getting back to your liquid and investing some other solid, whereas if you wait a little while and think – you and everybody else in the world – about methods of disposing spent fuel ultimately, it may turn out that other options appear preferable, may it not?
>
> CLELLAND: It is very easy to dispose of spent fuel. All you do is to dissolve it in nitric acid and convert it to glass. Then you are back to the general type of reprocessing system. You have a choice then. You can either remove the uranium or leave the uranium in the glass.
>
> KIDWELL: Let me just get this clear: so far as ultimate disposal of spent fuel is concerned, that is chemically and from an engineering point of view, something on which you so see no difficulty at all. Is that right?
>
> CLELLAND: It is not difficult? I am sorry, I did not catch you.
>
> KIDWELL: I understood you to be saying that it is very easy to dispose ultimately of spent fuel. That is right is it?
>
> CLELLAND: By reprocessing, yes.
>
> KIDWELL: But by reprocessing if you wish.
>
> CLELLAND: By reprocessing techniques. By using reprocessing techniques, you dispose of spent fuel.
>
> KIDWELL: No, what I am suggesting is this; that if you wait and see what research produces over the next 10–15 years, it may emerge that direct ultimate disposal of solid ceramic spent fuel is a preferable route to any route involving reprocessing. It may do. Do you accept that possibility?
>
> CLELLAND It is very doubtful indeed. If you have a method of doing it well I could visualize it.

During preparation for the inquiry, FOE had been aware that one of the claimed advantages of the glassification of liquid wastes during reprocessing was its low leachability. But there appeared to be no published material comparing the leachability of glassified waste following reprocessing with that of the simple storage of the spent fuel pellets. Shortly before Kidwell's cross-examination of Dr Clelland, we were able to obtain from the United States a summary of some new research examining the leachability of spent fuel. Kidwell had this in his hands but was unsure whether BNFL had access to more compelling comparative research on the issue. Earlier on in the cross-examination, Dr Clelland had already said there was plenty of published work on the area and that it was common knowledge that the spent fuel was easily leachable. But Kidwell now felt confident to press the point home.

> KIDWELL: Now, are you able to produce some published work on comparative leach rates over the weekend?
>
> CLELLAND: I do not think so, no. I am sure not.

KIDWELL: No. It all depends on your asserting that it is common knowledge, does it?

CLELLAND: No, information can be made available but I do not know if it can be over the weekend.

KIDWELL: Oh I see. You say that is obtainable.

CLELLAND: I think so, yes. I am sure it is. Well it is.

KIDWELL: Now what I am seeking to do is to ...

LORD SILSOE to the Inspector: (Lord Silsoe, representing BNFL was clearly intervening to protect the witness who was getting into some difficulty) Sir, you will be getting one of them, the leach rates of the glass in Mr Corbet's proof.

INSPECTOR: Well, as I understand it, what Mr Kidwell is interested is whether there are some leach rates for pellets.

KIDWELL: Yes, Well, of course there are, because I am going to produce them in a moment.

INSPECTOR: Well, I am on tenterhooks.

LORD SILSOE: Well, we have got one; and they have got the other (laughter).

The paper that FOE produced appeared to be the first published results of experiments on the leachability of spent fuel pellets, but research on the issue was so new it did not really have the impact we had hoped. Many considered that Sir Roger Parker's conduct of the inquiry itself was faultless and fair and, though probably the longest planning inquiry held in this country to date, he had maintained the pressure to avoid it becoming hopelessly over-extended. As a lawyer, I was rather proud to see the finest qualities of the British judiciary on display to my non-legal colleagues at FOE. But all that changed when his report was presented to the Secretary of State just under three months later on 26 January 1978. Reports of Planning Inspectors normally contained lengthy summaries of the evidence before reaching a conclusion but Sir Roger had adopted a different approach. Few doubted his integrity and independence in sifting and evaluating the evidence but, having reached his conclusions in favour of the application, his report then largely justified these with highly selective extracts from witnesses to prove his case. My colleagues were horrified and now felt the whole exercise had been rather wasted. Letters to the *Times* were published, followed by FOE producing a lengthy critique of Sir Roger's report, which concluded: 'For all its shortcomings, the Windscale inquiry was undoubtedly a landmark in British nuclear policy-making. It set standards for the public treatment of nuclear issues that are higher than those reached anywhere else in the world. It is thus all the more tragic that the hasty and erratic judgments of the report of the inquiry did no justice to the proceedings. The result has been a polarization rather than a moderation of the debate.'

We then decided that before the Secretary of State made his decision, there should at least be a parliamentary debate on the issue. This had never happened before after a planning inquiry, but the lack of precedent was of little concern to us. I could, though, see potential legal problem since planning inquiry rules and decisions of the courts indicated that if the Secretary of State took into account new evidence following an inquiry, he might have to reopen the proceedings to give objectors an opportunity to comment on the new material. I wrote a letter to the Secretary of State saying that these principles were unlikely to apply to a political debate held in public in parliament, but it remained a potential stumbling block. The pressure for parliamentary debate increased and, finally, the government itself came up with an ingenious legal solution. I was told later that the idea came from Peter Shore's political adviser, Jack Straw, a young barrister who was later to become Home Secretary and Foreign Secretary in Tony Blair's government. Despite Sir Roger's recommendation that permission for the reprocessing plant be granted, the Secretary of State would formally refuse the planning application, thus making any legal arguments for reopening the inquiry otiose. The government would then publish a proposed 'Special Development Order' under the Town and Country Planning Act which would grant permission for the development and it was this draft order that would be subject to parliamentary debate. The debate was held on 15 May 1977 and the order was approved by a majority of 144.

The Windscale Inquiry and its aftermath was FOE's most intense campaigning experience to date. Although it did not win the argument on the application at the time, FOE's profile and reputation changed immeasurably. As the *New Scientist* noted in its weekly account of the inquiry: 'By common consent, the closing speech made for FOE by Raymond Kidwell QC was a trenchant and propitious piece of advocacy; for the Friends, it marked a British turning point. No longer can FOE be regarded as an enterprising but rather unavailing conservationist lobby. After its case and this submission here, it will be seen as an important technical and political force.'[4] For those involved it was both exhausting and exhilarating and, for the London office of FOE, the enormous boost to the group's reputation brought its own challenges. Revenue increased and the staff rapidly doubled in size, but we initially failed to develop organisational structures appropriate for a much larger body. When the staff was just around ten in number, meetings and discussions were often held informally and in a local pub. All the staff were paid the same salary and, as with many of the new pressure groups that had been established during this period, there was a reluctance to introduce what were seen as 'conventional' organisational approaches such as line management. With the rapid increase in size, we resorted to having weekly all-day staff meetings so that everyone could feel involved in all aspects of decision making. I occasionally complained, arguing that this might be acceptable if we were a self-supporting community, but our salaries were paid for by donations and fund-raising efforts, and supporters would not be happy if they knew we were spending a fifth of our time simply talking to each other. The next year or so created difficult tensions between the staff, local groups and the FOE board of directors as we tried to resolve the best way of developing future organisational structures. It reflected the birth pangs of an organisation which was rapidly growing up; similar problems were being faced in

---

[4] New Scientist 'Opponents Wind Up Their Case against Expansion', 3 November 1977.

many other pressure groups at the time. They were eventually resolved and more sophisticated management systems and salary differentials to attract the best staff were introduced, but it was not an easy time.

The Windscale inquiry was followed by an even lengthier inquiry into a proposed nuclear power plant at Sizewell in Suffolk and the Heathrow inquiry into a third runway. It spawned a whole stream of academic research and innumerable conferences into the role of the so-called 'big public inquiry'. Indeed this was the issue that was the focus of the first conference I organised in my subsequent academic career.[5] As for BNFL's reprocessing plant, it was eventually built at a cost of £1.8 billion and opened for business in 1994, one of only two nuclear reprocessing plants in the world. In addition to the Japanese contract, it received waste from some nine countries, but the income never covered the costs. In 2012, BNFL took the decision to close reprocessing operations at Windscale, with the last batch of fuel being reprocessed there in November 2018 and the site is now to be used for the storage of spent fuel at least until the 2070s. As BNFL stated: 'The international market has shifted significantly since Thorp's construction with the majority of customers now opting to store rather than reprocess their fuel.'[6] At the Windscale inquiry, over 40 years before, a key argument of FOE had been that storage was environmentally preferable to reprocessing but, as with so much of the analysis the organisation was making during that period, it was a generation ahead of its time.

[5] See ch 4.
[6] 'Reprocessing Ceases at UK's Thorp Plant', *World Nuclear News* 14 November 2018.

3

The Emergence of Environmental Lawyers in the UK

On my bookshelf is a small paperback with a plain brown cover and the rather prosaic title, 'Report of Conference on Law and Science'. Organised by the British Institute of Comparative and International Law, the conference was held in July 1964. It is significant in being what must have been the first meeting of British lawyers and scientists to discuss environmental challenges. One of the country's most senior judges, Lord Hodson, chaired the proceedings and noted in his introduction that while the role of the law would vary according to the circumstances 'it should be possible to evolve a set of widely applicable principles'. Many of the topics considered at this conference over 60 years ago are still high on today's environmental agenda – oil pollution of the sea, air pollution and the control of pesticides – but other concerns were more a product of their time. A session was devoted to the climate but the focus of discussion was not on greenhouse gases but on the possible effects of rockets and their exhausts on the upper atmosphere. The mix of legal and scientific disciplines at the conference was admirable and, in my early years as an academic, I worked closely and productively with environmental scientists. At the end of the conference, though, the closing speaker noted that: 'It would seem that far from any marriage of true minds as between lawyers and scientists there is at the present time very little communication between them at all. They are proceeding on parallel lines it is true but without very many sparks escaping from one track to illumine the other, both speeding at a terrifying pace towards and increasingly uncertain future.'

At the time, there were few in the country who would have described themselves environmental lawyers as such. Those dealing in town and country planning had a cohesive specialism in planning law. Many of the origins of modern environmental law were to be found in the Victorian public health legislation. There were practitioner textbooks on the Public Health Acts and a loose-leaf, *Encyclopedia of Public Health Law*, covered many areas of pollution law. Individual lawyers, such as the indefatigable Jack Garner, a former local government solicitor and later an academic at Nottingham University, published regular treatises on specialised subjects such as sewerage and drainage law. The early 1970s saw the emergence of modern environmentalism at the highest international level with the UN Stockholm Conference on the Human Environment and, within the United Kingdom, the establishment of the Department of the Environment and the setting up of the Royal Commission on Environmental Pollution. These changing perceptions began to be felt in the legal world and, symbolically perhaps, in 1973, the *Journal of Planning Law* changed its name to the *Journal of Planning and Environmental Law*.

A year earlier, the *Law Society Gazette* had published a letter from a solicitor, Edward Moeran, pointing to the vital role that lawyers could play in helping to deal with the potential environmental catastrophes facing the world – 'Should we not form a group of interested and dedicated lawyers now, whilst there may yet be time, to make our own contribution to this crisis of humanity?'. As a result of the letter, the Solicitors' Ecology Group was established, later to be named the Lawyers' Ecology Group. There was considerable press interest in a major conference on environmental law organised by the group in 1974 at the Institute of Contemporary Arts in London, though *New Scientist* commented rather sourly that, knowing lawyers, it would all end in words and no action. In my early days as the staff lawyer for Friends of the Earth (FOE), I had regularly attended its meetings and found them an invaluable source of contact with a select band of practising lawyers interested in environmental issues. But it was a small group, whose main focus was an ambitious plan to establish a national environmental law advice centre. Perhaps it was ahead of its time – it proved impossible to obtain sufficient funding for the venture.[1] The meetings, though perfectly pleasant, seemed to drag on endlessly, at least to a rather impatient young lawyer such as myself. But the group's newsletters give an intriguing reflection on the concerns of lawyers at the time; some still have contemporary echoes. In 1975, the Labour Party had decided upon a referendum on whether the UK should remain within the then European Economic Community. The Lawyers' Ecology Group convened a working group on the environmental implications of remaining in or coming out of Europe, though it was noted that the report 'does not come to any overall conclusion since the issues are so complicated and the views of the contributors are so disparate'. Perhaps this was not so surprising since the development of environmental policies and legislation by the European Community had only just begun at the time[2] and few would have predicted the impact and significance that EU environmental law was to bring over the next decades.

Some ten years later, younger academics specialising in environmental law were beginning to emerge in British universities. In early 1986, two law lecturers, Stephen Tromans from Cambridge and Andrew Waite from Southampton, placed a piece in one of the legal journals asking whether it was not time for a new environmental law association to be formed. This led to a meeting at Southampton University attended by around 30 lawyers – some of the older guard from the

---

[1] Eventually, in 1992, the Environmental Law Foundation was established to provide free advice to the public on environmental law problems and continues successfully today.
[2] See further ch 12.

Lawyers' Ecology Group, a number of academics and a scattering of practising lawyers both from the private and public sector. Everyone felt that the time was right for a new environmental law group, but there followed some intense discussion as to what sort of body it should be. Some favoured an activist group, bringing test cases before the courts. The majority view, though, was that the new organisation, the UK Environmental Law Association, should be a non-partisan professional body able to embrace all those who worked in environmental law, whether in industry, academia, the private and public sectors or environmental groups. It was felt that more activist legal groups would develop in their own time and, indeed, in subsequent years, groups such as Friends of the Earth began taking many more judicial reviews in the courts and, in 2008, ClientEarth, an organisation dedicated to using the law to improve environmental protection, was established in this country. The Southampton meeting appointed a small committee to develop both a structure and an initial programme of events for UKELA. I had attended the conference but had kept a low profile, as at the time I was heavily committed in developing research and teaching at Imperial College and was Standing Counsel to the Council for the Protection of Rural England, an honorary position but one that was demanding. Involvement in a new organisation was the last thing I needed at the time, but I found myself on the committee and, as the only member with a London base, offered to host the first committee meeting at Imperial College. Chance seems to have often played a part in my career. I had assumed that Stephen Tromans and Andrew Waite would take charge as it had been their idea, but both had missed their trains and arrived very late. To fill the gap, I ended up chairing the meeting; it went well and at the end, to my surprise, I was proposed as the first chair of UKELA.

Over the next few months we developed a constitution and ideas for core activities and UKELA was officially launched on 12 December 1986 in London at a meeting attended by over 50 lawyers. I was keen that while UKELA would be a non-partisan and professional body, it should bring a fresh approach and not just be viewed as another conventional legal association. We therefore chose the convention centre at London Zoo for the launch as somewhere quite distinct from a more standard legal location such as the Law Society or one of the Inns of Court.[3] Against a background of roaring lions and chattering monkeys, UKELA came into being. British environmental lawyers could be somewhat insular at times, and over-concerned with the peculiarities of national law. I was anxious that members saw the new organisation in the wider international context of the growing interest in environmental law. So I arranged for messages of congratulation on the launch of UKELA from equivalent environmental law bodies all around the world

---

[3] Over 30 years, we adopted the same tactic in launching UKELA's work on Brexit and the Environment – see ch 13.

to be read out – including Mexico ('We joyfully salute the Environmental Law Association of your great country'), India ('It is indeed gratifying to know that the United Kingdom is having an Environmental Law Association'), Russia ('Wish you and all association members every success in your novel cause') and the United States ('Your organisation will surely play an important role in fostering dialogue and promoting education and communication on environmental law issues').

There were two important organisational principles that I advocated in the early days and which have since remained constant within UKELA. First, there should be a maximum term for the chair, two or three years at the most, allowing for the constant injection of new blood and fresh ideas. I had seen other bodies where the leadership had remained in place far too long; for example, the chair of one national environmental law association in Europe had remained in place for over 30 years and, though a highly distinguished academic and leading environmental specialist, I could not believe this was healthy in the long run. Even though I was reluctant to step down after two years and still felt full of energy and ideas, it was the right thing to do to ensure the future strength of the organisation. The second principle was that UKELA should hold an annual conference which would not be too expensive for most members. At the time, one of the few bodies holding events on contemporary environmental law issues was the International Bar Association Section on Energy and Environment, but their conferences tended to be held at expensive hotels, way out of the financial reach of many, especially academics, unless one was an invited speaker. We therefore decided that UKELA's annual conference would always be held in a university, where accommodation costs were much cheaper, if not very luxurious. The tradition continues today: the 2019 conference was held at Sheffield University. Since the 1980s, universities have improved their facilities but have also increased their charges; in response, UKELA has introduced various discount schemes allowing student and younger members to attend the annual meetings.

1987 had been designated European Year of the Environment and I concluded my opening address at the London Zoo conference by saying that, 'It could not be a more fitting time for the launch of this Association. My hope is that we can make it the Year of Environmental Law as well.' We were indeed able to make some significant inputs in that year, all designed at raising the profile of environmental law in this country as a serious and distinctive field of law. Sponsorship from a legal publisher allowed us to launch a prestige annual environmental law lecture, named after one of the pioneers of environmental law in this country, Jack Garner. Lord Nathan was a partner in a leading city law firm and a member of the Royal Commission on Environmental Pollution and had shown great interest in the subject of environmental law. He had been persuaded to become UKELA's first president and gave the first Garner lecture. The Garner lecture continues today and has given a platform to distinguished individuals to air their thoughts on issues of environmental law. Former speakers have included Ludwig Kramer from the European Commission, Lord Woolf when he was Lord Chief Justice and, more recently, in 2017, Advocate General Kokott from the European Court of Justice.[4] When the Chairman of ICI agreed to give one of the early lectures, I reckoned that UKELA was really beginning to make a mark in the wider world. Another important event held in the first year was concerned with the meaning of environmental law. While the core elements of what constitutes environmental law are reasonably clear, it has never been easy to define precise boundaries and probably never will be. At the Institute for Contemporary Arts (where the Lawyers' Ecology Group had held its first conference so many years before) we organised a deliberately provocative debate between two leading academics as to whether there really was such a subject as environmental law. Professor Patrick McCauslan from the LSE argued that while there were many laws concerning the environment, this did not amount a coherent field of law in its own right. Professor David Williams from Cambridge responded that there were now emerging underlying principles, such as public participation and the precautionary principle, which did bring a sense of a distinctive field of law. In truth, both could have argued each's other case and the purpose was to tease out important perspectives rather than come to a definitive conclusion. Such a debate had not been held in this country before, but we were so caught up in the intellectual excitement of the occasion that, sadly, we overlooked keeping a record of the discussion.

Before the days of the internet, it was a challenge to keep up with new developments in environmental law or even locate records of important decisions of the courts. There were then no specialised environmental law reports and UKELA launched a quarterly bulletin on environmental law for its members to help fill the information gap. The printing quality of the early bulletins might now look a little basic and, today, UKELA produces a far more sophisticated electronic version. But these early records provide an evocative of record of the concerns at the time – articles in the first four bulletins include subjects such as marine conservation, nuclear liability, the enforcement of European environmental law by the European Commission and access to environmental information. I took particular satisfaction in persuading the senior lawyer for Severn Trent Water and the in-house lawyer for the Anglers' Cooperative Association[5] to write a joint article on problems with the current state of water legislation. Although they had been on opposing sides in litigation concerning water pollution, both of them, being good lawyers, could agree on deficiencies in the law and ways of improving its effectiveness from a legal perspective. To me, it epitomised the best of what UKELA could achieve.

---

[4] There are currently 11 Advocate Generals in the European Court of Justice. Their main role is to provide opinions on cases before the Court and, while opinions are not binding, they are extremely influential and followed in around 70 per cent of cases. Advocate General Kokott has been especially influential in the environmental field.

[5] The Anglers' Cooperative Association was formed in 1948 to protect fish from pollution and initiated many leading civil actions against polluters. In 2009, it merged with a number of other fishing associations and now operates under the name of Fish Legal.

By 1990, UKELA had grown considerably, with membership approaching almost 1,000 and regional groups and working parties on particular subjects such as waste and nature conservation were being established. At the same time, the House of Commons select committee on the environment was beginning to have a substantial input on policy development. I had noticed the extent to which witnesses to their inquiries were dominated by partisan groups, be they industry organisations, environmental groups or government representatives who were normally very defensive in the face of criticism. The issues being investigated often raised difficult issues of law, but the committee received little in the way of detached and authoritative legal evidence. One of my ambitions was that UKELA would fill that gap and that has indeed proved to be the case. Increasingly, it was invited to give evidence to the Commons select committee, as well as House of Lords committees dealing with European Union environmental legislation, and UKELA's analysis, often based on experience of how the law was actually working in practice, was well received. Government, too, began to consult the association on a regular basis and, today, it continues to play an important role in policy development. UKELA's ability to provide impartial and informed legal analysis on environmental law has recently been especially significant in helping to shape the debate on the implications of Brexit on environmental law.[6]

An important internal dispute emerged a few years after UKELA came into being. Originally UKELA's constitution had allowed for two types of membership – full membership, which included voting rights, was confined to those with legal qualifications, while associate membership was available to non-lawyers such as planners or environmental scientists and, indeed, anyone who was interested in the subject. I had deliberately pressed for the distinction because I felt at the time UKELA's impact would be the greatest if it was seen as primarily an association with legal expertise rather than one composed of anyone with an interest in environmental law. However, a few years later, the non-lawyers fought back, led by a planning specialist Wendy Le-las and Christine Hill, then the Company Secretary of UKELA. It was an argument fought with some passion. I still was wary of UKELA's distinctive legal profile becoming diluted, although at the time the ratio of lawyers to non-lawyers was about six to one. But, as Wendy argued in one of her letters to my successor as chair, Andrew Bryce, the logic of those who argued against non-lawyers having full enfranchisement within the organisation was that they should be disbarred from high office or taking part in working parties. If that were to happen, 'the non-lawyers might be better off: it would end the indignity of having no say in the Association and, as second-class citizens, they might even have a reduced membership fee'. In the event I was on the wrong side of the argument and the legal members voted to amend the rules to remove the distinction between full and associate members. My fears about dissipation

---

[6] See ch 13.

did not come about and UKELA still maintains a reputation for its legal expertise and experience.

Wendy le-Las and Christina Hill still regularly attend UKELA meetings. Looking at early attendee lists of the annual conferences provides a fascinating perspective on the development of environmental law in this country. Over 100 people attended the 1991 conference and although some of the delegates, such as Jack Garner, Lord Flowers and Lord Nathan, have since sadly died, many such as Richard Buxton and John Bates are still familiar names practising in environmental law. Some younger attendees at that early conference have clearly progressed. Jane Holder, attending as a student, is now Professor of Law at University College London. Farhana Yamin attended as a trainee solicitor, later developed international expertise in climate law and, in 2019, attracted considerable media attention by aligning herself to direct action of civil disobedience organised by the Extinction Rebellion protest campaigns. Apart from some of the familiar names in the list, the other striking aspect of the 1991 list of attendees was the range of professional profiles. Practitioners from law firms predominated, but there were just three barristers. However, there were also lawyers working in industry such as ICI and British Gas as well as local authority lawyers. It is a very different mix today. There are still many practising solicitors but almost as many barristers. Sadly, local authorities, despite being responsible for many areas of environmental law, no longer seem to have the resources to send legal staff, though they have been replaced by a large contingent of lawyers from the Environment Agency which did not exist in 1991. In-house company lawyers no longer attend; the reason for this decline is more difficult to fathom and is a trend I would like to see reversed.

From its early beginnings, UKELA has been at the heart of reflecting the development of environmental law as a distinct and vibrant field. Two examples, one from 1990 and one from 2019 epitomise this change. Robert Carnwath, now a Supreme Court judge and Honorary President of UKELA, gave the 1990 Garner Lecture when he was a leading QC. He had started practice in the 1970s and noted that he and his colleagues were then content to call themselves planning lawyers. Later, with the growth of judicial review, some styled themselves administrative lawyers. In the 1980s, with the growth of litigation concerning local government finance, he said it became fashionable to call oneself a local government lawyer. But he concluded: 'In the nineties, however, the mood is changing and I for one will be proud to carry the banner of environmental lawyer.' His words proved personally prophetic and, in his various subsequent roles as a senior judge, chair of the Law Commission, and Senior President of Tribunals, Lord Carnwath has been one of the influential figures in the development of environmental law in this country over the past 30 years. The other and more recent change concerned *Halsbury's Laws*. This is a multi-volume definitive statement of existing law, first published in 1907 and regularly updated. In the early years of twentieth century, the term 'environmental law' did not exist as such, though the first volumes covered areas such as nuisance law, public health and, intriguingly, a volume devoted to Electric Lighting And Power. The Victorian Public Health Law represented one of the bedrocks of environmental protection in this country and its influence was still reflected in the title of the 2010 *Halsbury's* Volume, 'Environmental Quality and Public Health'. In 2019, however, a new edition was published and now, at last, was entitled 'Environmental Law'. I had been invited to be consulting editor to this volume and instinctively pressed for the change which, it seemed to me, would represent a significant, albeit rather belated, coming of age of the subject. Areas covered in the new *Halsbury's* include climate change law, environmental principles, environmental permitting, contaminated land, public participation, business management and the environment, and environmental civil sanctions. They truly reflect the breadth and importance of contemporary environmental law as well as the sheer amount of law that now exists – the two volumes extend to over 1,300 pages. Future editions will no doubt deal with significant new legal developments, but the notion of both environmental law and environmental lawyers seems now to be fully embedded in our legal system.

4

Environmental Law as an
Academic Discipline

Early Sparks

Shortly before I left Friends of the Earth in 1978, an academic from Imperial College in London, Gordon Conway, telephoned to say he wanted to discuss an idea with me and we duly met in one of the dingy meeting rooms in the basement of 9 Poland Street. I knew little of Imperial College and had had even less contact with academic scientists, let alone a Reader in Biology. Equally, I suspect this was the first time Gordon had encountered an environmental lawyer from an environmental group. He explained that Imperial College was planning to set up an environmental centre which would run a new one-year Master's on the environment, the first of its type in the country. The idea had the strong backing of the then Rector, Lord Flowers, a distinguished nuclear physicist who had recently been chairman of the Royal Commission on Environmental Pollution.[1] The experience of chairing the Commission had clearly brought home to him the importance of understanding the intricacies of governmental arrangements and the legal system for securing effective environmental policy. He felt strongly that scientists generally had little understanding of how law and policy worked and should be far more attuned to these aspects if they were to play a more effective role in society. Although the new MSc at Imperial would have a strong environmental science basis, it would also include courses on environmental law and governance as a key element.

Imperial College had no law school and Gordon said that he had approached some of the London University law schools for assistance. But at that time, while they ran courses on planning law, there was little in the way of environmental law being taught and they could not help. The then Department of the Environment had provided Imperial College with core funding for the new centre and

---

[1] The Royal Commission on Environmental Pollution had been established in 1971 as a permanent independent advisory body on environmental matters. Its chair had always been a leading scientist, but membership included other disciplines such as economics and law. It was closed in 2011. The 29 Reports produced over its lifetime have had considerable influence on the development of environmental policy and law in this country. See further ch 9.

they came up with my name as a possibility – my legal work at Friends of the Earth had clearly had some impact. Gordon invited me to contribute a short course on environmental law as a visiting lecturer. I had never taught at university level before, but it was an exciting idea, the fee would be a useful supplement to a meagre income and it was a challenge that I readily accepted.

The MSc in Environmental Technology was launched in 1978, with under 30 students. At the time, the concept of most MSc courses was to provide a specialist training following a university degree. The Imperial College course was quite different. Ideally, students would have a first degree in a solid science subject, but the MSc course was designed to broaden their horizons, exposing them to other disciplines important to environmental decision making. The innovative nature of the course meant that, despite the backing of the Rector, it had not been an easy process to secure approval from the more conservative members of academic committees within Imperial, with one engineering professor describing the proposals as a 'pap course for pap people'. The structure of the MSc was based on a first-term common course, including environmental law, which all students took. In the second term, they would take a specialist option such as water or energy and the final term was devoted to a lengthy research thesis. This basic structure was remarkably robust and has stood the test of time. It still forms the basis of the current Imperial College MSc course and has been followed by universities in many other parts of the world.

My initial role was to teach a 20-hour course during the first core term as a visiting lecturer. I explained at the start that my main purpose was not to turn the students into lawyers but to give them a better understanding how the law works and how lawyers think. At that stage, they had little understanding of the basic building blocks of a legal system such as distinctions between criminal and civil law, statutes and regulations and the fundamentals of European and international law and how they fitted into our national system. However, they were very bright students who quickly assimilated these core elements and we could move on the more substantive environmental law. Most of them were far more numerate and scientifically literate than I was and I learned much from them. They, in turn, began to appreciate the fundamental importance of language to the lawyer. Reading a piece of legislation, a lawyer's first instinct is to check whether it contains the terms such as 'must' or 'may'. The distinction is vital since the first implies a legal obligation to do something, while the latter is simply a discretionary power. These linguistic subtleties were all new to the students; they quickly became engaged and would sometimes ask highly pertinent and practical questions about legislation which I had never thought about. One example occurred during a lecture on town and country planning law and the Use Classes Order. This allowed a business to change its existing use to another listed within defined classes without the need for new planning permission. One class grouped especially unpleasant operations such as maggot breeding and included 'a cat's meat shop'. One of the students then asked what exactly was a cat's meat shop – he had never seen one – and why was a dog's meat shop not included? I had no answer and duly wrote to the Department of the Environment. The reply was that this category did indeed appear to be an anomaly; it must have come from old Victorian public health legislation and they would change the terminology under the next revision of the Use Classes Order. The current Order still retains a rather esoteric list of businesses under Special Industrial Group E including 'Boiling blood, chitterlings, nettlings or soap' and 'dressing or scraping fish skins' but the term 'cat's meat shop' has, perhaps sadly, now disappeared from the legislation. The students were naturally delighted to have brought about this change in the law, even if one, perhaps, of not the greatest environmental significance.

The experience of graduate teaching and working in a research environment was immensely rewarding and I was already having doubts as to whether full-time practice at the bar was for me. At this time, there appeared to be few openings for environmental lawyers in British universities and I asked Gordon Conway whether he knew of any opportunities in the United States where there was already a well-established community of environmental law academics. His reply was that my contribution to the Centre had been well received and it was possible that he could obtain funding for a two-year full-time appointment. He made it clear that this was not a probationary appointment and there could be no guarantee of any extension beyond the fixed term. A decision had to be made and I discussed the pro and cons with my wife. I was now doing my pupillage training as a barrister, a career at the bar could be intellectually stimulating and might eventually lead to becoming a QC or even a judicial appointment. But it would be tough going in the early years and more difficult to control one's life and hours – during the second half of pupillage I was already getting briefs at 6pm to prepare for a magistrate's court hearing the next morning. An academic career would bring fewer financial rewards and the fixed-term appointment at Imperial was still something of gamble. But it could provide far more creative opportunities to help shape the future development of environmental law and we both agreed that academia was the preferable option. It is a decision I have never regretted.

I was duly appointed to the two-year post. This allowed me to develop further teaching on the option courses but also brought me into closer contact with the College's research activities. Most of the academics teaching on the Master's course were based in other mainstream departments such as Engineering or Biology but had a particular interest in pushing the boundaries of their own discipline and were attracted to the Centre's intellectual ethos. The Centre itself had its own core research programme, funded by the Department of the Environment, exploring the dynamics of ecological systems, how they behaved under pressure and whether there were robust principles which could predict resilience, collapse or recovery. It became apparent to me that this area of research could have important implications on how one designed legal systems to protect the environment. One researcher, for example, was using data from bird surveys to determine whether a bird population would survive in a woodland that was reduced, say, by 25%, but would collapse if there was a 30% reduction. Based on theories of island biography,[2] one could immediately see how the insights and predictions of tipping points could be of immense practical importance to planners and other decision makers – for example, a proposal to cut down woods to build 20 homes might still allow its bird population to flourish, but an increase to 30 could destroy it.

The weekly meetings where the researchers, many from different disciplines, would meet were immensely stimulating. Gordon Conway was anxious to promote a truly interdisciplinary approach as opposed to one that was multi-disciplinary. The distinction was important but often overlooked and dictionary definitions still sometimes define the terms in the same way. Multi-disciplinarity essentially involves bringing the inputs of different disciplines to analyse particular issue, but with each discipline remaining, as it were, within its own black box. In contrast, a truly interdisciplinary approach means exposing the nature of one's own discipline so that it might change and be affected by insights from others. This is not easy to achieve. One technique we tried at Imperial College was to prepare a paper and then have someone from another discipline read it and summarise what they thought were the key points to the rest of the group. This often provided real insights into how an expert from a different discipline could process the information one had written in a quite unexpected way. Another approach that Gordon introduced was to ask each of us to describe a book or article in our own discipline which had proved especially inspiring and the reasons for its impact. I chose Michael Atiyah's *Accidents Compensation and the Law*.[3] This had been published during my second year as an undergraduate studying law at Oxford, when we had already studied in detail the principles of the law of torts dealing with private claims for damages. But we had been taught solely from a purely legal perspective. Atiyah's book, for the first time, put the whole subject in a much broader context by arguing that as a mechanism designed to provide compensation for those who have suffered harm, the law was inefficient and unfair and should be replaced by a statutory compensation scheme along the lines recently introduced in New Zealand. Aside from its penetrating analysis of case law developed by the courts, the book included references to insurance practice, government reports and social science in a way that was utterly different from any standard legal textbook I had read to date. It forced the reader to evaluate critically the purpose of existing legal structures and whether there might be other more effective ways of achieving its goals.

I was still the only legal academic at Imperial and needed to make my mark if there was to be any chance of an extension to my initial two-year contract.

---

[2] First developed some years before by Robert MacArthur and Edward Wilson in their seminal book, *The Theory of Island Biography* (Princeton, Princeton University Press, 1967). The theory examines factors that influence the population and diversity of species within largely insulated areas such as islands, forests, protected habitats and mountains.

[3] P Atiyah, *Accidents Compensation and the Law* (London, Weidenfeld and Nicolson, 1970).

There was little time to establish significant legal research so, in 1981, I decided to organise a conference of a type that Imperial College had never seen before – one that would bring together leading scientists, lawyers, civil servants, industry and the environmental group community. The conference was entitled 'Commercial Nuclear Power – Legal and Constitutional Issues'. The experience of the 1978 Windscale Public Inquiry into nuclear reprocessing was still fresh in the minds of many and a public inquiry into Britain's first pressurised water reactor at Sizewell had been announced in 1981 and was expected to commence at the end of the year. As Lord Flowers said in his opening address to the conference, 'The fact is that there comes a time in the development of any new technological enterprise when its acceptability by the public at large may be its dominating feature ... the development of nuclear power has raised acute conflicts in society, the resolution of which seems to me to require a parallel development of the legal and constitutional framework and of the practice of open government'.

There were many legal issues relating to nuclear power that could have been discussed but the focus of the conference turned on the public inquiry system. How, within a sophisticated democracy, could one develop frameworks for decision making where major and complex developments were involved, which allowed issues to be thoroughly examined within a reasonable timeframe and in a way that was considered fair by the general public? As such, the issues being explored went well beyond nuclear power and were relevant to any large-scale energy development or other developments such as airports or motorway schemes.

Jeffrey Jowell, Professor of Public Law at University College, began by quoting Lord Atkin's dictum that efficiency and justice were not always on speaking terms.[4] He noted the tensions between the objectives of a liberal goal to hold decision makers to account and those of management, seeking to achieve efficiency and effective implementation of its goals. The public inquiry, developed in the nineteenth century, provided a mechanism for straddling both objectives – allowing genuine public participation but improving the quality of managerial decision making – but he considered a lack of clarity about their real purpose often brought its own problems. Robin Grove-White, then director of the Council for the Protection of Rural England, provided a more sanguine and critical analysis of the political context of these inquiries, arguing that the reality was that there was already a government and industry committed towards the rapid development of nuclear power. He pointed to the recent emergence of a new range of independent and sophisticated research groups that were challenging the current orthodoxy of energy policy, but were largely disenfranchised within the official policy-making community. In that context, he concluded there was a growing danger that there would be a collapse in public confidence in the public inquiry and that 'it is increasingly difficult to square the official assurances given to manufactures in

---

[4] Lord Atkin (1867–1944) was one of the most influential British judges in the early twentieth century.

the nuclear field over the past 18 months and more with public expectations that public inquiries will be genuinely open'.

The star legal speakers were Sir Roger Parker who had chaired the Windscale Inquiry and Raymond Kidwell QC who had represented Friends of the Earth. It was somewhat of a coup to have persuaded Sir Roger to participate as, apparently, he had told Lord Flowers after the Windscale inquiry that he would never speak publicly on the subject. But for some reason he was persuaded by my letter of invitation to make an exception for this conference. Sir Roger noted that it was vital to understand what sort of public inquiry was involved – whether it was strictly a planning inquiry concerning local planning issues, a specific inquiry into the principle of some new technology or, as in the case of Windscale, what was nominally and in strict legal terms a site-specific local planning inquiry but, as he said, 'was clearly nothing of the sort'. He argued that government needed to be realistic about the timescales involved and should be honest about the terms of reference which he felt should be as wide as possible. Sometimes it may be acceptable that a decision on principle is taken in advance, but this must be made plain otherwise, he felt, it was unfair to all those taking part: 'What must not be allowed to happen is that they should be under the belief that they are taking part in a process of determining whether the project should go ahead at all when that is not a matter which is any longer in the field of controversy.' Raymond Kidwell, QC, who had represented Friends of the Earth at the Windscale Inquiry, provided a powerful analysis of the role of the lawyer and the power of cross-examination in a major inquiry. He felt the Windscale Inquiry had been set up far too late 'when a government was about as heavily committed as it could be to be the relevant policy. There were Japanese fountain pens full and poised waiting to sign a contract to which the government was virtually committed' and the time pressures on objectors with inadequate information had been intolerable. He urged that, in future, consideration should be given to appointing a counsel to the inquiry, not necessarily to replace the role of well-informed objectors but to provide neutral assistance.

Several significant themes emerged during the conference which are still of importance today. The provisions of the 1998 Aarhus Convention concerning access to environmental justice[5] have, over the last decade, posed significant challenges to the standard costs principles for judicial review. But the focus of the debates on Aarhus has been with court procedures rather than public inquiries. At Windscale, all objectors had to raise their own costs if they wished to have legal representation and, while planning inquiry rules allow for the award of costs after the event, these are largely confined where they have been incurred because one party has acted unreasonably. Here we were talking of providing funding for objectors before the inquiry to ensure the fullest representation. At the time of the conference there had been some recent experiments in Canada providing

---

[5] The Convention provides that members of the public must have access to administrative or legal remedies to challenge breaches of national environmental law by private or public bodies and these procedures must be 'fair, equitable, timely and not prohibitively expensive' (Art 9.4). See further ch 10.

government funding for objectors at nuclear-related inquiries. Sir Roger Parker observed: 'I am not saying that Government should always fund the opposition. That may be wholly unnecessary but what they should, I think, do is to ensure that, if an effective opposition can only be produced if it is funded, then funded it will be.' A consensus emerged during the day that government should take an initiative on the subject but, in the event, no progress was made. All the parties at the subsequent Sizewell nuclear inquiry which was even longer than the Windscale inquiry had to pay their own costs and it remains the case today that there is no public funding for objectors at planning inquiries.

Shortly before the conference, a new model for major inquiries had been proposed by an independent think-tank, the Outer Circle Policy Unit. Its idea was a two-stage inquiry with the first stage to examine the broader policy issues and largely be explored by a panel, with cross-examination reduced to a minimum. This would be then followed by a second and more conventional site-specific inquiry that was focused on the actual development proposed. This had a superficial logic, but the reality for those who had been involved in significant inquiries was that often it was only by exploring in detail the specifics of a project that one could begin to properly understand and critique higher policy issues. Certainly, both Sir Roger Parker and Raymond Kidwell were highly sceptical of the two-stage inquiry proposal.

Two years before the conference, the highest court in the country, the Judicial Committee of the House of Lords, had decided the case of *Bushell v Secretary of State*.[6] An inspector at a public inquiry into a proposed motorway had refused Bushell the right to cross-examine government witnesses on their methodology for predicting traffic growth. As described in Chapter 1, I had met Mr Bushell when I was the staff lawyer for Friends of the Earth and advised him not to take the case. The ambiguities in the current rules could be exploited by environmental organisations and the danger of litigation was that a court would have to come down with a black-and-white decision on the issue. Indeed, that is precisely what happened. In the lead judgment, Lord Diplock held that it was acceptable that government policy should be excluded from the ambit of an inquiry concerned with a single stretch of motorway. The detailed traffic forecasting methodology could not be described as policy as such, but fell within a grey area so closely connected to policy that it was fair that cross-examination on the issue was excluded. The implications of the *Bushell* decision featured heavily during the Imperial College conference, with Jeffrey Jowell feeling that the decision narrowed the role of the public inquiry to preclude a full examination of policy. Raymond Kidwell, though, argued that while the decision had caused grave concern it could be confined to its particular set of facts and should not affect the nature of larger inquiries such as Windscale where government had deliberately drawn expansive terms of reference of the issues for examination.

---

[6] [1981] AC 75.

On its narrowest interpretation, *Bushell* was concerned with rights of cross-examination and it was clear that Lord Diplock has set in motion arguments concerning its value. As he noted, 'It would, in my view, be quite fallacious to suppose that at an inquiry of this kind the only fair way of ascertaining matters of fact and expert opinion is by the oral testimony of witnesses who are subjected to cross-examination on behalf of parties who disagree with what they have said. Such procedure is peculiar to litigation conducted in courts that follow the common law system of procedure; it plays no part in the procedure of courts of justice under legal systems based upon the civil law, including the majority of our fellow member states of the European Communities'. At our conference Roger Parker strongly defended the power of cross-examination: 'It is a process which is very unpleasant if you are at the wrong end of it but it is exceedingly efficient at getting to the real guts of the problem.'

Yet 30 years later, the idea of major public inquiries and the extensive cross-examination of witnesses being used to explore and inform the development of policy for major infrastructure planning and new technology has all but been squeezed out of the system. The Windscale public inquiry lasted 100 days, at the time the longest of its sort. But subsequent major inquiries such as the Sizewell inquiry and the Heathrow public inquiry lasted much longer. It is arguable how far this was really due to poorly designed terms of reference, or over-indulgent management by the Inspector in charge of the inquiry, but it was the panoply of lawyers representing objectors and engaged in detailed extensive cross-examination that appear to have taken the major blame. Rights of cross-examination still exist at local inquiries concerning planning appeals for development proposals, though the vast majority are now decided by written representation. Public inquiries concerning Local Plans, though, no longer employ the adversarial system and, as the planning inspectorate's current procedural guidance notes, 'hearing sessions will be inquisitorial, with the Inspector probing the issues as opposed to an adversarial approach'. An Inspector may allow cross-examination of witnesses but 'this will only happen in very exceptional instances where the Inspector is convinced that a formal approach is essential for adequate testing of the evidence'. The Planning Act 2008 introduced new procedures designed to speed up decision making for projects deemed to be of national significance such as power stations, airports, or highways. The relevant procedural rules provide that those in charge of the hearings – the examination authority – shall identify the matters to be considered and will be responsible for the oral questioning of those giving evidence unless they feel that questioning by others is necessary to test a representation or ensure a fair chance of presenting a case. National Policy Statements are now issued by government in relation to classes of infrastructure project and section 87 of the 2008 Act provides that the Examining Authority may disregard representations which relate to the merits of policy set out in such statements. It is true that there are consultation requirements for draft policy statements and they must be laid before parliament, and parliamentary select committees now take a greater interest in scrutinising such statements. But Jeffrey Jowell's concept of managerial efficiency has come to dominate procedures and the papers from the Imperial College conference now almost read as from a different age and a different vision of the notion of a participatory democratic society.

My own contribution to the proceedings was a detailed and fairly learned examination of the legal procedures concerning nuclear power stations which, now seems rather too legalistic. But I was young and trying to establish my credentials as a legal academic and I delivered a carefully written paper which was later published in a law journal. But the experience revealed the extraordinary powers of the brain under stress. The procedures for nuclear power stations were then, rather surprisingly, governed by provisions of the Electric Lighting Act 1909. But, I noted, this was not as bizarre as it might first appear, because the early twentieth century had seen a massive amount of legislation dealing with the then new technology of electricity. I concluded my presentation with a lengthy quote from Lord Hershall in Parliament in 1888 pressing the case for new laws – in colourful language he had noted, 'in the South Seas island the electric light is more used than in London'. Standing at the lectern, I turned to the last page and to my horror it simply was not there. My mind began to race as I wondered where it was (it turned out, as often happens, I had left it in a photocopier) thinking this was the end of my brief academic career and wondering whether to just walk off in disgrace. Somehow the brain reactivated; I was able to complete, from memory, the full quotation from Lord Hershell. It had seemed at least a 30-second pause to me, but one of my students later told me he was not aware of any gap in my presentation. I had, in fact, been experiencing what brain research has later termed as the 'oddball effect' where a stressful situation can create an internal, slowed-down perception of time that is quite different from the external reality.[7]

The conference raised the profile of the Centre for Environmental Technology on the wider policy and public stage and no doubt helped to secure my appointment as a full-time lecturer in environmental law at Imperial College later in the year. The then European Economic Community had initiated an environmental programme in 1973 and emerging Community legislation was beginning to impact on the UK. I found my developing research was increasingly drawn into this area of law. A particular issue of controversy at the time was the European Commission's proposal for a directive on environmental assessment. The UK government was not against the concept of environmental assessment as such and forms of assessment were already being employed in the planning system where significant developments were being proposed. British Gas, for example, were cooperating with planners in Cheshire County Council in using environmental assessment techniques in relation to new gas field proposals. But it was very case-specific and largely conducted by agreements between developers and planners to ensure the best environmental outcomes. What alarmed the British government was the

---

[7] See, for example, P Tse, J Intriligator, J Rivest and P Cavanagh, 'Attention and the Subjective Expansion of Time' (2004) 66(7) *Perception & Psychophysics* 1171–89 (October).

European Commission's proposal to put environmental assessment requirements into hard law. It went against a prevailing British philosophy that one could not determine in advance those classes of project requiring assessment procedures since the location and context was all important in determining potential environmental impacts. The spectre of the enormous amount of litigation concerning environmental impact statements in the United States loomed large in the background. At the time, unanimous voting by all Member States was required to agree an environmental directive[8] and, for many years, the UK resisted giving its consent.

The initial proposals and drafts for the directive had, in fact, been prepared for the European Commission by two British academics, Norman Lee and Chris Wood of Manchester University who were well aware of the nuances of the British planning system. Their first proposal in 1976 contained no specified list of projects but provided that whether a proposal required assessment would be determined by guidelines. A very British approach, but one that was considered too flexible and imprecise by the European Commission who preferred the more explicit listing approach of mandatory and discretionary projects advocated by the US Batelle Institute. Succeeding drafts of the directive were being regularly leaked and, in 1979, the Department of the Environment asked the Centre's research team to examine Draft number 18. The Centre's environmental scientists recognised that there was a potential internal illogicality in having a discretionary list that provided that projects falling within it and which were likely to have a significant effect would require environmental assessment. But how could one judge whether a project was likely to have such effects without first conducting an assessment? They rejected the mandatory/discretionary listing approach and proposed a more methodical screening approach based on ecological principles which would apply to all projects – probably more logical from an environmental perspective, but one which did not meet the prevailing politics.

The British government continued to resist the proposals and industry, in particular, was concerned that the directive would give rise to a massive amount of litigation. A conference was organised at the Royal Geographical Society in 1982 to examine the Commission's latest draft and I gave a paper challenging the view that we would see litigation on the scale seen in the United States concerning environmental impact statements. I explained that the short section in the key US legislation on environmental impact statements[9] was incredibly open-textured, requiring the judiciary, through subsequent case law, to interpret almost every word that had been used in the provision. In contrast, the European proposal had

---

[8] The environmental assessment directive was based on the common market provisions of the Treaty and it was not until 1987 that the Treaty was amended to allow such measures to be agreed by qualified majority voting by Member States. Legislation based on the specific environmental provisions of the Treaty introduced in 1987 still had to be agreed unanimously until the Treaty was amended again in 1992 allowing most environmental measures to be agreed by qualified majority voting.

[9] National Environmental Policy Act 1969, s 102(C) requiring an environmental impact statement for 'major Federal actions significantly affecting the quality of the human environment'.

deliberately confined itself to projects (though with a promise that environmental assessment of plans and policies would come later) and these were expressly listed in the draft of the proposed directive. I argued that while there would inevitably be some litigation, it would be on a much smaller scale and British judges, applying normal principles of judicial review, would be far less intrusive than their US counterparts. There were then few independent academic lawyers providing such a perspective on the issue and I was told later that my contribution had some effect on assuaging fears within both industry and government. The UK dropped its objection to the proposal and, three years later, the directive was agreed by all Member States. I now rather blush at my optimistic predictions since the directive has, in practice, given rise to an enormous amount of litigation in this country – though still nowhere near the scale of that in the US. And it has taken the UK courts some years to try to put a break on legal challenges, with senior judges emphasising that environmental assessment should be seen as an aid to decision making rather than a legal obstacle course and stressing that judgments as to significant effects were a matter for planning authorities rather than the judiciary.

Despite the use of explicit listings, some of the terminology of the project classes still remains somewhat unclear. Some ten years later, when I was working for the European Commission, I was wrestling with the meaning of one of the discretionary classes, 'land reclamation for the purposes of conversion to another type of land-use'. It was a concept that did not seem to resonate in this country. All the language versions of a directive have equal legal force and it is sometimes helpful to look at the text in different languages to see if that assists in understanding what is meant. The French and the German versions did not help, so I turned to the Spanish text. To my surprise, there was no mention of land reclamation, but in its place the phrase, 'roturaciones que permitan la conversión con vistas a otro tipo de exportación del melon' (ploughing up that allows conversion with a view to another type of melon export). I informed Commission officials who seemed remarkably untroubled at what must have been the work of a translator having a very bad day and the Spanish version was later corrected. But I still was rather astonished that such an error could remain in the law unnoticed for over ten years and wondered how many Spanish melon exporters had been innocently subjecting their projects to environmental assessment, while their competitors in other Member States had no such worries.

The European directive may have been inspired by the US legislation but while this was focused on a written environmental impact statement, the underlying approach in the directive was that environmental assessment was a process of decision making requiring the provision of environmental information and consultation with relevant authorities and the public. Even the term 'environmental impact statement' never appeared in the directive. The final version of the proposed directive, published in 1982, was deliberately non-prescriptive as to methods of public consultation, simply providing that the competent authority shall decide the best means for 'giving information to the public within a suitable time limit and for ascertaining the views of the public'.

Nigel Haigh, then director of the Institute of European Environmental Policy, proposed a research project that would compare public consultation procedures that already existed within Member States and which would probably be used for implementing the directive. As he noted in the introduction to the final report of the study: 'It seemed all too possible that people might come to believe that different countries were doing something similar merely because on paper the procedures looked similar, while in practice they were doing things really rather differently.' He felt that a national expert might write coherently about their own system but could all too easily miss important features that would seem distinctive from another country's perspective. He had the imaginative idea that more revealing results would be gained from sending an expert from one country to experience the system of public consultation in another country and vice versa. To keep the project without bounds, just two countries were chosen – the UK and France – where similar-sounding procedures, the public inquiry and the enquête publique, both conducted by independent government inspectors, were often used in planning projects.

Nigel commissioned me and a French expert to carry out the study, my first significant research project at Imperial College. I was duly sent to experience at first hand an enquête publique into a proposed housing development on the south coast of France. It was totally different from any British planning inquiry I had attended and essentially provided an opportunity for members of the public sitting round a table to write down their comments in an official book presided over by a rather bored inspector. There was no oral evidence or questioning. One of the objectors was trying to write down the names of those who had already made written comments, the Inspector said this was not allowed and the meeting became very heated with everyone shouting over each other. The proposed development was for new houses in a coastal resort town and some of the local residents argued that these would simply be holiday homes for foreigners. At that point, a young man sitting quietly in the corner said he was a representative of the developers and claimed the houses would only be for local people. This caused more anger and confusion and there was none of the careful questioning of a witness that I would have expected to tease out the true facts. Some months later, I saw an advertisement in the *Sunday Times* promoting the opportunity to buy holiday homes at the development concerned.

We arranged for my French counterpart to visit a small planning inquiry lasting a couple of days concerning a similarly sized housing development in Surrey. She found the British procedures as astonishing as I had done in France. Just before the inquiry opened, we met a quiet middle-aged man who was to give evidence on behalf of a local environmental group. He had done so before at a previous inquiry and explained he was deeply apprehensive about being exposed to the developer's cross-examination. The French researcher had no idea what he was talking about, but true to form, the developer's barrister, in the best style of a quiet but persistent series of questions, demolished the objector's arguments. My French researcher was outraged and at the end of day tackled the barrister asking him how he could have behaved in such a way – 'Just doing my job' was the reply.

The resulting report was well-received and at least established that the terms 'enquête publique' and 'public inquiry' should never, in future, be translated as the same without considerable qualification. Although we deliberately did not tackle the difficult question as to which system produced better planning decisions by whatever criteria one used, it was very revealing about different administrative cultures that exist within Europe. The French researcher was struck by how the British inquiry managed to combine both a degree of formality and informality with the Inspector displaying a dry sense of humour and in a way she felt would never happen in France where procedures were either very serious or very informal. And it would have been all too easy to be rather smug about the British system. I experienced another, though rather more orderly, enquête publique where the Inspector sat in an empty room for two days. Individual members of the public came in, quietly explained their concerns and the Inspector assisted with maps and plans to help his understanding of the issues they were raising. It had echoes of a confessional in a church. While I still advocate the power of cross-examination in complex cases of controversy, I wondered whether for an ordinary member of the public, unused to speaking or being questioned in public, this was not a better and more attractive procedure of engaging the public rather than having to appear at a standard British public inquiry.

I continued to develop research on various aspects of environmental law, including nuclear decommissioning, pollution control and environmental assessment. My full-time position also allowed me to develop specialised law courses on the various options, including energy, water and ecology, but this was quite challenging as there were no textbooks on these subjects. Again, it often led to stimulating discussion on legal issues with bright and engaged students largely from scientific backgrounds. My unusual position at Imperial College meant that I often found myself contributing papers on the law at non-legal conferences of environmental experts such as the National Society of Clean Air and the British Association for the Advancement of Science. But the challenges of accommodating the growing amount of EU environmental legislation within our domestic legal system became a particular focus of my research. In 1983, the Centre held a major conference to mark the tenth anniversary of the beginning of the European Community's programme on the environment. Once again, we were able to attract a range of high-level speakers including the Director General of the Environment in the European Commission, the Chief Scientist of the Department of the Environment and the then chair of the Royal Commission on Environmental Pollution. As a lawyer, I was especially pleased that Sir Gordon Slynn, then one of the Advocate Generals before the European Court, accepted the invitation to speak about the role of the European Court.

The audience was an equally impressive range of expertise and disciplines, including environmental scientists, academic and practising lawyers, local authority and government officials and representatives from the community of environmental groups. Even Lord Diplock, then a Law Lord, attended. He had recently raised concerns about the legality of European Community environmental legislation. At the time there were no explicit environmental provisions in the Treaty giving the power to make such laws and EU environmental legislation was being based either on single market provisions relating to trade or a reserve catch-all provision which, many argued, still required the laws to be related to economic aspects of the single market.[10] Lord Diplock had argued that whatever the public good in some directives such as bathing water or drinking water, it was legally dubious whether they could really have an impact on competition within the single market. He was probably correct, but as he pointed out at the conference, since all directives then had to be agreed unanimously by Member States, there was very little likelihood of anyone questioning their legality. Politics essentially had ousted the law and one would have to wait another four years before the European Treaty was amended to include specific sections on the environment. At the time, of course, no-one in the audience would have contemplated that, almost 30 years later, our national politics would be so dominated by Brexit. Yet many of the speakers were concerned to unpick prevailing myths about EU environmental law and policy – producing the lowest common denominator, requiring uniform emission standards, a top-down approach and so on – and their contributions remain as pertinent today. As Konrad Von Moltke, director of the Institute of European Environmental Policy, put it in his address to the conference: 'The European Community is frequently seen as a "foreign institution" which the countries of Europe have somehow become involved with. This is true not only of the United Kingdom but also of other countries. Ultimately, however, all national institutions are potentially European ones. Hence, European policy begins at home; it does not, however, end there.'

---

[10] The text of the reserve provision read: 'If action by the Community should prove necessary to attain, in the course of the operation of the common market, one of the objectives of the Community and this Treaty has not provided the necessary powers, the Council shall, acting unanimously on a proposal from the Commission and after consulting the European Parliament, take the appropriate measure' (Treaty Establishing the European Economic Community, Art 235).

5

Practising Environmental Law
as a Barrister

Most of our judges were vaccinated against the dangers of speculation by their
careers at the Bar

Alexander Roche (Law Lord 1935–1938)

I had qualified as a barrister immediately after reading law at university but
delayed the 12-month pupillage period until I left Friends of the Earth. In the
1970s, securing pupillage was far less organised than it is today and it was largely a
question of writing to individual chambers. Today, the process is far more rigorous
and transparent. I had worked with Raymond Kidwell QC during the Windscale
inquiry; he had appreciated my input and was happy to arrange pupillage with one
of the brightest of the younger barristers in his chambers, Michael Harvey. The Bar
was then a lot more formal than is now the case and it was something of a culture
shock coming from the far less inhibited atmosphere of environmental pressure
groups. I was advised, ever so politely, to shave off my beard which had almost
been de rigueur for the male staff at Friends of the Earth and, on the first day, when
I introduced myself to one of the barristers and offered to shake hands, I was told
in no uncertain terms that barristers never shook hands with each other. Environmentalism had still not entered the mainstream culture and, to many, Friends of
the Earth had the aura of a rather strange sect. Several times, during my pupillage,
barristers would come up to me saying, in rather patronising tones, 'I understand
you came from the Flat Earth society'.

But working with Michael Harvey was stimulating and intense and his practice,
mainly in the field of civil litigation, was taking off. I was amazed at the stamina he
showed and the relentless hours involved – appearing in court all day in a complex
case, a short tea break followed by a two-hour conference with clients on an
equally challenging matter and rounded off by further written opinion and pleadings work in the late evenings and at weekends. As a pupil I was involved in three
especially memorable cases in the courts, though only one was truly environmental. The first arose out of the collapse of the Emley Moor Transmitter tower during
high winds on 19 March 1969.[1] The mast was a new design and the case involved

[1] *Independent Broadcasting Authority v British Insulated Callender Cables* (1980) 14 BLR 1.

complex legal issues concerning contractual warranties and negligence. It eventually reached the House of Lords, but my only role was to take notes for Michael Harvey during several days of hearing in the Court of Appeal. I was intrigued that the QCs representing the opposing parties, David Kemp and Harvey McGregor, were the authors of the two leading legal textbooks on damages. They brought a wealth of knowledge and expertise to the subject and at times it felt like two eminent professors arguing with each other. In those days, apart from the basic written pleadings, all the arguments were conducted orally and there were no written skeleton arguments which are now an essential part of civil litigation.[2] David Kemp had been preparing to make some complex submissions on the legal principles of negligence and independent contractors and produced a one-page bullet point summary of his key points which he handed to the judges to assist them as they followed his argument. This was, in fact, probably the first written skeleton argument ever seen in the Court of Appeal and I can still recall vividly Lord Justice Roskill, a fairly intimidating judge of the old school, handling the piece of paper with some distaste and asking David Kemp what he was expected to do with it.

Lord Denning had been one of the most influential post-war judges and was still sitting in the Court of Appeal, though by now in his eighties. For a law student, Lord Denning's judgments were written in clear and compelling language and his readiness to ignore strict legal precedent in favour of his own sense of justice had always been especially attractive. But when dealing with practical legal issues, I began to appreciate that predictability in legal outcome was essential in some areas of law if commercial arrangements were to have any certainty. I remember a conference where Michael Harvey was advising one of the national car park companies. They were concerned with their potential liabilities should a car parked on their land be damaged or have goods stolen from it and we were asked to advise on the legal effectiveness of contractual clauses which would limit their liabilities with customers. Michael Harvey was able to say that on the existing state of the law the wording we suggested would be legally sound, but if the case came before Lord Denning the result would be totally unpredictable. This made things very difficult for practical commercial and insurance arrangements and the old adage that one Lord Denning is essential in a legal system but two would be disastrous began to make much more sense.

As a pupil, I saw Lord Denning in action in an important medical negligence case which is still quoted today.[3] There had been a difficult birth resulting in the baby being born paralysed and the doctor involved was sued for negligence. The hearing in the Court of Appeal gave rise to the bizarre sight of three elderly male judges trying to understand the difference between various forms of breech

---

[2] According to the current procedural rules: 'The purpose of a skeleton argument is to assist the court by setting out as concisely as practicable the arguments upon which a party intends to rely.'

[3] *Whitehouse v Jordan* [1980] I All ER 650.

birth and each took turns in manipulating a dummy baby in various positions through a plaster cast of a woman's hips. Lord Denning was clearly concerned to stem an excess of medical negligence claims in this country and, at the end of the first day, asked the barristers whether there was a distinction between professional negligence and a simple error of judgment where there should be no liability. He wanted us to come up the next day with appropriate tests for distinguishing the two and I was sent overnight to explore the issue. But it was not easy and there was no precise case law on the point. In the event, Lord Denning made a robust case for distinguishing a mistake from negligence. Starting his judgment in a typically eye-catching sentence, 'Being born is dangerous for the baby', he warned against the spectre of US medical malpractice litigation: 'We must say and say firmly, that, in a professional man, an error of judgment is not negligent. To test it, I would suggest that you ask the average competent and careful practitioner: "Is this the sort of mistake that you yourself might have made?" If he says: "Yes, even doing the best I could, it might have happened to me", then it is not negligent.'[4]

There was little in the way of environmental law then being practised by barristers at this time, with the exception of the specialised planning bar. But the third major case I was involved in as a pupil, *Budden v British Petroleum and others*,[5] was a distinctive and unusual example of environmental litigation at the time. The *Budden* case arose out of concerns about the effects of leaded petrol on children's health. For over 60 years, organic lead compounds had been added to petrol to improve its effectiveness but worries about the health implications of lead in vehicle emissions had begun in the later 1960s. In 1972, the UK government announced a British Standard, voluntarily agreed by industry, to slowly reduce the level of lead to 0.84 g/l. Further reductions were planned but then delayed by the 1973 oil crisis. Four years later, regulations were made under the Control of Pollution Act 1974 prescribing a statutory limit and, in 1978, an EEC Directive had been agreed setting an upper limit of 0.4 g/l.[6] The whole issue of lead in petrol had attracted intense media interest in the UK and there were many calls for the complete phase out of leaded petrol.

Political and legal progress at governmental and EU level seemed agonisingly slow. The parents of several very young children living in Paddington near the overhead motorway felt that the only way to speed up action and protect their children was to initiate their own litigation. Rather than attempt a judicial review against the government, they decided bring a civil claim in common law against

---

[4] The finding of no negligence was upheld in the House of Lords but mainly on an examination of the evidence. Lord Russell of Killowen, though, criticised Lord Denning for suggesting that an error of judgment could never give rise to negligence: 'I would accept the phrase "a mere error of judgment" if the impact of the word "mere" is to indicate that not all errors of judgment show a lapse from the standard of skill and care required to be exercised to avoid a charge of negligence.'

[5] (1980) 124 SJ 376.

[6] The Directive permitted Member States to set lower levels provided these did not go beyond 0.15 g/l, though, in practice, all countries stuck to the higher limit.

those industries they felt directly responsible for the damage. The claimants were the children but represented by their parents as 'next friends' while their chosen defendants were Octel, the company which supplied leaded petrol, two major manufacturers and retailers of leaded petrol, Shell and BP, and the Ford Motor Company whose cars made up a significant proportion of those driving on the motorway near them. Action was commenced in the Mayor's and City of London county court on 5 July 1978, but gradually worked its way to the Court of Appeal.

Michael Harvey was representing Shell. I had now left Friends of the Earth but remained a board member and although FOE was not running a campaign against lead in petrol at the time, I offered to withdraw from the case. But Shell was content for me to be involved though obviously I was under a duty of legal confidentiality and the FOE Board was also relaxed with my position. Initially, the case was based on nearly every type of civil claim one could imagine – trespass, private nuisance, public nuisance and negligence and the arguments involved examining a mass of case law from the last 100 years. It was a bizarre atmosphere in the lower court with the defendant companies all represented by senior QCs with supporting solicitors. In contrast, one family was represented by Patrick O'Connor, a young barrister with a radical reputation but wearing a formal dark suit. The next family was represented by my predecessor at Friends of the Earth, David Pedley, a solicitor immensely learned in the law but dressed in his customary white linen suit, with shoulder-length blonde hair and an earring in one ear. Finally, Nicholas Albery, the father of one of the claimants, appeared in person. He was bright and engaging and persuaded the court that he should be able to tape-record proceedings. Every so often, Albery would jump up and ask if he could change the batteries of the recorder and rearrange the microphone. His timing was always impeccable – just as a senior barrister for one of the defendants was starting a submission, he would then be thrown off his stride as adjustments to the recording equipment were made.

The defendants had applied to strike out the proceedings as disclosing no cause of action and an abuse of the process of the court. In striking out proceedings, detailed evidence is not considered; the court had to assume that the damage caused by lead in petrol would be proved if the case went to full trial. The question was whether, as a matter of law, there was a claim and proceedings were very much concerned with pure legal principles. Judges at that time were unimpressed if they felt their courts were being used for wider political goals. There was no social media then, but one of the defendant companies obtained a newsletter put out by supporters of the families where it was stated that the claimants did not really expect to win but they would have made a public point. The judge was furious at the thought of his court being used for a political campaign and said he would be minded to strike out the claim there and then, but as the actual claimants were the innocent children, he decided it would inappropriate to do so at this stage.

Much of the case really turned on concepts of responsibility for environmental harm. On the first day, the Ford Motor Company submitted that their current cars could, in fact, run on lead-free petrol without any engine modification and the court therefore excluded them as defendants. Ford helpfully added that, at the time, British Leyland cars could only run on leaded petrol, but the judge refused the claimants' request to add them as a defendant at such a late stage. Both sides accepted that if there was a problem with lead being emitted from motor vehicles, it related to built-up areas and the sort of dense levels of traffic seen on an urban motorway. Shell argued that, in those circumstances, even if damage could be proved neither the manufacturer nor the seller of the petrol should be held liable in law and that an analogy would be carbon monoxide poisoning in a tunnel under the Thames due to inadequate ventilation. Car-owners might have a legal claim against the highway authority responsible for the tunnel but not the car manufacturers – so here, Shell argued, if anyone was to be liable it should be the highway authorities who had permitted the dense traffic levels in urban areas. The families then applied to include the Greater London Council – the relevant highway authority – as a defendant but, again, the judge refused. The companies then argued that the action was akin to holding the manufacturer of a gun legally liable for injuries caused by the owner of the gun shooting someone at a later date. The families countered that the analogy was unsound as someone who bought a gun then had a choice as to how they used it while, in contrast, drivers of motor vehicles had no option but to purchase and use the leaded petrol that was sold by the manufacturers.

The case finally case reached the Court of Appeal some 12 months later; by then the causes of action had been whittled down to one of negligence. Once again, this still being a striking out action, the court had to assume that the claimants would be able to prove at full trial that that they had suffered some physical injury caused by the leaded petrol. The question, as the court put it, was whether at this stage it could be shown that the action had no chance of success. The critical issue turned on the fact that there were statutory limits on the amount of lead in petrol and that the defendants had, at all times, complied with these limits. In certain cases where a statute explicitly authorises an activity which causes harm, this can give rise to a defence of what is termed 'statutory authorisation'. The Court had doubts as to whether this defence could be raised in respect of the Control of Pollution Act limits and felt it would not appropriate to strike out on those grounds alone.

Nevertheless, compliance with the statutory limits still turned out be crucial to the outcome of the case. There was no suggestion that the Secretary of State's decision on the limits was illegal and the Court said it had to assume that the conclusions he had reached were in the public interest having regard to potential dangers to health and other relevant factors. But the families argued that the true analogy was with a statutory speed limit of 30 mph. There were circumstance such as driving near a school or in a congested area where it would be no defence to a claim in negligence for the driver to say that he had driven at 29 mph. A driver might still be obeying the criminal law on speeding, but a much slower speed might be expected of the non-negligent driver in particular circumstances.

The same principle applied here; the companies could not claim that compliance with the statutory limits for leaded petrol was sufficient to relieve them of liability. In giving the lead judgment, Lord Justice Megaw accepted that a court might well hold a motorist negligent even though he was within the statutory speed limits. Here, any limitation of lead had to be of general application and, in effect, the court was being asked to prescribe a lower general limit than that contained in the regulations and implicitly approved by parliament. As he said, if the action succeeded, 'the permissible limit thus ordained by the courts, to be enforced as being orders of the courts, would be different from and inconsistent with, the permissible limit prescribed by the authority of Parliament. This would result in a constitutional anomaly which in our view would be wholly unacceptable.' In his view, the question the defendants would have asked themselves for the purpose of negligence was the identical question which the Secretary of State had to decide. They could not be negligent if the limit they adhered to was one which they were reasonably entitled to believe was consistent with the public interest and the action to strike out the claim therefore succeeded. Striking out claims take place before full discovery of documents, where parties must reveal all the relevant information they hold. If discovery had shown that the defendants had a lot more internal information about the dangerous effects of lead than the Secretary of State had received (there was no hint to us from Shell that this was the case), the result might have been different. But without discovery or a significant leak from a whistleblower, claimants in such a case are essentially in something of a Catch-22 situation.

Shortly after the case, the Campaign for Lead Free Air (CLEAR), was launched, funded by a property developer, Godfrey Bradman and headed by Des Wilson, a former director of Shelter. In 1983, the Royal Commission on Environmental Pollution decided to examine the whole issue of lead in the environment and concluded that it was technically possible to produce lead-free petrol without undue cost to the economy. It accepted that there was continuing unscientific uncertainty about the effects of lead at low concentrations on children and called for further research. In an almost classic application of the precautionary principle – though the term was not then used – the Commission stated: 'It would be prudent to take steps to increase the safety margin of the population as a whole.' It advised that leaded petrol should be phased out and the government accepted the recommendation within half an hour of the report being published.

The issue of lead in petrol may have been resolved by political pressure rather than the judiciary as the claimants in *Budden* had hoped. But re-reading the decision in the case and my contemporaneous notes, it is striking how many of the themes emerging in that case, now nearly 40 years old, have become of relevance again. The last few years has seen a growth in litigation in the courts concerning climate change, both in Europe and other jurisdictions. As with the *Budden* families, climate change litigation is driven by a frustration that government action is too slow and that the courts might offer more effective solutions. Judicial review against government is never easy and, so far, legal action in this country seeking the government to introduce lower greenhouse gas reduction targets has not been successful.[7] It is noteworthy that in perhaps the most successful climate change litigation in Europe to date, the Dutch *Urgenda* case,[8] the claimants, as did the families in *Budden*, decided to avoid action in the administrative courts, where they felt judges tended to be too deferential to government, but instead brought a claim in the civil courts in respect of the damage caused by the state. It may not be too long before litigation directly against fossil fuel companies and other industries will be seen in this country, as is already happening in the United States. Once again, the companies will no doubt argue in their defence that they are complying with all the statutory requirements concerning greenhouse gases and should not be legally obliged to go further. If this happens, the arguments in the *Budden* case may well need revisiting.[9]

Towards the end of pupillage, I had decided that full-time practice at the Bar was not for me and I had moved to Imperial College to develop an academic career in environmental law. Almost ten years later, I met a fellow pupil who had recently joined European Law Chambers, a new set of chambers established by Claire Tritton QC. I felt at the time that most chambers would not really relish the involvement of an academic, but he said that my expertise in European environmental law would be welcome. I was interviewed and duly joined as a part-time member. At the time, the implications of new EU environmental directives, such as those relating to large combustion plants, access to environmental information and environmental assessment, were increasingly being felt by industry and I found myself in demand for legal opinions on the meaning of these new laws and how they would impinge on operations. At the time, I had not fully appreciated the drive and determination that Claire Tritton had needed to set up a new set of chambers, one that was solely devoted to European law and situated just outside the traditional area of the Temple. This was almost unprecedented at the time. But those very qualities were perhaps not best suited to managing the chambers once established and it soon became apparent there was considerable unhappiness with her style of leadership among the full-time barristers who had joined her. As a part-time door tenant, I remained semi-detached from what was happening – and indeed my perceived neutrality meant that I often received late night phone calls from Claire, followed the next night by the second most senior barrister, each cursing each other in most un-barrister-like language. European Law Chambers eventually collapsed. David Vaughan QC had already established a European law group within Brick Court Chambers and invited me to apply to be

---

[7] See *Plan B and others v Secretary of State* Ref C1/2018/1750 25 January 2019 where the Court of Appeal upheld the decision of the High Court to refuse leave for a judicial review.

[8] *Urgenda Foundation v State of Netherlands* Case 200.178.245/01 (Hague Court of Appeal, 9 October 2018).

[9] *Budden*, though, was concerned with a product put on the market, rather than with emissions from a process and the reasoning of the Court of Appeal may not be so compelling.

a door tenant there and where I remain today. Since then, most of my legal work has taken the form of written legal opinions on various aspects of environmental law. Running litigation in the courts, though, is not easily compatible with a full-time teaching job and, in any event, requires a detailed knowledge of procedure as well as substantive law. My skill and experience have mainly been concerned with issues of law and I would probably forget to ask for costs if I was running a case on my own. Nevertheless, I was later involved in two major environmental cases which reached the courts.

The first concerned the privatisation of water. Water privatisation had been brought into effect by the Water Act 1989 and I had already become immersed in the subject because the legal publishers, Sweet and Maxell, had invited me to produce an annotated version of te new legislation for their *Current Statutes* series. This involved analysing every section of the Act to explain what it meant and including cross-references to all the definitions. I followed the style of previous works in the series but decided to include many more references and extracts from parliamentary debates on the legislation to explain the policy background – something of an innovation at the time. It was a gruelling task because one could not really start until the Act had received Royal Assent and Sweet and Maxell wished to publish as soon as possible. It effectively meant a three-month summer period getting up at 5 am and continuing late at night, methodically going through all 194 sections in the Act, together with some 20 detailed schedules attached at the end. I had a stroke of luck when I was told that the parliamentary draftsman of the Water Act was a technical enthusiast and had done the drafting on his computer – something unprecedented for the draftsmen in those days. I wrote to him and he kindly supplied his disc containing the text of the final version presented to Parliament. This immeasurably speeded up the process of cross-referencing such a complex and lengthy piece of legislation. The resulting book was published just four months after Royal Assent.

British Waterways Board v Severn Trent[10] was concerned with a fairly narrow but important legal issue of water law. Water authorities had long had a legal right to discharge unpolluted surface water into canals and other watercourses, but the British Waterboards Board now claimed that, since privatisation, this right no longer existed. In future, Severn Trent would need to negotiate a licence and pay for the privilege. I appeared for Severn Trent and was led by Michael Beloff QC. The case involved tracing the complex history of drainage law starting with the Public Health Act 1875 which contained a general duty of local authorities to provide a system of drainage and gave them express powers to lay pipes. The legislation then contained a proviso that no discharges from the pipes should contain pollutants. There was no statutory provision expressly giving a right to authorities to discharge from the pipes, but in a Victorian case,[11] the Court of Appeal had

[10] *British Waterways Board v Severn Trent Water* [2001] EWCA Civ 276.
[11] *Durrant v Branksome UDC* [1897] 2 Ch 290.

held the combination of the existing statutory provisions gave an implied right to discharge to rivers and other watercourses, subject to the proviso in the legislation that they contained no polluting matters. These statutory provisions had been carried over in the Public Health 1936. The research into the statutory history was challenging and, in a fit of rather overzealous preparation, I drove over to the second-hand bookshops in Hay-on-Wye to buy an 1887 edition of Lumley's *Public Health Law* and the 1936 edition of Glenn's *Public Health Act 1936*. They provided an invaluable understanding of how contemporary experts interpreted the legislation.

The Water Act 1989, which privatised the water authorities, contained various schedules which appeared to continue to apply the relevant provisions of the Public Health Act although they were not entirely clear on the point. However, the 1989 legislation was shortly replaced by the Water Industry Act 1991. This was what is known as a Consolidation Act, intended to bring together previous legislation on the subject without introducing major changes to the law. Once again, the 1991 Act provided the authorities with express pipe-laying powers and contained an equivalent to the Public Health Act proviso against discharging polluting matter. But, for some reason, this proviso applied to other functions of the authorities but not to the pipe-laying powers – a critical step in the reasoning of the Court of Appeal back in 1892. Our argument was that this omission was not legally significant since modern environmental controls would prohibit any discharges that might cause pollution and that the implied right of discharge for a water authority therefore survived.

In the High Court, Mrs Justice Arden, as she then was, was prepared to look at the history of the water legislation right back to the Victorian Public Health Acts and agreed with our argument that the implied right to discharge survived. British Waterways Board appealed, and it was striking how a different set of judges could analyse the issue in a completely different way. Essentially, they looked at the Water Industry Act 1991 as a complete and coherent set of statutory provisions on the subject. The general approach of the courts to a Consolidation Act is that they should look at the words of the Act itself rather than construct it by reference to previous legislation, but that principle is subject to exceptions where there is ambiguity. But they felt that there was no such ambiguity here and that Mrs Justice Arden had been incorrect in delving into the history of the legislation. The Court concluded that the 1991 Act contained no discharge right from pipes and that it would not defeat the intention of Parliament if authorities had no such rights to drain water into canals or watercourses owned by someone else. Severn Trent could purchase a licence to do so as British Waterways were demanding but, in any event, could still perform its statutory duties to make provision for drainage of its sewers without such rights. As Lord Justice Peter Gibson put it: 'It can do this by discharge into rivers or the sea (provided that it does not cause pollution or offend environmental controls), by discharge onto its own land ... There is nothing in the evidence to suggest that the sewerage undertaker is inevitably left at the mercy of an overgreedy landowner.'

We then sought leave to appeal to the House of Lords on the grounds that this was an important issue of legal principle that should be determined by the highest court in the land.[12] Normally, one first sought permission from the Court of Appeal itself which, in practice, it hardly ever grants, leaving the decision whether or not to grant leave to the House of Lords. Michael Beloff was abroad and ask me to take the lead, the first time I had spoken in the Court of Appeal. I took advice from colleagues in chambers and was told it was best to be extremely succinct. One of my problems was that I knew a little too much about the history of the legislation. In examining an Act of Parliament, the courts constantly talk of the parliamentary intention behind the provisions, but I was aware that here this was somewhat of a myth. Many of the detailed provisions in the original 1989 Water Act, including the all-important schedules, had never been debated in parliament as it had been subject to guillotine procedures;[13] as a Consolidation Act, the 1991 Water Industry Act had received even less line-by-line parliamentary scrutiny. When I was writing the annotated commentary on the Water Act 1989, I had met one of the civil servants responsible for the legislation who told me they had got into quite a muddle over the detailed schedules (the problems in our case had arisen from provisions in one of the schedules) using a lot of scissors and paste late at night. This was not the sort of legal argument one could put before the Court of Appeal, though, at one point, I asked if I could wear my academic hat for a moment. This caused a wry smile on the part of the judges and I told them that I had read all the parliamentary committee proceedings on the legislation and never was this apparent significant change in the law discussed or raised, suggesting it really was a very important point deserving leave to go to the House of Lords. But as expected, the Court of Appeal refused leave and, in a permission for leave hearing before the House of Lords, we were given equally short shrift.

Some years later there was an important follow-up to the case which again shows how different courts can come to the same issue in a quite distinct way. In *Manchester Ship Canal Company Ltd v British Waterways Board*[14] a similar question about implied rights to discharge was raised, but here it was argued that while the Water Act 1991 may have taken the right to discharge away, this only applied to pipes constructed after that Act came into force. Manchester Ship Canal argued that pre-existing pipes continued to possess an implied right to discharge non-polluting water and, though it was an argument Michael Beloff and I had considered raising in the *British Waterways* case, we had not felt it was legally strong enough to run. But the High Court accepted Manchester Ship Canal's interpretation, only for the Court of Appeal, applying the *British Waterways* decision, to hold no such rights of discharge survived the 1991 Act, whether they were from pre-existing or

---

[12] In October 2009 the Supreme Court replaced the Appellate Committee of the House of Lords as the highest court in the United Kingdom.

[13] Guillotine procedures allow the government to limit the amount of time for Parliamentary debate on stages of a Bill.

[14] [2014] UKSC 40.

new pipes. The case then reached the Supreme Court in 2014 and Lord Sumption conducted an analysis of what he described as 'the labyrinthine scheme of amendments, repeals and re-enactments in the legislation of 1991'. The Supreme Court concluded that sewerage undertakers possessed and continue to have the right to discharge from pipes existing at the time of the 1991 Act but not from any pipes created subsequently. It was essentially pragmatic solution to a difficult issue and Lord Sumption was able to locate a rather obscure provision in the legislation to justify his conclusion. But, in many ways, it was an unsatisfactory case in terms of statutory interpretation. The High Court in the *British Waterways* case had thought it appropriate to look behind the history of the legislation leading up to the 1991 Act. The Court of Appeal said it was not, while in the *Manchester Ship Canal* case, Lord Sumption said that this was a case where the history needed to be explored. There seemed to be uncertainly amongst the judiciary as to whether the 1989 or the 1991 Water Act had changed the situation. Lord Sumption was clear that it was the latter, but it seems strange that what was purported to be a Consolidation Act should have changed the law in such a significant way. The doctrine of parliamentary intention continues to hold powerful sway in the courts, but here I still wonder here whether there was any conscious decision by government or parliament to have altered the discharge rights in this way or whether it really was due to late-night confusion on the schedules.

Contaminated land began to feature as a significant environmental issue in the 1990s and I had been a specialist adviser to the House of Commons Select Committee on the Environment which made the first major report on the subject.[15] This helped to lead to specific legislation on the subject introduced in 1995 and contained in Part IIA of the Environmental Protection Act. Apart from deciding whether land is contaminated, a critical legal issue is determining who should be liable for any clean-up, especially as the actual contamination may have been caused many years before. The 1995 legislation was reasonably clear by providing that, initially, it is the person who caused or knowingly permitted the contaminating substances to be present. If they cannot be found, then the current owner or occupier is liable, the justification being that the land would increase in value following remediation. Provisions were provided to relieve current owners or occupiers where this would cause financial hardship, in which case the Environment Agency and, essentially, the public purse, would pick up the costs.

National Grid Gas v Environment Agency[16] tested these provisions for the first time. Contaminated land had been found in several private gardens in Bawtry, North Yorkshire in 2001. The site had been used by for the manufacture of coal gas since the early nineteenth century and had passed through various gas companies including, on nationalisation of the gas industry in 1948, to the East Midlands Gas Board. No one could be certain quite when the contamination occurred, but it

---

[15] See ch 6.
[16] [2007] UKHL 30.

must have been before 1952 when coal gas production ceased. The East Midlands Gas Board had sold the land for housing development in the 1960s. The Environment Agency had spent over £1 million on remediation work at the site, but the gas companies who had actually caused or permitted the contamination no longer existed. The developers who may have been aware of the contamination and therefore also liable under the 1995 Act had also long ceased to exist. So, the Agency now sought to recover half their costs from National Grid Gas (formerly Transco) on the grounds that it had inherited the liabilities under the various pieces of legislation relating the re-organisation of the gas industry, including privatisation in 1986.[17]

Transco resisted the claim. Their solicitors had instructed Richard Gordon QC at Brick Court Chambers and decided that it would be helpful to include me on the team as someone familiar with the legal and policy background. The case was initially heard in the High Court and Mr Justice Forbes accepted the logic of the Environment Agency's two main arguments. First, given the context and aim of the contaminated land scheme in the Environmental Protection Act, it was acceptable to interpret the term 'person' in the statutory provisions on liability in a generous way not just to include the original company who caused the contamination but any successor company in order to ensure continuity. But if that was incorrect, in any event the various statutory re-organisations over the years had transferred existing liabilities to successor companies. This was one such liability.

The case clearly had significant financial implications for many industries and Mr Justice Forbes granted leave for the case to leapfrog to the House of Lords, by-passing the Court of Appeal. The appeal was set down for a two-day hearing. Richard Gordon had prepared a lengthy speaking note, but Lord Hoffmann immediately opened by saying to him that this seemed like a very simple point of interpreting clearly drafted statutory provisions. I turned to the other junior for Transco, Martin Chamberlain[18] and whispered to him whether this was good sign for us. He thought it was. One of the attributes of a good advocate is to be able to read the court. Richard Gordon quickly realised that their Lordships were with him and managed to compress his all-day submission to under an hour. Counsel for the Environment Agency could also see that it was a losing battle and the hearing was concluded by lunchtime.

In the lead judgment, Lord Scott noted that the language of the statute clearly placed primary responsibility on the actual polluter. The original gas companies would have been liable, as might be the developer who had knowingly permitted the contamination on the site. But he asked how could that make Transco, who had never actually owned the land in question, liable? He felt that an extended interpretation of the term 'person' in the legislation was 'a quite impossible

---

[17] The Agency had decided that if the developers had still existed they would also have been liable for half of the remediation costs, hence they sought 50 per cent from Transco.
[18] Martin Chamberlain was appointed a High Court judge in 2019.

construction to place on the uncomplicated and easily understandable statutory language'. As to the statutory transfer of liabilities under the various pieces of legislation re-organising the gas industry over many years, he felt it was perfectly clear these related to existing liabilities at the time of the transfers. Liabilities transferred to Transco's predecessor, British Gas, on privatisation under the Gas Act 1986 could not include liabilities that were to be created nine years later under the new law relating to contaminated land.

In preparation for the case I had looked at a number of court decisions in the United States concerning liability of successor companies for environmental contamination. Some judges were clearly adopting creative solutions to impose liabilities to ensure that companies who had considerable resources would pay the costs involved, whatever the actual terms of the relevant legislation said – a good example of the so-called 'deep pocket' theory of liability. The approach of the House of Lords showed a quite different judicial approach. The language of the statutory provisions was clear and if parliament had wished to extend liabilities further that was matter for parliament, not the courts. The truth was that despite some ambiguous ministerial statements in parliament during the passage of the bill, neither government nor parliament had properly addressed the issue of successor liability in the statutory provisions. Perhaps they had hoped this issue would be handled by the courts, but the *Transco* decision indicated that the courts felt it was for government and parliament, not the judiciary, to take on that responsibility.

In the course of the argument, one of the core environmental principles, written in the European Treaty, the 'polluter pays principle', was mentioned at several points as underlining the contaminated land regime. Lord Scott had no quarrel with the principle, as such, but simply said Transco was not the polluter, so it was not relevant. In a rather more nuanced judgment, Lord Neuberger accepted that in the current awareness of environmental contamination it might seem justifiable to extended the notion of polluter pays to include a company who had acquired assets from another company which had actually caused the pollution. But, he concluded, 'Whether and, if so, in what circumstances and on what basis, it would be right to extend the concept of a polluter paying in such a way is a matter of policy for the legislature, not for the courts. The role of the courts is to interpret the relevant statutory provisions which the legislature has enacted, in order to determine whether they have that effect'.

Just over ten years later, the government intends to include a number of environmental principles, including in the polluter pays principle, into its proposed environmental legislation concerning Brexit.[19] I have always found some difficulty with the principle in that it sounds compelling on first reading, but does not really assist in defining who is the polluter in any particular circumstance. As the *Budden* lead-in-petrol case demonstrated so many years before, the polluter might

---

[19] See further ch 13. The precise legal terms for introducing these principles into national law have recently been subject to considerable political and legal debate.

be considered to encompass a range of actors – in that case the makers of petrol, retailers of petrol, the designers of urban road schemes, or even those choose who drive in cities. But now that the principle is likely to be given some statutory recognition in national law, it will be intriguing to see in the future the extent to which the judiciary will feel more equipped to use the principle to develop and expand existing notions of environmental liability and responsibility.

Practising as a lawyer, especially at the Bar, is challenging and demanding but brings its own rewards. I found writing opinions intellectually satisfying in that one of the reasons an opinion is sought is precisely because the relevant legislation or case law is not very clear as to how it might apply to the issue in hand and one often has to go back to first principles to decide the best answer. While academics can often conclude that a question is complex and needs further research, here one cannot duck the issue as the client needs a firm and clear answer, whatever the legal difficulties involved. On the few occasions I have been involved in litigation before the courts, the experience has been intense and equally fruitful in giving me a real feel for how law works in practice. As we were developing a case, I often found that my understanding of the wider policy context involved could provide a positive contribution. It was constantly striking how difficult it is to predict how a court will receive the arguments put forward and just how significant is the personality of the judge dealing with the case. But I have few regrets in deciding not to commit my whole working life as a practising barrister. Constantly representing clients and arguing for positions which one does not necessarily feel will provide the most effective solutions is not really in my nature, and litigation is often dealing with a fairly constrained set of issues. I doubt whether full-time practice would have given me so many opportunities to try to influence the wider development of environmental law and policy.

6

Influencing Public Policy

Parliamentary Select Committees

The modern shape of parliamentary select committees derived from reforms introduced in 1979 when select committees were established in the House of Commons to track individual government departments. These committees could choose their own areas for investigation and while their recommendations have never been binding on government, a response to their reports is obligatory under parliamentary rules. The standard practice of the committees has been to invite calls for evidence on the subject chosen, followed by oral questioning of invited witnesses including civil servants and the relevant government minister. As an academic, I had found many of the early reports of the select committee on the environment invaluable sources of information on detailed thinking about environmental policy and law, not least because they contained full transcripts of the oral question and answer sessions, as well as all the written evidence submitted. And, wherever possible, I would attend the sessions. The first I visited was the committee's inquiry into pollution from nitrogen dioxide, an issue that is still one of intense concern in this country. The key government witness was Michael Howard, then Secretary of State for the Environment. The public are normally admitted before the witnesses and I duly took my place in the front row behind the seat reserved for the Secretary of State. But I had not realised that, by convention, this row is reserved for the civil servants advising him and when they arrived they were far too polite to remove me so I stayed in my position, now surrounded by half-a-dozen government officials. Sitting just a few feet behind the Secretary of State as he was being questioned gave me a vivid sense of being present at the highest level of political exposure. Michael Howard was fluid and confident; only at one point did he falter when questioned whether the government's transport policies were consistent with the UK's commitments to reduce transboundary emissions of NOx under a recent international treaty. He clearly assumed that I was one of his department's senior advisers and turned to me whispering 'What's the story?'. With a vague shrug of my shoulders, I said that I had no idea. He was able to bluff an answer, but as he left at the close of the session, I caught his eye and received a daggers look. He clearly still thought I was a civil servant and was preparing my demotion.

Select committees are supported by parliamentary officials but often also appoint one or more specialist external advisers to assist them on a particular inquiry.

In 1990, Sir Hugh Rossi, a conservative MP, was chair of the Select Committee on the Environment. A lawyer by training, he was a robust character and was not afraid to probe and criticise government policy on the environment, even when it was his party in power. In the previous year the committee had carried out an inquiry into toxic waste which had thrown up evidence of extensive historical contamination of land in the country, both from abandoned landfill sites and old industrial processes. As a result, in 1990, the committee decided to launch an inquiry that would be focused on contaminated land. One of my colleagues at Imperial College, Roger Perry, Professor of Environmental Control and Waste Management, had been appointed a scientific adviser to this inquiry, but it was clear that legal issues of some complexity would be involved. No doubt because of the Imperial College connection and my increasing visibility in environmental law, I was invited to be a specialist advisor to the inquiry.

It was my first official involvement in public policy work. A key role of the specialist adviser was to advise on the key issues to be explored, sift through the written evidence and prepare questions to be put to witnesses. One of my first impressions was the extent to which the members of the select committee largely ignored party politics when sitting on the committee; to an outsider, it was near impossible to tell to which party they belonged. The extent to which the committee could act a cohesive, cross-political group was largely due to the skills of the chair and the choice of subject matter. Hugh Rossi repeatedly refused to let the committee investigate the controversial poll tax that had been introduced by the Conservative government in 1990 in England and Wales because he knew it would simply split on party lines. He has since been criticised for this decision, but there is no doubt that reports that are unanimously endorsed by members from all political parties have considerable weight because of that very fact. I only saw him once put pressure in a private session on a Conservative MP who disagreed with the rest of the committee and wished to put in his own minority report. It was done with extreme politeness, with Rossi saying that he was entitled to do so, but reminding him it would be rather sad as it would be the first ever report of this committee that had not been unanimous. The MP quietly withdrew his objections. The second main impression was that while the chair and the clerk were fully engaged in the subject matter of the inquiry, this was not necessarily the case with all the members of the committee, some of whom had been placed at the behest of party whips. I had assumed that before each oral session there would be an intense discussion by the committee on the questions and issues to be raised but, in reality, members often would arrive late just before the session began and the list of questions was rapidly distributed amongst them almost by random. It was frustrating as a specialist adviser, because one could not guarantee that a member would follow up witness answers with more searching questions of relevance. There were exceptions of course and one could readily spot the those who fully understood the issues and were able to pursue a line of questioning with confidence. But they were the exception and often found themselves soon promoted to government positions, which meant they had to leave the committee.

At the time of the inquiry there was no specific legislation concerning contaminated land. If land was to be redeveloped, land use planning controls provided the legal mechanism for securing decontamination and the extent of clean-up required to be achieved was dependent on the proposed end use of the land in question. There was no general duty on an industry to clean up land it had contaminated, to ensure it was decontaminated when sold on, or even inform the purchaser of the condition of the land – *caveat emptor* ('let the buyer beware') was the prevailing principle. The committee was concerned at the lack of a coherent approach to the subject and, in particular, wished to see a duty of local authorities to prepare registers of contaminated land within their area. One of the effects of a select committee investigation can be to concentrate the minds of government. Over the six-month period of the inquiry there was a notable development in departmental thinking from the initial evidence from civil servants at the start of the inquiry to the final session involving the Minister for the Environment, David Trippier. He indicated that the government was now prepared to take a far more proactive approach to the issue than had hitherto been the case and was contemplating the possibility of local authority registers. As Sir Hugh Rossi noted in response: 'That is a welcome statement. It indicates a complete departure from the thinking in the department as we perceived it when I began this inquiry to what has now evolved.'

Contaminated land is a complex issue, but the committee's report stimulated policy and legal development, though it took some years to emerge. One of the government's immediate responses to the report was a provision in the Environment Protection Act 1990 for establishing public registers of land which had been subject to contaminative use, but their introduction was delayed because of concern about creating blight at a time of economic recession. The government published a consultation paper in 1994,[1] which eventually led to a dedicated specialist legal regime contained in amendments to the 1990 Environment Act that were introduced in 1995.

Specialist advisors are normally appointed just for a specific inquiry but Hugh Rossi and the subsequent chair of the select committee, Andrew Bennett, clearly welcomed the involvement of a specialist environmental lawyer and, over the next few years, I became, by default, a quasi-permanent adviser to the committee in a number of subsequent inquiries. In 1990, the committee carries out an inquiry into Northern Ireland and the environment, the first on the subject by a select committee and one in which I was particularly pleased to be involved because of long family connections in the region. The report identified that the natural environment was one of Northern Ireland's greatest assets but acknowledged that it had not been given high priority given the troubles that were still existing – it would still be eight years before the Good Friday Agreement. The committee

---

[1] *Paying for our Past: The Arrangements for Controlling Contaminated Land and Meeting the Cost of Remedying Damage for the Environment* (London, Department of the Environment, 1994).

was especially concerned that Northern Ireland appeared to have a record of late transposition of European environmental directives and wanted much more proactive work on the issue. Other inquiries where I remained a specialist adviser included those on beaches, eco-labelling, eco-products and waste.

By then, I had experienced working for a short time within the Environment Directorate of the European Commission and had been involved in the early development of a proposed landfill directive.[2] The proposals would heavily restrict the types of waste that could be landfilled in future and were clearly going to have immense implications for waste management practice in the UK where landfill predominated. Since the committee had had a long interest in waste management, in 1991, I urged them to hold an inquiry before the final draft of the landfill directive was published by the European Commission. The latest version of the draft directive was already in wide circulation within government and the British waste industry and was causing considerable concern. I felt that by conducting an inquiry on the draft, the committee might have some real influence on thinking within the European Commission which was still fairly fluid. At the same time, I spoke with the relevant officials within the Commission and explained the role of a parliamentary select committee, a body they had never heard of before. I told them it was independent from government and it could be extremely valuable if they were to give evidence to explain their current thinking behind the proposals. They readily agreed, the committee launched an inquiry into the draft landfill directive (the first time it had investigated proposed EU environmental legislation in this way) and invited the Commission officials to give oral evidence. But quite unwittingly I had set in motion a quasi-constitutional European row of epic proportions. Once the final version of the proposed directive was officially published by the Commission, the European Parliament would then, under the EU legislative process, have an opportunity to be involved. The chair of the European Parliament's Environment Committee, Ken Collins, a forceful Scottish MEP, was outraged that a committee of a national parliament was taking evidence on a proposed environmental directive before his committee had been formally involved. He was not persuaded by the fact that the select committee was inquiring into what was still work still in progress by the Commission and proceeded was to block the Commission officials from giving evidence. Not surprisingly, the MPs were furious at the perceived arrogance of a European institution and I was told that the row had reached the ears of the Prime Minister, John Major. The officials never appeared before the committee and the situation became even more bizarre because it was perfectly acceptable for them to come to London to have discussions with the representatives of the British waste industry. Industry then gave evidence before the committee and recounted at second hand what the Commission officials had told them the day before about

---

[2] See ch 12.

their proposals. The sad story did not help to improve how British MPs perceived European Community procedures for law making which seemed to largely ignore the input of national parliaments. At the time, Member States were involved in discussions on revising the Treaties governing the EU and the committee's report noted, in fairly restrained tones: 'We hope that as the Inter-Governmental Conference proceeds, the various European institutions will adopt a consistently positive attitude towards the informal involvement of national parliaments in the policy-making and legislative processes that the Commission makes greater use of the significant body of knowledge and experience which has been built up by the Parliamentary Select Committees.'

A year later, in my role as editor of the recently launched *Journal of Environmental Law*, I asked Richard Hawkins to review the committee's report in the journal. I had long felt that select committee reports and similar official reports deserved to be subject to the same critical analysis in journals as were books on environmental law and this was a deliberate initiative. But I also knew that my choice of reviewer was somewhat of a risk because Richard Hawkins was a characterful environmental lawyer advising the waste industry and was not afraid to give robust views. His review was largely complimentary of the select committee's report, but laid into the European Commission in typically colourful language – '... this ill-drafted directive, incompletely researched, with little or no scientific balance and inconsistently related articles'. Shortly after his piece was published, I received an angry telephone call from Ken Collins, denigrating the review and making veiled threats about the future viability of the journal. I maintained my temper and replied that we did not censure reviews and that if he wanted to submit a considered response I would welcome its inclusion in the next issue. Nothing was forthcoming and the journal continued to thrive. But the whole experience was a valuable lesson that in trying to be helpful and assist discussion and debate, one can sometimes unleash quite unexpected institutional sensitivities.

The landfill directive inquiry was unusual as it was rare at the time for a House of Commons select committee to hold an inquiry focused on EU legislation. That role had largely been undertaken by the House of Lords Select Committee on the European Communities, which had a number of sub-committees including one on the environment. They consistently produced valuable reports on many areas of EU environmental policy and law, and senior European Commission officials told me that for all the apparent Euroscepticism within the UK, the British Parliament, and especially the House of Lords committee, was the only national legislature within the European Union which took such a close and detailed interest in the development of EU environmental policy and law. Their authoritative reports had considerable influence on thinking within the Commission. In 1991, the House of Lords environment sub-committee decided to hold an inquiry into the general subject of the implementation and enforcement of European Community environmental legislation. I had already written on the subject and had worked for a short period within the implementation unit in the European Commission dealing with environmental law.[3] I was duly appointed a specialist adviser to the committee along with Nigel Haigh, then director of the Institute for European Environmental Policy.

Apart from government witnesses, including Michael Heseltine, Secretary of State for the Environment, the committee received evidence from the European Commission, the European Parliament, the European Court of Auditors and many national bodies including environmental organisations, trade bodies and the recently formed UK Environmental Law Association. The final report of the committee stills makes valuable reading and much of the analysis could apply as much in a purely national context as it did to European law. The committee felt that, to date, there had been insufficient attention paid to the issue of implementa- tion and enforcement of Community environmental law, but that in the field of the environment it was especially vital to do so – 'since, in general, economic forces do not act so as to create vested interests in environmental protection – quite the contrary – administrative and legal deficiencies threaten to frustrate the very objectives of policy'. The time had come for a substantial change in attitude: 'First, member states together and separately must pay more attention to implementation and enforcement; its place on the political agenda should be given more promi- nence. Second, implementation should be seen as a continuous process spanning not only the execution of Community obligations but also their formulation and evaluation of their effectiveness. And third, perhaps most importantly of all, the whole system should be made more transparent so that it can be properly scruti- nised at each stage.'

The report highlighted important issues on which there have since been some developments, both good and not so good. It stressed the key importance of ensur- ing effective transposition of EU Directives into national law if implementation was to have real impact. In this context, the committee favoured more systematic procedures that would allow national authorities to discuss draft transposition proposals with the European Commission, thereby helping to identify problem areas before positions were fixed. Generally, the practice was to send the transpos- ing legislation to the Commission only after it had been were finalised at national level and, at that stage, national governments will naturally resist criticism since the loss of face in having to amend existing national law is considerable.[4] Unlike directives, the other main form of EU law, regulations, are largely 'self-executing' in that they do not require transposition to have legal effect within national systems. The European Parliament wanted greater use of EU regulations to avoid problems of non-implementation but the committee did not feel a wholesale move to regulations was the answer: 'We believe the requirements of environmental

---

[3] See further ch 12.

[4] EU Directives contain provisions requiring Member States to send the Commission the text of national transposing legislation within two years (and sometimes three) of the Directive coming into force.

protection can best be met by providing member states with the opportunity to tailor Community requirements and policies so as best to meet particular environmental conditions and so as to accord, as far as possible, with national and local legal and administrative arrangements. Directives give member states the opportunity to do just this and they should remain the main form of legal instrument for Community environmental policy.' In this context, the committee was critical of the growing practice of some Member States to simply copy out the provisions of directives word-for-word in their national law.[5]

Full transposition will have little effect unless there are effective national enforcement procedures. At the time of the inquiry the European Environment Agency was about to be established but its role was largely confined to data analysis and assessment and it had no direct enforcement powers within Member States. The House of Lords committee considered that the new agency could play a stronger role in reviewing the measures taken by Member States to monitor and enforce compliance. I was uncomfortable with powers of direct inspection but Michael Heseltine, the Secretary of State, had recently proposed the establishment of a Community 'audit inspectorate' which would examine and monitor the performance of environmental regulatory authorities in Member States. The committee supported the idea and considered the logical home for such an inspectorate would be within the European Environment Agency but, sadly, the idea never came to fruition. Some environmental directives now include provisions about inspection and enforcement and in the last few years the European Commission has been making proposals for improving best practice amongst Member States. Informal networks of environmental regulators such as the Environment Agency and their equivalents in other Member States have since developed and these provide valuable fora for the exchange of information. But we still lack the more systematic arrangements envisaged by the idea of an audit inspectorate.

The Committee also recognised that access to the courts by individuals or non-governmental bodies was vital to ensure legal accountability of government and public bodies with environmental responsibilities. In the UK, such procedures were largely confined to judicial review applications in the Administrative Court which were highly costly and appeared unfavourable compared to those existing in other countries such as the Netherlands and Denmark where specialised, low-cost environmental tribunals existed. The debates on the need for a specialised environmental court or tribunal had only just begin in this country and the then Lord Chief Justice, Lord Woolf, had given an important public lecture arguing the need for change. As the committee noted: 'As far as the United Kingdom is concerned costs might also be reduced and associated benefits realized if a specialist environmental tribunal were to be created, as recently suggested by Lord Justice Woolf.' It would be another eight years after the report was published before an environmental tribunal was finally established in this country.[6]

[5] See further ch 12.
[6] See further ch 10 on the development of environmental courts and tribunals in this country.

The committee recognised the importance of the European Commission's own procedure for taking enforcement action against Member States and the citizen's complaint procedure it has established to alert it of potential problems areas. However, it recommended that the implementation unit within the Environment Directorate needed more staff (at the time it had just 10 lawyers dealing with enforcement) and that it needed to establish clearer priorities for the type of cases it would handle rather than trying to investigate every complaint. Since then, staff levels have been increased and clearer prioritisation strategies have been established with a greater emphasis on ensuring that full and effective transposition has taken place. Where an infringement cannot be satisfactorily resolved by discussion with a Member State, the Commission can eventually take the matter to the Court of Justice of the European Union. There had been a number of cases in the 1980s, though not in the environmental field, where Member States had blatantly refused to comply with judgments of the court and, at the instigation of the British government, amendments had recently been introduced under the Maastricht Treaty[7] giving powers to the Court to impose financial penalties on a Member State which did not comply with a judgment. I had real concerns that it seemed a rather regressive step to resort to fining a government in the same way one might deal with a recalcitrant industry and the committee's report reflected this view: 'The imposition of a fine by the Court against a member state might also in an insidious way devalue the moral authority of Community law and the Court.' Perhaps I was overly pessimistic. There have since been a number of number of cases in the environmental field where the European Court has indeed imposed large financial penalties on Member States who have not complied with its judgments (the United Kingdom to date has received no such fine) and its authority has not diminished as a result. Certainly, by all accounts, the very threat of fines has helped to concentrate the minds of governments and especially Treasury departments, to take the necessary steps to avoid a financial sanction from the Court.

The 1991 House of Lords report was a product of its time but it is striking how many of the issues discussed are now of relevance in discussions on the implications for the United Kingdom leaving the EU. Michael Heseltine's proposal for an audit inspectorate monitoring the performance of national environmental regulators echoes in many ways the proposed Office for Environment Protection.[8] The whole question of whether our courts should have the express power to impose financial penalties on government and public bodies for failures to comply with their environmental duties is high on the agenda. Thirty years ago, when the House of Lords considered the issue in relation to the new powers given to the European Court of Justice to penalise Member States, there were conflicting opinions on the issue and similar arguments have now re-emerged, with equally different views. In addition to specific enforcement powers, it is proposed that the new body will

---

[7] The Maastricht Treaty was agreed in February 1992 and came into force on 1 November 1993.
[8] See further ch 13.

have a general duty to monitor the implementation of environmental law. We have never done this systematically in our national environmental law and it is a role I welcome. The House of Lords report contained important material considering the wide number of factors that come into play when one is considering what is meant by implementation which goes well beyond the simple application of legal controls by a regulatory body. I hope it will be read by those in the new body responsible for considering how to carry out this important new duty.

7

A National Environmental Agency

The creation of the Environment Agency in 1995 as the core national environmental regulator in England and Wales owed its origins to water privatisation some 15 years earlier. In the Victorian era, local authorities had the main responsibility for ensuring water quality and effective sewerage treatment but, during the twentieth century, their powers were increasingly transferred to larger public bodies with more specialised functions. Rivers and water bodies areas do not respect local administrative boundaries and, over the next 40 years or so, there was a period of further consolidation to ensure that new authorities had increasing jurisdiction over a whole river system from source to estuary. By 1973, there were just ten water authorities in England and Wales based on the country's main water catchment areas who were responsible for the whole water cycle, including pollution control, water abstraction, flood management, fisheries and sewerage treatment.

As part of the Thatcher Government's policy on privatisation, the government published a White Paper in 1986 proposing to privatise these water authorities. It was reluctant to breach the integrated approach to water management that had been developed over so many years and therefore proposed transferring nearly all the functions of the river authorities[1] to the new privatised bodies. This included their powers to grant water discharge and abstraction licences and the bodies would also be responsible for the enforcement of the controls. These regulatory functions would now be set against a much tighter framework of legally binding environmental standards made by government. There was concern amongst many in industry and the environmental sector as to whether it was appropriate for a private body to regulate and enforce legal controls in this way, but the government argued that there were other areas, such as the financial sector or professional standards, where regulation was often in the hands of the private sector. With a much clearer legal framework of environmental standards, together with protective appeals mechanisms, there should be no concern. However, in a letter published in *The Times* on 13 May 1986, Nigel Haigh of the Institute of European Environmental Policy pointed out that many European directives in the field of water pollution required Member States to appoint 'competent authorities' to carry out certain functions including the issuing of consents to discharge pollutants into rivers or estuaries. The term 'competent authority' was not defined in the

---

[1] Flood control and land drainage were excluded.

EU legislation but he queried whether as a matter of EU law it could encompass a private body.

I was then Standing Counsel to the Council for the Protection of Rural England, an honorary position where I was asked from time to time to give legal advice to the organisation. Its director, Robin Grove-White, was an acute environmental tactician and was well aware that simply publishing a legal opinion from a senior QC could have considerable impact on government thinking. He decided to commission an opinion on the question of EU law that had been raised by Nigel Haigh. I did not think that my views on the legal issue would carry sufficient weight and, in any event, was not sufficiently familiar with wider aspects of EU public law that would inevitably be involved in any analysis. We therefore engaged one of the country's leading experts in EU law, Francis Jacobs QC.[2] There was no clear case law in the European Court on the issue. His opinion[3] considered that where EU legislation referred to operational matters such as monitoring or taking samples, these tasks could be carried out by a private body. But when it came to issues such as the issuing of licences or carrying out enforcement functions being carried out by a 'competent authority', he concluded that, were the issue to come before the European Court of Justice, it might well decide that these functions had to be carried out by a public body. It was, at the very least, a seriously arguable case. The Opinion was published and sent to government and the European Commission. The legal uncertainty that it raised, together with the prospect of potentially lengthy litigation before the European Court and the effect this might have on any flotation of shares, clearly unnerved government ministers.

Shortly before the 1987 General Election, the then Secretary of State for the Environment, Nicholas Ridley announced a major rethink. Ridley was known to be a strong believer in the free market but was also very much an independent thinker who was not afraid to grasp political realities. He decided that privatisation of the industry would still go ahead, but no longer based on the integrated water management model. Instead, a new non-departmental public body, the National Rivers Authority (NRA), would be established to carry out the regulatory and enforcement functions, with the new privatised water authorities responsible for the delivery of services, including water and sewerage operations. As he said in Parliament on 21 October 1987 about the regulatory functions: 'After further consideration and having listened carefully to the arguments, I came to the conclusion that these functions are essentially a public responsibility. I could not accept the principle that one private body should determine what another can take out of a river or put into it or how much it should be charged for so doing.' The NRA came into existence in 1989 under the strong chairmanship of Lord Crickhowell, a former Conservative MP. He rapidly helped to establish the new body as a truly independent environmental regulator in the water field.

---

[2] Later to become an Advocate General of the European Court of Justice.
[3] Written jointly with Murray Shanks of his chambers.

Meanwhile, changes were taking place within the Alkali Inspectorate, a small specialised agency of central government that had regulated emissions into the air from a range of designated industrial processes since the 1860s. In its 1976 study on air pollution, the Royal Commission on Environmental Pollution had praised the technical expertise of the inspectorate but felt that in a contemporary climate requiring greater openness and public engagement, it needed to conduct its business in a far more transparent manner than had hitherto been the case. The Royal Commission had also called for a change in the law to allow the inspectorate to regulate all emissions from the designated processes whether to air, water or onto land to allow a more integrated approach to pollution control. It recommended that the overall criterion for decision making should be the best practicable environmental option and that a new body to be called Her Majesty's Pollution Inspectorate be established to replace the old Alkali Inspectorate and reflect its wider remit. The government initially responded by simply calling for greater coordination between the different environmental regulators but, in 1987, the Alkali Inspectorate was renamed Her Majesty's Inspectorate of Pollution. The change anticipated a new system of integrated pollution control from designated processes which would cover all the emissions from a process whether to air, water or land.[4] I was told later that the change of name from that proposed by the Royal Commission was a last-minute decision by a civil servant who was clearly a stickler for precise grammar and who had felt that the title 'Her Majesty's Pollution Inspectorate' might suggest it was just dealing with pollution from royal palaces.

David Slater was appointed chief inspector of the new inspectorate on 1 May 1991. Coming from the environmental consultancy world, he brought a fresh openness to the position and was anxious to engage with the wider environmental community. We had met at a conference and he invited me to give a talk to his senior staff on the changing world of environmental law. I explained to them that there had recently been a rapid growth in specialist environmental lawyers, the substance of environmental law was becoming more complex and formalised and that EU environmental law was becoming much more significant in its legal impact on our national system. Environmental groups were becoming more active in bringing judicial reviews against government bodies and the inspectorate could expect such challenges in the future. At the time, the inspectorate numbered around 250, but there were no in-house lawyers. The lack of legal staff was understandable in that, in the past, highly technically qualified inspectors were largely dealing and negotiating with their counterparts in the industries that they regulated. One striking illustration of this non-legalistic approach concerned the core criterion in the legislation that had existed since 1874 until 1990 that industries must use the 'best practicable means to prevent and reduce pollution from air emissions'. The term was described by Alfred Fletcher, the Assistant Inspector, in 1876 as legally

---

[4] Integrated pollution control was introduced in the UK under Part I of the Environmental Protection Act 1990.

superior to fixed emission standards 'for it is an elastic band and may be kept tight as knowledge of the methods of suppressing the evil complained of increased'. But to a lawyer, the phrase was clearly full of ambiguities and was crying out for judicial interpretation. Does one take into account technologies developed in other countries to judge what is 'best' at any particular time? And when a Chief Alkali Inspector in the 1980s wrote in one of his reports that 'what would be uneconomic would not be practicable', did that mean uneconomic for the particular process operator, or for the whole sector? Yet, in over 100 years, there had never been litigation on these provisions, a fact that was completely incomprehensible to my US environmental lawyer colleagues.

This did not mean that the system was ineffective, but I argued at the meeting that, rightly or wrongly, we were now in a new era of environmental law where the old style of closed regulation would not survive. I urged David Slater to hire an in-house lawyer to work with the inspectors to address these new challenges. The inspectorate was then an agency within the Department of the Environment but housed in a separate building and David explained that he could always go the government lawyers for specialist legal advice. But while this might be valuable in some instances, I felt this was bound to be a rather detached and formal process and from my experience as the staff lawyer at Friends of the Earth working on a daily basis with campaigners, it made all the difference to have an in-house lawyer who could work closely and informally with individual inspectors. A few months later, I heard that my views had clearly resonated and that a lawyer in the Department of the Environment, Rik Navarro, had been transferred to the Inspectorate as their first staff lawyer.[5]

In 1991, the government finally accepted the need for a new national environment body with John Major, the Prime Minister, announcing on 8 July the intention to establish an Environment Agency. Although the principle of the new organisation was established, there followed considerable discussion as to the precise scope of its functions and in its consultation on the proposal, the government set out four possible options: (i) the Environment Agency to take over waste regulation from local authorities and the responsibilities of Her Majesty's Inspectorate of Pollution (HMIP) but with the National Rivers Authority (NRA) continuing in existence; (ii) the Agency to be an umbrella body coordinating the work of both the HMIP and NRA; (iii) the Agency to take over waste regulation, the water pollution functions of the NRA and HMIP; and (iv) the Agency to take over waste regulation and incorporate both the NRA and HMIP. The House of Commons Select Committee on the Environment established an inquiry into the proposed options in 1992 and I was appointed a specialist adviser to the committee. On hearing the evidence, I advised the committee that it would be preferable that the new Agency focus on regulatory aspects of the environment, leaving the NRA to handle flood defence and other operational aspects of water management. Otherwise, there was a danger

---

[5] Rik Navarro later became the first head of legal services at the Environment Agency.

that the new Agency's work would become overly dominated by its water manage-ment responsibilities, both in terms of staff numbers and finance. The committee agreed and advised accordingly, but the chairman of the NRA, Lord Crickhowell, vigorously resisted the idea, arguing that this model would be the final break-up of the integrated approach to water and river catchment management planning. His views prevailed.

The Environment Agency (The Agency) was established under the Environment Act 1995 and took over the responsibilities of the NRA, HMIP and the waste regulation authorities in local government. It was not an easy marriage in the first few years, with staff coming from three very different types of organisation and with three separate trade unions representing their interests which added enormous complications for pay structures. The Agency is what is termed a non-departmental body. As such, it is independent in law from central government and its staff offic-ers are not civil servants but employees of the Agency. Independence, though, is a relative concept. Board members and the chief executive are appointed by govern-ment and a large proportion of its finances are derived directly from government. Section 4 of the Environment Act 1995 gave power to ministers to give guidance to the Agency with respect to the objectives to pursue and, under section 40, a minister could give the Agency legally binding directions of both a general or specific character in relation to any of its functions. During my time, very few such directions were, in practice, issued and those were of a non-controversial nature, mainly relating to EU environmental legislation. In theory, government could use these powers to, say, require the Agency to refuse a particular licence application or a block a controversial prosecution. But the political protection against such a degree of control is the legal requirement that directions must be published. It would be a brave government minister who would abuse their power to interfere with such specific Agency decisions.

The Environment Agency had been in existence for four years when in 1999 I applied to be a board member. It was a competitive process and, during the inter-view, I explained that despite my environmental law expertise, I did not want to be seen in any way as a rival or threat to the in-house legal team; rather I would try and bring a strategic dimension to the legal side of its work. I was duly appointed and one of the most striking aspects I found in the discussions and paperwork for board meetings was the amount of time given to income streams and funding. My academic lectures on environmental law focused on the legal powers of the Agency but paid very little attention to how it derived its income. But my experi-ence on the board brought home just how critical finances are to organisations of this size. They were complex and came from a variety of sources. When I joined the board, just over a quarter of the Agency's income came from direct grant from government known as 'grant-in-aid'. The grant was not in a single block, but ring fenced into various categories such as environmental protection, water resources and navigation and fisheries, and money could not be transferred from one to another. Income for flood defences, coming from various precepts and levies and capital grants from government, was a higher proportion. The remaining income came from industry and other non-government sources through charging schemes such as those for environmental permitting, navigation fees and fishing licences. These external sources of income gave the Agency a greater degree of resilience from government, especially when it began to put a squeeze on resources and contrasted greatly with the position of the other key national environmental regulator, England Nature (later to become Natural England) which was almost wholly dependent on government funding. It was striking how much flood defences and water dominated the Agency's activities; in my early days on the board, over 45 per cent of the Agency's money was spent on flood defence, some 20 per cent on water resources and just about 30 per cent on other areas of environmental protection. Sitting on the board, I still had concerns whether it would have been preferable, as the House of Commons select committee had originally recommended, to have constructed the Agency to be focused almost exclusively on environmental protection, but was constantly assured that, in practice, the large engagement on water operational issues brought wider environmental benefits.

For my first few years on the board, meetings were held in private. There was no statutory requirement to hold the meetings in public, nor were board papers published. In May 1997, the board discussed the issue of openness and confirmed the current arrangements, which were consistent with the relevant government code of practice at the time. But the board agreed that a summary of its deliberations and decisions should now be posted on the Agency's website after board meetings. Nevertheless, pressures were building for more transparency. Later that year, Michael Meacher, a Minister at the Department of the Environment, met the board and while he accepted that it had taken some steps to make its decisions more transparent, he urged that its meetings should be more open and that the public should have full access to board papers. In 1998, the Labour government had published a White Paper[6] proposing that the boards of all public bodies should, as a minimum, hold annual meetings to improve public understanding of their work. Meanwhile, the Environment Agency's counterpart in Scotland, the Scottish Environment Protection Agency, had moved to holding its board meetings in public, putting pressure on the Agency to follow suit. Marek Mayer, the editor of the influential environmental journal, *ENDS Report*, had regularly requested access to board papers and had equally regularly been refused. He now began a sustained campaign of criticism of the board's lack of openness, making his feelings public at the Agency's Annual General Meeting in September 1998.

The debate continued within the board on the issue. Some members argued strongly that if meetings were held in public, Agency officers would no longer be as candid with us about problems and challenges. My own view was that the time was right to move to a more transparent system. There would still be opportunities for informal discussions outside the board meetings and, in any event, we would

---

[6] *Quangos: Opening the Doors* Cabinet Office (London, Office of Public Service, July 1998).

not always be told the full story by officers, whether operating meetings in private or public. In 1999, we eventually agreed, in principle, that board meetings should be conducted in public and held a dummy run of a public board meeting, watched by a number of assessors, including an official from the Scottish Environment Protection Agency, a trade union representative and the Agency's Head of Public Affairs. One of the main comments of the assessors was that if the meetings were to be held in public, we should no longer have board members and officers sitting together as had been the previous practice. The public needed to see that that the officers were reporting to the board and the two groups needed to be physically separated from each other. We were also advised that board members should be wary of making witticisms as that could be seen by the public that we were not taking issues seriously. I was probably as guilty as any as I do, sometimes, employ a flippant sense of humour as a means of tackling a difficult issue, but I had to learn to restrain myself.

Although there were some areas such as personnel issues or ongoing legal disputes that were reserved for a closed session, we decided that most of the board's business should be conducted in public. Local authorities often agree positions beforehand in advance of conducting business in public, but we never had a pre-discussion on the items in the open agenda and the board meetings involved a genuine and unrehearsed exchange of views. The first open board meetings were well attended by the press and members of the public and it was, initially, an unsettling experience to know that whatever one said was being listened to by a silent but attentive audience. But gradually the meetings became more natural and less inhibited and, at the end of the day, I felt it was a healthy experience. The press and the public had in front of them copies of all the board papers that we were looking at and I could honestly tell them afterwards they were seeing the decisions being made as they happened and there were no secret agendas in play.

Normally, the chair and chief executive would take questions from the public after the formal meeting was completed and there were two particular occasions where proceedings became especially uncomfortable. After the board meeting held in Swansea, we met members of the local community who were extremely concerned about a waste incinerator planned to be built very close to where they lived. Suspiciously, it was just within the boundaries of a neighbouring local authority, which had already granted planning permission for the project. The Environment Agency now had to consider an application for a waste operating licence. After the fairly prosaic discussions of finance and pensions at the board meeting the experience of meeting the local residents brought home to me the very real world in which the Agency operated and the pressures that its individual officers often had to face in dealing with an antagonistic and suspicious public. At a crowded public meeting held a few weeks before, the leader of the local authority had opened by saying that the officer from the Environment Agency would now explain how many people would die if the licence was granted. This was not a middle-class community of professionals and the internet had now given them access to the latest scientific papers on the effects of dioxins and other emissions from incinerators, including those published in other countries. They expected the board members and the Agency officers to be fully up-to-date with the literature.

But the toughest public board meeting I experienced was near Doncaster where a local action group had been agitating about a nearby landfill site for waste. There was an exceptionally high public turnout and we suspected there would be trouble. Sir John Harman, the chair of the Agency, opened proceedings, carefully explaining that this was not a public meeting of the Agency board, but a meeting of the board in public. He was immediately interrupted by the leader of the action group who demanded that we discuss there and then their concerns about the waste disposal site. Sir John explained this was not an item on the agenda but, when the meeting was over, he and the chief executive would take questions and could discuss the issue with them. The leader of the action group refused to back down, saying they were not prepared to wait for three hours while all the ordinary business of the board was discussed. There was a stand-off and Sir John finally called us to leave the hall. I was spat upon as we left to a jeering crowd and the board retired to a small back room. Rik Navarro, the head of legal services and I suggested that perhaps we should go and meet the group to discuss their concerns but Barbara Young, the chief executive, argued this would simply be caving into mob rule. The agenda had been made public beforehand, clearly stating there would be a question and answer session for the public after the close of the board meeting and we must stick to this. We therefore carried on with our business, against a background of jeers from the crowd as they occupied the main hall. The police had been sent for and arrived in the form of a one young policeman who was horrified to see we were still conducting our board meeting, but now in private. The crowd had assumed they had forced us to abandon our meeting. If they realised this was not the case, there would be even more trouble. Nevertheless, unbeknownst to them, we carried on for several hours and, by the time we had finished, most of the objectors had left out of boredom. In retrospect, Barbara Young was correct not to change the planned agenda, but the experience was a vivid reminder of the very real passions and concerns the public can feel on environmental issues. The practice of open board meetings being held in various locations around the country continued for a number of years, but, apart from occasional exceptions such as the Doncaster meeting, the public attendance was small and it was an expensive exercise, especially in times of increasing financial constraints. In June 2016, the board decided that the practice was no longer justifiable and board meetings are now held in closed sessions in London. Minutes of the meetings and board papers, though, continue to be available on the Agency's website and the board holds more informal public events to discuss particular areas of public interest. I have some regrets, though, that the practice has discontinued, especially as the Scottish Environment Protection Agency continues to have open board meetings. But perhaps, like the major public inquiries of the 1970s and 1980s, it was a brave exercise in open democracy that, in times of austerity, was now past its sell-by date.

The experience of open board meetings also raised questions as to the precise role of board members. Chief executives and senior officers often seemed to treat the board as a sort of non-executive advisory group, but, according to the Environment Act 1995, the chairman and the board members 'were' the Agency: 'The Agency shall consist of not less than eight members nor more than fifteen members.'[7] But what did this really mean in law and who were we representing when we were in the public arena? Initial job descriptions were fairly ambiguous on the point. One board member during my time clearly felt he was there to represent the public, with his main role to hold the Agency and its officers to account. During site visits he would readily tell members of the public about internal weaknesses of the Agency and, in the board meetings, would take some delight in humiliating or catching out Agency senior officers with surprise questions. This did not seem the correct approach to me. In public I felt it my role to defend the Agency as far as I could and, while at the board meetings I would question officers on papers, I generally give them advance notice of my concerns as I did not feel that springing surprises was the most productive method of teasing out information on complex issues. But it was not always an easy balance to maintain.

Another piece of the legislation concerning the board was frustrating and was typical of legal provisions being drafted with the best of intentions but having perverse effects. There had been concern in the 1980s that some hospital trusts had awarded contracts to firms in which trustees had undisclosed interests or relatives who ran the businesses concerned. As a result, statutory provisions for declarations of interests in non-departmental public bodies had been tightened up. In the case of the Environment Agency, Schedule 1 of the Environmental Act 1995 stated a board member who 'is any way directly or indirectly interested in any matter that is brought up for consideration' must declare that interest. I had no problem with this, nor that the board member was disbarred for voting on the matter in question. But the provision then went on to say that once the interest was declared, the member must not take part in any deliberation or decision of the Agency relating to that matter. This seemed perverse. The board, for example, might have been discussing the regulation of chemicals and a member, who had a relative working in the chemical industry, might have some pertinent observations on the subject. Once the interest was declared, others could judge whether the contribution was of value or biased because of the connection. Similar interest provisions existed in local authorities and Sir John Harman, who had been leader of Kirkless City Council, told me he was disbarred from taking part in any discussions on education because his daughter was a teacher. Worse still, because of the draconian consequences of declaring an interest, the Agency legal advice was to interpret what was meant by 'an interest' extremely narrowly. It seemed to me it would be far preferable to have as generous approach as possible to declaring interests and then permit involvement (but not voting) by the member concerned who might have something useful to contribute because of their interest in the matter.

[7] Environment Act 1995, s 1(2).

These provisions about declarations of interest remain in force and I still consider them unhelpful.

Board members, of course, did not confine their contribution to just the monthly board meetings. There were various sub-committees in which we were expected to participate and a good deal of informal interaction with officers on particular issues. I was asked to be the 'Legal Champion'. Lawyers in organisations such as the Agency are often perceived as having a negative influence, frequently having to explain to the chief executive and other officers why a particular course of action was legally impossible. I felt at times it was not always appreciated by the board quite what an impressive team of environmental lawyers has been developed within the Agency. In 2003, the legal publishers Butterworths published a textbook on new pollution legislation that had written by three Agency lawyers – Julia Farthing, Bridget Marshall (who later became the head lawyer for the Scottish Environment Protection Agency) and Peter Kellett (currently head of legal services at the Agency). At just under 500 pages, it was impressive legal work providing a detailed commentary on the background and the provisions of the legislation and the authors did not hold back from their own criticisms where they felt the law or policy was misguided. It was a book that any academic or practitioner would have been proud to have written and I brought it to the attention of the board as an important endorsement of the Agency's legal expertise.

As the only lawyer on the board at the time, I had a particular interest in how the Agency went about the enforcement of environmental law. This was ten years before civil sanctions became available to the Agency[8] and, when it came to dealing with breaches of environmental law, the Agency at the time had a number of possible responses. The most serious was a criminal prosecution and, unlike its counterpart in Scotland, the Agency had the power to initiate its own prosecutions without going through the Crown Prosecution Service. Instead of a prosecution before the courts, it could issue a formal caution, which required an admission of guilt and, though carrying no sanction, would go on the company's record. In some areas of environmental law it could serve a notice requiring compliance within a specified time or it could simply issue an informal warning or advice. Although, technically, nearly all breaches of environmental law were strict liability offences, meaning that the mere act of the breach was an offence without the need to prove intention or recklessness, it was clear that not all breaches were prosecuted. The Agency had to exercise a professional discretion as to how to respond. Re-reading one of my early board papers, we were told that, in 2001, there were just under 45,000 reported incidents of potential breaches. Technically, these were all criminal offences, but many were extremely minor and needed no formal response – in that year there were 717 prosecutions, 360 cautions and 371 notices, with prosecutions focused on what were considered to be the most serious incidents. In the early 1970s Keith Hawkins of Oxford University had carried out

---

[8] On civil sanctions see further ch 11.

some pioneering socio-legal research on how the then regional water authorities exercised their discretion to initiate a prosecution and found that choices were often made by individual officers, applying their own perceptions of what seemed fair and just in the circumstances. In deciding whether to prosecute, the Environment Agency itself had to follow the Code of Crown Prosecutors[9] and still does. This contains a two-stage test: first, it had to be satisfied that the evidence for a prosecution was reliable and credible and that there was a realistic prospect of conviction; second, that the prosecution had to be in the public interest. These are pretty broad criteria and, in 1998, the Agency decided to publish a detailed Environment and Prosecution Policy which contained the principles on which the Agency made its enforcement decisions and it has continued to do so to this day. A published enforcement policy is valuable in that it can help ensure consistency in approach within a large organisation and sends important signals to industry and the general public. For example, the policy can indicate that voluntarily owning up to the offence and taking immediate remediation steps can significantly affect the Agency's likely response. The Agency was somewhat of a pioneer in making public its enforcement policy. When I later conducted the Sanctions Review for the Cabinet Office in 2006, I found that out of 53 national regulators within the scope of the review, only 17 had a published enforcement policy.[10]

The board received regular reports on the number of prosecutions made and initially officers made much of their 100 per cent success rate. I pointed out that this was not necessarily a good benchmark, since it implied that the Agency might not take a case to test a point of difficult law where the result might be uncertain, or where the evidence was not absolutely clear cut but the case still worth pursuing. A 90 per cent success rate might be a better goal, provided one knew the reasons for the failures and that they were not down to poor case management. My advice was accepted and I was pleased to hear from the head of legal services some years later that he had recently congratulated the legal staff on a prosecution they had just lost on an interpretation of the law. He had reassured them that the Agency's actions had been entirely justifiable and it was not a black mark to have been on the losing side. Nevertheless, during my period on the board, it was clear that when criminal cases came before the courts, the fines imposed were extremely small – in 2000/2001, the average prosecution fine was just £3,758. For some companies, the damage to its public reputation from a conviction, however small the fine, might be a sufficient deterrent, but for the less scrupulous, the profit being made for breaking the law often outweighed any fine imposed. I even heard rumours that within the newly privatised water authorities, calculated comparisons between the costs to the company of compliance, the likelihood of detection and levels of fine were sometimes being made. The reasons for the general level of low fines were varied. Magistrates' courts were often unfamiliar with environmental

---

[9] The Code of Crown Prosecutors was introduced under the Prosecution of Offences Act 1985, s 10.
[10] See ch 11.

prosecutions and had to take account of the financial means of the offender, many of whom, especially in the field of illegal waste disposal, were small businesses or even single operators. It was not until 1999 that the Court of Appeal[11] provided general guidance on the level of fines to be imposed in health and safety prosecutions, with the court noting that, 'A fine needs to be large enough to bring that message home where the defendant is a company not only to those who manage it but also to its shareholders'. Many of these principles could be read across to environmental law, but it was only in 2014 that the Sentencing Council issued detailed guidelines for sentencing in environmental offences. This has since had a dramatic effect on increasing the overall level of fines.[12]

Back in the 1990s, the level of fines being imposed by the courts was immensely frustrating for the Agency. In 1999, it decided on a new approach to bring home the importance of compliance – the publication of annual league tables which would 'name and shame' companies guilty of the most serious pollution offences. At board level, we had an intensive discussion as to how best to rate the gravity of the offences, but eventually decided that rather than impose the Agency's own judgement, we would simply list them by the level of fine imposed by the courts. We recognised that the quirkiness of sentencing practice by individual judges and magistrates meant that these tables did not necessarily reflect the comparative reality of the seriousness of the breaches, but at least no-one could question the figures. The 'Hall of Shame', as it was dubbed by the press, captured the attention of the national media and was a lead item on both the BBC and ITV news. *The Guardian's* report was headed 'Worst polluters named in official list of shame', *The Time's* headline was 'ICI heads list of worst polluters' and local radio and newspapers focused on polluting companies in their own regions. It was a bold move and many of the companies listed resented the publicity, though some responded by saying how much they had invested in environmental protection. ICI had come out top of the list with three fines at different plants totalling £382,500. In public it claimed that this was unfair and, in any event, old news. But I was later told that ICI's Chief Executive had privately met with senior staff at the Agency to discuss the steps they should take to avoid appearing so high on the list in the future. The report became an annual fixture, but the next year the Agency decided that, rather than totally focus on the negative, they would also include lists of companies who had gone beyond that statutory minimum in terms of environmental protection and renamed the report 'Spotlight on Business Environmental Performance'. Interestingly, some companies appeared in both lists.

Securing sufficient resources from government for effective environmental enforcement was a continuing battle and the Agency made several responses.

---

[11] *R v Howe & Son (Engineers) Ltd* [1999] 2 All ER 249.

[12] Courts are obliged to follow the guidelines unless satisfied it would be contrary to the interest of justice to do so (Coroners and Justice Act 2009, s 125). In the review I conducted in 2006 for the Cabinet Office on regulatory sanctions, I had recommended that the Sentencing Council publish sentencing guidelines for regulatory offences: see further ch 11.

In 2000, Barbara Young, then the Chief Executive, put up a paper to the board suggesting that the Agency approach the Treasury to request that the income from fines imposed by the courts and which went to them (then around £2.8 million) be returned to the Agency and ear-marked for enforcement activities. I was some-what surprised to find that I was the only board member to have real doubts about the wisdom of such a move. The Agency had always exercised discretion in how it responded to breaches of the law and its judgements and its reputation could be easily undermined if either industry or the public felt that a decision to prosecute rather than take another course of action was being influenced by the prospect of extra income coming to the Agency. I argued my case strongly but found no support from the rest of the board. The proposal went up to the Treas-ury who resoundingly rejected the idea – not on any high-sounding principles about enforcement discretion, but because they wanted the income. They replied that if the Agency received income from fines, the sum would simply be deducted from any government grant-in-aid to the Agency, resulting in no net benefits. The idea was revisited in 2003 in the light of that recent legislation[13] which permit-ted the Lord Chancellor, with the consent of the Treasury, to make regulations allowing fines imposed by magistrates to be paid to another body rather than central government. There was already a precedent in relation to fines for road traffic offences which could now go directly to local authorities, provided the income was directed towards road safety matters. The Agency's case for change confirmed that prosecutions would still only be undertaken in accordance with its enforcement policies and the Code of Crown Prosecutors and that the fine income would be directed towards enforcement activity including giving greater advice to business, especially small and medium-sized enterprises. But the proposal was never followed through. The whole issue of whether regulators should receive any direct financial benefit from sanctions imposed became particularly acute when I was considering the possibility of introducing civil sanctions (allowing a regulator to impose a financial sanction without going to court) during the Review of Regulatory Sanctions I conducted for the Cabinet Office in 2006. I favoured the use of civil sanctions as a sensible response to some types of breaches of law but continued to feel it unwise that the regulator imposing the sanction received any of the income. My recommendation was written into the legislation that followed the Review, which provides that all income from civil penalties goes to the Treasury.[14]

Another potential source of income was charges. From its inception, the Environment Agency had the power to impose charges in respect of licences and consents and over the years an increasing proportion of its income concerned with environmental protection has come from charges as government grant-in-aid was being reduced. The extent to which these charges could reflect not just the costs of granting the licence and monitoring the regulated process in question but also the

---

[13] Justice of the Peace Act 1967, s 60A inserted by the Access to Justice Act 1999.
[14] Regulatory Enforcement and Sanctions Act 2008, s 69. See ch 11.

wider financial burden on the Agency for carrying out enforcement activity against illegal operators raised both legal and political issues. From the legal perspective, charges were made in accordance with a charging scheme approved by the Secretary of State. According to the current government guidance on Environment Agency fees and charges: 'You may have to pay an Environment Agency charge to cover the costs of regulating your activity. The amount you pay depends on the activity you carry out and the regulations that apply to you.' This suggests that charges cannot reflect the costs on wider enforcement carried out by the Agency. Yet, in relation to sewerage charges imposed by privatised sewerage undertakers on industry, the Court of Appeal in 2006[15] held that charges did not have to relate only to the actual cost of regulating the discharge in question but could also reflect the wider costs on the undertaker in providing an effective sewerage system in its area. The charges in that case were made under different legislation, but the statutory provisions relating to the Environment Agency charges appear even more flexible. Yet, whatever the legal position, there is clearly a political dimension. I have long felt that it should be in the economic interests of law-abiding industries to see effective enforcement action taken against illegal operators in the same sector and that they should be prepared to contribute to the costs of so doing. Equally, they could argue that that enforcement activity is a matter of public interest and should be paid for by the taxpayer. In practice, it is not easy to judge the extent to which charges schemes do, in fact, include an element of cross-subsidy for enforcement. With government grant-in-aid to the Agency for environmental protection ever decreasing – it reduced by nearly 60 per cent between 2005 and 2017 – the pressure to make up the short-falls by increasing charges will be all the stronger. However, there will come a point where the legality of doing so may well be tested in court.

A more promising and, in the end, more profound approach towards dealing with financial constraints was the development by the Agency in 2001 of what is termed 'risk-based regulation'. In essence, it implied concentrating the Agency's enforcement activity on those sites and processes considered to pose the greatest environmental risk. A traditional inspection regime for landfill sites, for example, would require all sites to be regularly visited at the same intervals. In contrast, risk-based regulation meant evaluating sites in advance and focusing inspection on those posing greater risks, while well-run sites operated by law-abiding operators would require only the occasional inspection and could even largely rely on self-reporting. It was not a term I had come across before and, when the proposals were first presented at a board meeting, I queried, rather cynically, whether 'risk-based regulation' was really a euphemism for cut-price regulation. The director of operations replied that in a time of financial pressures it certainly would help to use limited resources more efficiently, but that even if he had unlimited finance

---

[15] *Thames Water Utilities v Ministry of Defence* [2006] EWCA Civ 1620.

it was a still direction that was sensible to take. Initially I remained sceptical, but I was comforted by the fact that as the programme was being rolled out, the number of serious incidents at regulated sites was declining. Correlation never necessarily implies causation, but if there had been an increase in environmental incidents I would have had serious concerns. As part of the approach, the Agency developed a fairly sophisticated methodology for evaluating risks, known as Operational Risk Appraisal (OPRA), based in part of the environmental and physical sensitives of a site, the complexity of the process and the operator's track history of performance and compliance. Sites were then banded as a result of the evaluation.

I became convinced that risk-based regulation was indeed the right way to develop and, in many ways, the Environment Agency was ahead of the game compared with most regulators at the time. When the Hampton Review on regulation was carried out by the Treasury in 2005, the Agency's approach was commended and the review[16] advocated that risk-based regulation should be adopted by all regulators. Financial incentives were introduced to encourage industries to obtain higher OPRA scores by varying the charges imposed – those on the lowest band being charged three times the standard charge and those on the highest receiving a modest reduction. Though I endorsed the concept, at the time I had – and still have – two main concerns about the system. First, the decision on banding is essentially as administrative decision made by the Agency, but one with significant consequences for the industry concerned, both in terms of reputation and financial costs. But there is no formal appeal mechanism if an industry queries the decision, other than raising the issue with the Agency or possibly complaining to the local ombudsman. Second, I suspect that very few members of the general public fully understand the implications of risk-based regulation nor are they formally engaged in the decision-making on banding. Almost by its very nature, risk-based assessment will sometimes fail and a serious incident could occur at a site previously judged by the Agency to be low risk. Local residents are unlikely to be impressed to learn that that there have been very few Agency inspections and a great deal of self-reporting because the site had been given a high OPRA score. Engagement with the public at the earliest stages to understand the rationale for the approach, as well as its potential pitfalls, is important if wider confidence in the system is to be sustained.

The concept of a national governmental body which is part of the state yet, at the same time legally and operationally independent from government, was developed in Britain in the nineteenth century and I often found it one that was difficult to explain to my environmental law colleagues in other European countries. In 2004, I was commissioned by a coalition of Northern Irish environmental groups to study the arrangements for environmental governance in the region. At the time – and it remains the case – the equivalent to the Environment Agency,

[16] *Reducing Administrative Burdens – Effective Inspection and Enforcement* (London, HM Treasury, March 2005). See ch 11.

the Environment and Heritage Service,[17] was an executive agency of the Northern Irish government and, unlike arrangements in other parts of the United Kingdom, had no independent legal status. I was asked to look at the position of equivalent environment agencies in other parts of Europe with the presumption that the Northern Irish position was wholly out of step with arrangements elsewhere. In fact, rather to my surprise, the research proved the opposite. With the exception of Sweden where the Environment Protection Agency was legally independent from government, in nearly every other country national environmental agencies were essentially part of the relevant government ministries.

For the Environment Agency, determining the balance between its functions of implementing government policy and acting independently was not always easy. Soon after I joined the board, we received a briefing from the Permanent Secretary of the Department of the Environment, Food and Rural Affairs[18] on how he viewed our role. He was very clear that we could be as critical of government policy as we wished and publicly so, provided there were no surprises. Government expected to have advanced warning of what was to be published by the Agency but would not interfere in any way. In strict legal terms, the government had the powers to direct the Agency on any matter, including how it went about enforcing environmental controls, but it wisely refrained from doing so. As a board member, the closest I saw to government pressure on a specific prosecution concerned the Sea Empress disaster. On 15 February 1996, a loaded oil tanker, the Sea Empress, was sailing towards an oil refinery near Pembroke when she became grounded, causing a major oil spill, the third largest to date in the United Kingdom. At the time, the ship was under the guidance of a pilot employed by Milford Haven port authority and there was evidence that he had been negligent. The Agency considered prosecuting the port authority for causing the pollution, but government began to pressurise the Agency to desist, because any fine would simply come out of the public purse. At the same time, Friends of the Earth was mounting a high-profile campaign on the issue and threatened that if the Agency did not prosecute, they would mount their own private prosecution against the port authority, shaming the Agency by so doing. Despite considersble pressure from government, the Agency decided to prosecute and the board supported the chief executive's decision. In January 1999, the port authority pleaded guilty at Cardiff Crown Court and the judge imposed what was then a record fine of £4 million with an award of £825,000 costs to the Agency.[19] The decision to prosecute was, I am sure, correct, though it did not necessarily mean that the Agency got the public credit for doing so.

---

[17] In 2008, it was renamed the Northern Ireland Environment Agency.

[18] DEFRA had been formed in 2001 when the Ministry of Agriculture Fisheries and Food was merged with the Department of the Environment, Transport and Regions (DETR) In its turn, DETR had been created in 1997 subsuming the former Department of the Environment and Department of Transport. The frequent change in departmental structures since the 1970s has not helped to secure a more integrated approach to environmental policy.

[19] The fine was later reduced to £750,000 on appeal.

One of the board members was sitting in a Welsh pub when the report of the judge's sentence came up on the television news. He heard a group of students praising Friends of the Earth for bringing the prosecution, but one of them said he thought it was actually some organisation called the Environment Agency. The majority, though, had never heard of the Agency and they all agreed that it must be Friends of the Earth who were responsible for bringing the case and should be congratulated for their boldness.

In May 2000, the House of Commons Select Committee on Environment Transport and Regional Affairs published a report on the Agency urging it to take a more high-profile role on environment issues: 'As an important advisor to Government on environmental issues, we would like to see the Agency engage more vigorously in public debate and raise its profile on matters of importance where protection and enhancement of the environment and sustainable development are concerned. Clearly, the Agency must conduct itself in accordance with Government policy, but it should also play an important role in influencing that policy as it is formed'. The Committee wanted the Agency to become a 'champion' of the environment and sustainable development. In evidence to the committee, the minister, Michael Meacher, seemed comfortable with such a role: 'I have always taken the view – and I have to be careful because I am not sure this is necessarily shared by all my colleagues – that I do believe in open discussion. I would not expect the chairman of the Agency to make an outright attack on the government. If he felt the need to make that kind of criticism, I would expect him to come to me and say it very frankly to me. If any of these public officials at a high-level wish to take a view which was different from the government's, perhaps particularly where they had given forewarning that they wished to do that, I see no reason why they should not do so. I think the important thing is the genuine frankness of public debate and there are issues, as we all know, where there is more than one view, which is perfectly reasonable.'

The Agency remains legally independent but the political times have changed. Tucked away in the Coalition Agreement between the Conservative and Liberal Democrats in 2010 was a commitment to reduce the number and cost of quangos. The reforms, headed by Francis Maude in the Cabinet Office, led to the Public Bodies Act 2011, which as initially drafted gave wide power to ministers to make regulations to abolish, merge or change the status of a large list of bodies specified in the legislation. The extensive powers being given to government caused controversy in the House of Lords where many peers questioned the constitutionality of the proposals. Amendments were introduced to allow wider consultations before the exercise of the powers and to introduce a sunset clause so that they did not remain permanent. The Environment Agency had survived any proposals to abolish it on the grounds that it was exercising functions requiring impartiality and technical expertise. However, the government proposals were not simply about cost-saving and there was an underlying philosophy that, in future, policy should more clearly be a function of government. As Francis Maude put it in the House of Commons in 2014: 'A major part of the programme of public bodies reform has been bringing policy functions back to the government in a way that provides direct accountability to parliament. The Agency is empowered to give advice and assistance to the Secretary of State as requested[20] and its operational and technical expertise can clearly be of immense value to government in developing policy. But it seems that the trend is moving away from the Agency acting as an environmental champion in the sense of publicly critiquing the general direction of government thinking on the environment. The government regularly produces what it terms as a 'Framework Document' setting out the respective responsibilities of government departments and their non-departmental bodies. The most recent Framework Document, agreed between the Environment Agency and the Department of the Environment Food and Rural Affairs, describes its role as including being a 'technical adviser of the state of the environment'. Government ministers began referring to the 'DEFRA' family as including the Environment Agency, Natural England and other bodies it sponsored. Common services in many areas are now provided by DEFRA rather than each being carried out by the independent bodies and the Agency's London office has been transferred into the same building as DEFRA. Furthermore, the creation of the 'gov.uk' information website in 2012 means that the Agency's own online presence has considerably diminished. In a recent report concerning Natural England, a House of Lords select committee[21] commented: 'Non-departmental public bodies, while playing a part in the processes of national government, should operate at arm's length from ministers and departments. We share the concerns of witnesses who have told us that Natural England no longer has a distinctive voice. We urge the government to recognise these concerns and to take steps to enable Natural England to operate with the appropriate degree of independence.' Unlike Natural England, the Agency has yet to lose its own press and communications office, but nevertheless there remains unease as to how far its independence will be further compromised. As is often the case, much will depend on the character of the chair and chief executive in how they handle the sensitivities that are inevitably involved. As a lawyer, I remain comforted by the fact that the Agency still maintains a large team of in-house lawyers, probably the largest group of environmental lawyers in the country. There are, as yet, no proposals that these lawyers should be transferred to general government legal services or, indeed, that the Agency's legal work be put out to private tender, even though this would be likely to impose more costs on the public purse. If either of these developments were to occur, I would have grave concerns. For the future, it may be that the role of providing independent and critical analysis of the effectiveness of government environmental policies will be taken up by the post-Brexit proposed Office for Environment Protection.[22] But the Environment Agency's influence on policy development is bound to continue, even if not quite so visibly as before and, no doubt, the new body will find itself drawing on the Agency's information and expertise to assist it in its work.

[20] Environment Act 1995, s 37(2).
[21] *The Countryside At A Crossroads – Is the Natural Environment and Rural Communities Act 2006 Still Fit for Purpose?* (London, House of Lords, Report of Session 2017–2019 HL Paper 99, 2018).
[22] See further ch 13.

8

Academic Environmental Law
Comes of Age

By the mid-1980s there was now a growing, though still small, band of environmental law academics within a number of British universities. Richard Hart, then head of legal publishing at Oxford University Press, began consulting as to whether there was now an appetite for a new specialist journal in this country devoted solely to the subject of environmental law. Compared to the number and range of such environmental journals in the United States, there was little in the United Kingdom at the time. The monthly *Journal of Planning and Environment* was focused on national law and largely aimed at the practitioner, with planning law still dominating much of its content. Academic articles on environmental law had to be placed in more general legal journals such as *Modern Law Review* or the *Cambridge Law Journal*. I responded positively that the time was indeed ripe for such a journal in this country and, to my surprise, was told by Richard Hart that the consensus of others he had consulted was that I should be the first editor. I was clear in my mind that I wanted a journal that would help environmental law to be seen as a subject of serious scholarship in this country, but one that would be distinctive and would appeal to both the academic community and the more thoughtful practitioner. Even the choice of cover design was important in this context – this being well before the days of journals appearing on the web. Green was somewhat of an environmental cliché, as were pictures of windmills and trees. I spent a morning with designers at OUP with swathes of colour charts and chose a deep blue to reflect that this was not some lightweight legal subject and a typeface and gold lettering for the wording on the cover which hinted at modernity. The editorial board also reflected my interest in engaging both lawyers and non-lawyers in the subject. In addition to distinguished legal academics such as Dick Stewart, then of Harvard Law School and Jeffrey Jowell at UCL, Nigel Haigh of the Institute of European Environmental Policy joined the board and, a little later David Fisk, then chief scientist at the Department of the Environment. The initial editorial board also included the vice-chancellors of both Oxford and Cambridge universities – Professor Richard Southwood, a scientist and chair of the Royal Commission on Environmental Pollution and Professor David Williams, a specialist in public law with a growing interest in environmental law. I suspect that attracting both vice chancellors to the board of the same journal was a first.

Initially, it was largely a question of commissioning articles and it was only as the journal gained its reputation that it would enjoy the luxury of many uninvited submissions and a high rejection rate. I had considerable admiration for the scale of environmental law scholarship in the United States, but less so for the enormous length of many articles published in the journals. Writing succinctly, but with authority, is a challenge in itself, but with the support of the editorial board we encouraged submissions that seldom strayed beyond 5,000 words. I also wanted to be somewhat provocative and expose British environmental lawyers to some of the best of legal thinking from continental Europe. The first issue, published in 1989, included two articles from non-British lawyers which address fundamental issues that are still worth reading today. Ludwig Kramer's 'The Open Society, Its Lawyers and the Environment' was based on the Garner lecture he had given to the UK Environmental Law Association in London that year. Ludwig was a senior lawyer working in the European Commission and he provocatively challenged environmental lawyers to be far more active: 'Lawyers know the rules of the game in our society, they are trained and paid for that. So they should voice their knowledge and not just contribute by commentaries alone on the adopted rules, to a government of environmental expertocracies. We take the luxury of leaving much of the public debate on environmental problems to bodies such as Greenpeace, Friends of the Earth, Green Alliance, World Wildlife Fund and others with the inevitable emotionalism which encompasses their action. Lawyers too easily sit back, complacently, taking these groups as alibi, showing some sympathy but seldom join in the debate. And yet they have the possibility of knowing, of having access to data, to hard facts, to studies and findings. They could and should form the missing link between the governing environmental expertocracy and everyone, combining knowledge with information and practice.'

The second article, entitled 'Perspectives on Environmental Law', was by Professor Gerd Winter of Bremen University. This contained a stimulating, though at times intellectually demanding, account of the way that law had developed over the centuries. The nineteenth century had seen the development of laws designed to release the inventiveness and energy of the individual operating in a free market – company law, patent laws, freedom of trade and so on. He termed this 'emancipatory law' and felt that modern environmental law was essentially to be seen as an interventionist approach sitting on top of this body of law. While environmental law had secured some progress, there was now a danger of it becoming bogged down and overloaded, unable to fulfil its overall ambitions. Gerd Winter argued that we should now try to reduce the burden of the task environmental law is expected to undertake: 'The way out of the situation can only be to build solidarity with the environment into the mobilising, subject-emancipating law itself … the emancipatory law must be inoculated with ecological considerations. The one-dimensional pursuit of economic goals which established itself with this law must be expanded, so that ecological interests are immediately represented in it and not merely mediated ex post facto via controlling administrative programmes.'

He described this as the fourth phase of environmental law, but it was one that had yet to be achieved. Gerd Winter's vision of employing laws that encourage individual initiative and energy but are truly embedded with an environmental orientation is surely worth revisiting at a time, in light of Brexit, when there are opportunities for a fundamental rethinking of the way we structure and design environmental law.

The *Journal of Environmental Law* was not a one-man show and, in addition to the editorial board, there was a skilled and supportive band of environmental academics and lawyers giving their time for free. I remained the editor-in-chief for ten years, still immensely enjoyed the role and the challenges involved and would have happily continued in post. But I had seen other journals where the editor remained in place for far too long and thought it best to step down. Chris Hilson of Reading University succeeded me and both he and the current editor, Liz Fisher of Oxford University have introduced effective innovations and changes without losing the initial vision of the journal. It continues to be one of the preeminent academic journals in the field.

In pre-internet days there were real challenges in finding information on the latest developments in environmental law and policy, but the one exception was the monthly ENDS report. This had been started in 1978, the idea of Max Nicholson and a businessman, David Leyton and was initially edited by John Elkington. Its aim was to provide up-to-date and authoritative analysis of what was happening in UK and European environmental policy – a sort of *Economist* for the environment. It rapidly became a key resource for anyone involved in the environment and civil servants often read it to find what was happening in other departments; it was one of those initiatives where it was difficult to imagine how one coped before it appeared on the scene. John was succeeded by Marek Mayer who brought an extraordinary eye for detail and critical scepticism together with the ability to unravel and explain complex issues in an intelligible manner – a specialist journalist of the best sort. He sadly died too young of cancer in 2004 but I got to know him well. In 1982, I persuaded him that there were now in increasing number of important decisions on environmental law being taken by the courts and that ENDS should reflect these. He commissioned me to write a monthly case-analysis, something that I continued until 2019. Writing to a limit of 1,000 words on a complex new case and in language that would be intelligible to both lawyers and non-lawyers was often not easy and, from a purely academic perspective, I knew the column would not be considered 'real' scholarship. But I took immense satisfaction in finding how widely the reports were read both within and beyond the legal profession and sometimes would meet government ministers who had clearly found the column of value.

Within Imperial College I continued to develop research initiatives and expanded the teaching. I remained the only lawyer at the College and Lord Flowers had wisely warned me of the dangers of becoming too isolated from my own core discipline. Maintaining contact with environmental law academics at other universities was important and editing the *Journal of Environmental Law* was of great value in this context. But leading firms of solicitors were now beginning to see the potential of developing an environmental law practice and to kick-start their initiatives they poached some of the leading academics, such as Stephen Tromans, Owen Lomas and Andrew Waite, leaving me feeling a little more isolated. I had always maintained that, aside from patent law, environmental law was one of the few legal areas where the interaction with science was essential and working with some of the best academic environmental scientists continued to remain rewarding. I was able to capitalise on my base at Imperial by holding a conference on environmental science for environmental lawyers, attended by the new wave of environmental law practitioners. With one or two exceptions, most of the lawyers had not studied science since their early days at school and the conference was designed to give them the opportunity to ask some of the best environmental scientists at Imperial all the basic questions they might have otherwise been afraid to raise at a more conventional meeting. New environmental legislation emerging from Europe often contained critically important but, to the non-scientist, well-nigh unintelligible, schedules of chemical terms and sampling methodologies. What, for example, was the difference between organic and inorganic chemicals (this turned out to be rather less clear cut than one might have first imagined) and equally important what was the significance of the distinction for the environment? It was a stimulating and eye-opening day and a number of those who attended still tell me today they remember it well and have found it of immense value for their work.

In 1989, I was promoted to Reader, a rigorous process within Imperial requiring evidence of national and international research and excellence in teaching. Two years later, I felt that environmental law was developing so rapidly that I needed to find funding for another legal post to support my work. I approached the London firm of solicitors Denton Hall (as it then was) with whom I had had contact at the Windscale inquiry during my time at Friends of the Earth to see if they would fund a five-year post for a legal researcher to assist me. I mentioned that doubling the funds would secure a professorship and, to my surprise, they replied that this was their preferred option. I explained there was no guarantee I would be the candidate, but Imperial College insisted my name was put forward. Again, it proved a very tough process since one now had to show international standing and leadership and I had the added burden of satisfying both a scientific and legal academic community. In those days, Imperial College was part of the University of London and candidates had to go through both the College and the University process, with a different set of national and international referees for each stage. Imperial College considered I was suited for a professorship as did the London-based legal academics on the legal committee at the University of London. But one of the committee members from outside London thought that while I would be professor in time, it was a little too soon. In truth, he or she (I never knew the name) was probably correct. One had to show significant contributions since the appointment as a Reader and I had given myself at least five years before I would apply for a promotion rather than just the two-year gap that had, in fact, happened. The news infuriated Eric Ash, who has succeeded Lord Flowers as Rector of Imperial and he was almost persuaded to secede from the University of London there and then.[1] In fact, the University of London legal committee then sought another round of national and international references – almost everyone I met in environmental circles seemed to have contributed – and the appointment was confirmed in 1991. At the same time, the University of Kent were also recruiting for a professor of environmental law and Bill Howarth, an expert in water law, was appointed there just three months later. As he still likes to tell me, I may have been the first professor of environmental law in the UK, but his was the first professorship in the subject that had been advertised and was subject to a competitive process.

The funding from Denton Hall allowed Imperial College to make another legal appointment and Nicola Atkinson, an Australian lawyer with both practical and academic experience, was appointed. Over the next few years we secured research contracts on various aspects of environmental law, including contaminated land, chemical regulation and climate change and built up a small team of very bright legal researchers including a young Irish barrister, Martin Hession. He had one of the most febrile and creative legal minds I had come across to date and eventually moved to a senior position in climate change in the European Commission. I had now been at Imperial College for over ten years and was beginning to feel that if I did not move soon, I would be there for the rest of my working life. Gordon Conway and other key figures with whom I had worked at the start of my academic life there had moved on and I was conscious that I still was rather isolated from mainstream legal academic communities where environmental law was developing apace. Oxford University had recently set up an Environmental Change Unit (ECU), designed to bring an interdisciplinary approach to the subject with a new Masters' Course. Its first director left halfway through his five-year term and the directorship was advertised. I was encouraged to submit my cv in a rather informal manner and was surprised to be telephoned a few months later by the vice-chancellor of Oxford to say that the appointments committee had unanimously decided I was the right person for the job. It was not quite what I was looking for, but a professorship at Oxford was a strong temptation: I already lived near the city and I knew I could bring a legal and policy dimension to the unit which they were lacking at the time. But the then Rector of Imperial, Lord Oxburgh, advised against me taking the post. He told me he had been a professor both at Oxford and Cambridge and I would find it unrewarding, as there would be far too much internal politics and the constant search for funding would be draining. I replied that I had been told in writing that core funding was not something I need be concerned about.

Risk-taking at certain points in one's career can be valuable and I felt if I did not take the position, I might always be kicking myself later. I therefore accepted,

[1] Imperial College eventually did secede from the University of London in 2007.

moving to Oxford in 1994, but realised within a few weeks that this was going to be a major challenge. The ECU was in a far more vulnerable state than I had been led to believe. I had studied law at Oxford but then had little idea of the delicate relationship between the University and the Colleges. Colleges were legally independent and could establish their own initiatives and compete with the university for research contracts. Some were already doing so in the environmental field and the ECU, being a university initiative, had no powers of coordination. The ECU itself did not formally come within any faculty within the university – making it very exposed. Core funding was essential if it was going to have any real momentum, but it became clear on my arrival that, despite what I had been told, it was, in fact, competing with many other calls on the university development office.

The ECU already had around 15 researchers working on reasonably long-term contracts concerned with climate change and energy conservation and I brought with me two legal researchers from Imperial College working on existing contracts. At Imperial, tenured academics and researchers on fixed-term contracts were largely treated as equals. Oxford was very different and, with the exception of two senior research leaders, the main band of researchers had no access to colleges and felt largely that they were second-class citizens, excluded from the core element of university life in Oxford. My chair was linked to Linacre College which had long shown an interest in the environment and one of my proudest achievements was to have persuaded Linacre to give researchers at the ECU automatic dining rights should they so wish. It may sound a rather trivial initiative to those outside Oxford, but to the researchers it gave them, at long last, a recognised status and connection within the system and I was roundly applauded when I told them the news. No college had done this before with a university research institute and the arrangement continues today. The current principal of Linacre told me last year that it remains a unique set-up within Oxford University.

In the year I arrived, the ECU had launched its own one-year Masters' course on environmental change – similar to the MSc at Imperial but with differences. It was slightly weaker on the physical science but stronger on subjects such as anthropology and social science. At Imperial College, there were transparent financial procedures concerning the proportion of fees a department running a course would receive, but this did not seem to exist at Oxford at the time and all arrangements were subject to individual negotiation. I was somewhat shocked to find that, far from receiving any fee income, the ECU was expected to fund the administrative costs of running the course from its own research grants. I explained to a relevant university committee that this was really intolerable and that the ECU's teaching costs should be paid out of fee income, only to be told I was a little ahead of my time. Looking back, I realise that there may have been some method to the madness. I had had a long interest in film making and was then chairman of Merchant Ivory Productions. The company's ebullient producer, Ismail Merchant, once explained to me that, with independent film making, one often had to start making a film without all the finance in place otherwise it would never get made. I expect the same had happened here and the new course would have taken years to launch if all the financial issues had been sorted out beforehand. In the event, despite the unhappy financial arrangements, we launched the course and it remains today one of the most successful of its type in the country.

Despite some notable achievements, including a one-day conference on transport at a packed-out Sheldonian Theatre and involving the Secretary of State for Transport, I found much of my experience of directing the ECU frustrating and exhausting and felt unable to play to my strengths. I expect I was rather too impatient and the university decision-making procedures were far too cumbersome for my tastes. After just over a year, I went to the Vice Chancellor to explain this really was not for me, but that if some of the fundamental arrangements concerning the ECU were not resolved, they would be unlikely to find a third director of any standing. Rather than making public my concerns, I penned a memorandum explaining what I thought was needed (including proper association with a faculty, guaranteed income from the Master's course and so on). The Vice Chancellor was both sympathetic and apologetic and said there was a tendency in Oxford to sow a thousand seeds of new initiatives without proper long-term support. Many of my recommendations were acted upon before a new external director was appointed and I was later told that, by leaving, I achieved what would otherwise have taken at least ten years to secure if I had remained. The ECU subsequently became the Environmental Change Institute and is now a flourishing and world-leading academic research institute.

Imperial College welcomed me back (Lord Oxburgh resisted telling me 'I told you so') and together with Andrew Blazer, a former environmental adviser at the CBI, we developed a new specialist option on the MSc Course called Business and the Environment. Pioneering in many ways, it covered environmental issues directly affecting businesses such as company law, eco-labelling, sustainable development and life-cycle analysis. Nevertheless, I was becoming increasingly aware of the extent to which environmental law was impinging on other areas of substantive law such as trade, competition and even company liquidation and felt, that, intellectually, there was now more to be gained from the company of legal scholars. I had already been approached by one London Law School, but discussed my plans with Jeffrey Jowell, then Dean of the Law Faculty at University College London. I explained that, at the time, I had heavy commitments with bodies such as the Royal Commission on Environmental Pollution and the Environment Agency and it was only fair that I should seek a part-time appointment. Jeffrey replied that this, in fact, met his personal vision for a modern law school. He wanted a mixture of full-time and visiting academic appointments but with one or two academics employed part-time – treated as full members of the Faculty with their own rooms and administrative support staff – but also fully engaged with the outside world. He encouraged me to apply but I first discussed the possibility with Jane Holder, then the only lecturer at the Faculty specialising in environmental law, in case she was uncomfortable at the prospect of my joining. But she was very supportive and I moved to UCL in 1999. I was a little wary following my Oxford experience but, in the event, UCL provided everything that had been promised to me and has since proved to be an immensely supportive and friendly academic environment.

At the time I moved to UCL, legal regulation as a method of securing environmental outcomes was being denigrated in government and policy circles, both at national and EU level. Tony Blair had just given his first speech on the environment as prime minister and the word 'regulation' received just one scant mention in what he said. Other approaches such as voluntary agreements between government and industry, economic measures such as taxes, emissions trading and liability regimes were being promoted as being more effective and less cumbersome than the more conventional regulatory methods of licensing, legally binding emission standards and similar control regimes. For my 2002 inaugural lecture as a professor at UCL I therefore decided to make what was, at the time, a rather bold defence of the power of traditional regulation – the title, 'Regulating in a Risky Environment', was intended to refer to the prevailing political climate rather than environmental risks as such. I was not opposed to the use of different forms of policy instrument, but felt they were not being subject to the same level of critical scrutiny as was traditional regulation and, with one or two exceptions, where they had been used, the results were not as positive as their proponents had predicted. They also tended to lack the requirements for transparency and rights of public involvement that were now built into more formal regulatory processes. But I reserved my main criticism for the term 'command and control', which was frequently being used in the legal and policy literature to describe conventional methods of regulation. The phrase had emerged from the United States and was clearly intended to be pejorative, implying an approach that was unnecessarily bureaucratic and prescriptive and capable of stifling innovation. I felt the term was now burdened with so much critical baggage that it should be ditched in future and that, as I put it, 'new terminology should be developed to provide a space for a more detached appreciation and relocation of the appropriate role and development of future environmental regulation'. I came up with the phrase, 'determine and direct', as a substitute for 'command and control'. 'Determine', I felt, was preferable to 'command' in that it still implied that it was government, rather than science or economic theory, that had the responsibility for deciding the goals of environmental policy. But in a modern society, government could no longer simply dictate these goals but needed to involve new procedures and processes to give legitimacy to the policy choices being made. 'Direction' was intended to indicate a rather more flexible concept than control, implying that regulation should be outcome focused, harnessing the inventive power of industry and the market but within clearly defined boundaries endorsed by legal sanction. I rather hoped that my concept of 'determine and direct' would enter the literature and become the new paradigm, but it was not be. The distinguished twentieth century British scientist, Sir Lawrence Bragg, once said that the secret of writing a good paper was to assume one was giving evidence on oath and had to justify the accuracy of every word but that, for a good lecture, 'the force of impression depends upon a ruthless sacrifice of unnecessary detail'. In retrospect, it was a mistake to have left my idea of 'determine and direct' to the end of a long and rather dense presentation – if it was to have changed the language of the debate it should have been up front at the beginning and remained a clear and powerful drumbeat throughout.

Jane Holder and I decided to establish a centre within the UCL Faculty of Laws to provide a focal point for environmental law teaching and research. We deliberately called it the Centre for Law and the Environment rather than an environmental law centre. The term 'environmental law' can be treated as a fairly confined set of laws and it seemed to me that what was of most interest was how all areas of law (eg energy, transport, competition or company law) impact on the environment – hence our name for the initiative. Ned Westaway, a recent LLM graduate and now one of the rising stars of the environmental law bar, became the Centre's administrative coordinator for its first year. Over the next few years, the Law Faculty made several appointments bringing together a rich range of academics who could cover national, European and international environmental law. They included Joanne Scott, an expert in European law, Catherine Redgwell, a specialist in international energy and environmental law (who later moved to Oxford to the Chichele chair in international law) and Phillipe Sands, a barrister and international environmental scholar, who, like me, was a part-time appointment. A few years later, they were joined by Maria Lee from Kings College. I would like to claim credit for attracting such an impressive body of expertise and many at the time thought I was consciously empire-building. But it was far from the case and in fact I knew nothing of the applications being made, though, of course, welcomed their presence and involvement in the Faculty.

At Imperial College, all academics was expected to regularly secure research contracts and I had already transferred several existing contracts to UCL and took with me Ray Purdy, a young researcher who had initially joined me in Oxford. Contracts included a number from the European Commission concerning the compatibility of national law with European environmental directives and these required a painstaking examination of complex national legislation with an article-by-article analysis of the relevant European law. Our reports were well received and sometimes formed the basis on infringement proceedings brought by the Commission against the UK. Many of these contracts were fairly short-term, but there were two which developed into larger projects and tackled issues still of relevance today.

The first concerned the potential use of satellites in the enforcement of environmental law. It was an area that Ray Purdy and myself had initially developed at Imperial College under EU funding and involved a number of European research institutes. At the time, imagery from satellites was still fairly broad in scale, but it could detect changes in land patterns and was being used by the European Commission to monitor farmers claiming subsidies under agricultural support programmes. Ray and I were especially interested in the extent to which satellite imagery could be used to assist the enforcement of environmental law. We were conscious that the technology could raise issues of privacy – there was emerging case law in the European Court of Human Rights concerning the use of CCTV images and privacy – and it seemed somewhat of a contradiction that while there were detailed legal rules concerning the use of search warrants to enter premises, as well as case law concerning trespass by low-flying aircraft, there was nothing in law to inhibit satellites flying over private and public property and taking images. At the time, the resolution of the imagery (car number plates or individual persons could not be detected) was probably not powerful enough to raise privacy problems, though increasingly it might in the future as the technology is constantly improving. We wanted to explore how a court might consider the evidential value of satellite imagery in litigation (eg photographs had been accepted by the British courts since the late nineteenth century). We worked closely with remote sensing experts who were confident that their imagery could be of value in environmental disputes. In Greece, for example, there had been many forest fires where, somewhat suspiciously, the boundaries of neighbouring farms seemed to expand after the fires had burnt out. Satellite imagery taken before and afterwards could precisely reveal the changes that had taken place. Another group of our experts claimed that the technology could detect illegal waste disposal operations. We decided to test the claims being made by the technical experts by organising a mock court in Italy involving three practising judges from England, Greece and Italy. They were totally unfamiliar with the technology (as would be many judges) to an extent that was surprising to the scientists – one judge even asked whether there was someone in the satellite taking photographs. I arranged for a British criminal barrister to cross-examine the technical experts to test their assumptions and as would happen in a real case, he was briefed by one of the experts on the scientific weaknesses that existed but were not being made very apparent by those promoting the technology. Imagery from satellites is derived from digital data with various technical interventions and adjustments applied subsequently to produce a recognisable picture and the barrister was able to probe these undisclosed interpretative interventions to undermine the reliability of the images as acceptable evidence.

In many ways, this early research was a little ahead of its time. The resolution and coverage of satellite imagery has now developed rapidly and continues to do so. We were able to continue the research at UCL under a major research council grant working with remote sensing experts in the college and since then, Ray Purdy has gone on the establish a consultancy specialising in the use of satellite imagery especially in the field of environmental law enforcement. At a time when environmental regulators are increasingly under financial pressure, its potential value is even greater and is beginning to be recognised officially. In 2017, the European Commission launched proposals to improve environmental governance and enforcement and specifically mentioned the potential of satellite technology in this context. In the same year the Commission presented satellite imagery to the European Court of Justice for the first time in infringement proceedings. The case concerned habitat and birds protection in the Bialowieza forest in Poland and the Commission presented satellite imagery to demonstrate that the government had breached an interim injunction imposed by the court prohibiting further forestry management operations until the final court hearing. The Commission has no direct powers of inspection on the ground in environmental infringement cases and clearly the satellite imagery they had obtained was enough to challenge Poland's assertion that the forestry operations had ceased. As the Court noted, 'While the Republic of Poland may deny that those satellite images have any evidential value, they are nonetheless sufficient, taken together, to raise doubts that Poland has complied fully with the order of the Vice-President of the Court of 27 July 2017'.[2] Failure to comply with the interim injunction resulted in a financial penalty being imposed. I remain convinced that the value and potential of satellite technology in the enforcement of environmental law has yet to be fully realised. But as Ray Purdy has since found out, there are those in government and the regulatory bodies who appear to be uncomfortable with exploiting a technology that might reveal that, say, the extent of illegal waste disposal is far worse than expected. 'FOFO', or the fear of finding out, is often a powerful disincentive in official circles. There also remain important issues such as the development of stringent codes of practice concerning data collection and analysis (such as has been developed with DNA evidence) if satellite imagery is to have rigorous evidential value in legal proceedings. And there should be much closer collaboration between those developing new satellite technology and those engaged in law enforcement so that both understand more fully at an early design stage the requirements that would be of most practical value. But I expect that for the next generation of environmental lawyers, satellite imagery may become as familiar and compelling as CCTV and photographs are in today's legal proceedings.

The other main area of research at UCL that engaged my interest was carbon capture and storage, a technology designed to extract carbon dioxide from power stations and other industrial processes to prevent it being emitted into the atmosphere. The carbon dioxide is then liquified and stored deep underground. I had first encountered the term when I was a member of the Royal Commission on Environmental Pollution during its seminar study on energy and the environment in 2000.[3] Carbon capture as a technology dealing with climate change was still then in its very early stages and, although the Commission advocated much greater investment in renewables and energy conservation, it was likely that baseload power stations would be a key part of any realistic future scenario. Some of the members considered that nuclear power would be the only option in that context, but other scientists on the Commission were far less convinced and in the various future energy scenarios developed by the Commission fossil power stations involving carbon capture were presented as an alternative to nuclear power.

It was already apparent that there were legal issues of some complexity that would be involved and I organised a conference on the subject at UCL. Initiatives were already been made in various areas – the UK government was planning a

[2] *Commission v Poland* C-441/17 R 20 November 2017.
[3] See ch 9.

new regulatory framework on carbon capture, the European Commission was beginning plans on a directive on the subject and at international level, there were concerns about whether the existing provisions in international treaties on marine pollution would unintentionally prohibit carbon storage beneath the sea. But it became apparent at the conference that it was difficult even for the specialists involved to have an overall sense of all the developments taking place and it struck me it would be valuable to create a programme focusing on the legal aspects of carbon capture – one that would provide comprehensive and freely accessible information on legal developments taking place round the world for anyone engaged in the subject whether at national, European or international law. There was an immediate need for such an initiative and securing sufficient funding from research councils would have taken far too long. I therefore approached several industries and public bodies see if they would support to our proposed programme. Carbon capture was already an area of controversy amongst some environmental groups who felt it simply allowed the continuance of fossil fuel and I was anxious that our programme was seen to be completely detached and neutral. UCL advised seeking what was termed a donation research model under which there were no contractual deliverables to the sponsors who gave us complete freedom to develop the programme as we wished. Securing research funding is never easy, but with industry and commercial organisations it was a completely different process from writing lengthy research grants and a challenge in its own right. We had to make succinct presentations to senior executives and be absolutely clear in what we were proposing to do and why it was needed. But decisions were made quickly, often within a few weeks and, after some months of hard work, we were able to secure sufficient funding from organisations such as Shell, Rio-Tinto and the Crown Estate to launch the UCL Carbon Capture Legal Programme in 2010. The programme continued for five years and was able to create a comprehensive legal resource library, commission a series of research reports, organise two major conferences in London and New York and produce an edited book on carbon capture and the law, the first of its kind. Legal understanding of the issues involved has developed considerably over the period and new bodies such as the Global Carbon Capture Storage Institute, initially funded by the Australian government, have since been established. We worked closely with the GCCSI and the International Energy Agency, especially in the creation of their regulators network which met annually at their Paris headquarters. Regulators implementing existing areas of environmental law often meet and discuss their work in various networks, but this initiative was distinctive in that regulators from many different countries were coming together to consider an emerging technology and what would be needed in terms of designing an effective regulatory framework to handle its future development. Universities should be at the forefront of research and after five years I felt the programme had fulfilled its initial goal and that governments and other bodies now had the resources and expertise to address and develop the legal and regulatory issues involved. My leading collaborative researcher on the project,

Ian Havercroft, moved to the Global Carbon Capture Institute where he is currently senior consultant on legal and regulatory matters.

At the time of writing, there were 22 large-scale CCS facilities in operation around the world, but commercial progress in Europe remains tantalisingly slow. There is some irony in that it was the European Union which in 2009 developed the first piece of legislation in the world addressing the complete process of CCS from initial capture and transport to final storage. But public opinion in many European countries remains largely sceptical of its value and while developing a sound regulatory framework that addresses environmental concerns without stifling the technology is essential, it is clear that law by itself cannot deal with the policy, economic and public acceptance issues that must also be addressed if carbon capture is to fulfil its potential. At one stage UK industries had been world leaders in the technology and the country still has immense potential for storage in former oil and gas fields under the North Sea. But government has failed to provide sufficient and consistent support during the last decade, though its recent commitment to a zero-carbon goal in 2050[4] may signal a change. Certainly, the UK Climate Change Committee has recently described carbon capture and storage as a necessity, not an option, if this goal is to be achieved.[5]

Directing the UCL Centre for Law and the Environment was exciting and rewarding but it is always sensible to refresh and renew and I was delighted when, in 2017, Professor Maria Lee agreed to take over its directorship. New academic appointments have since been made, including Professor Eloise Scotford and Steven Vaughan (now co-director of the Centre), bringing in a younger generation of environmental law scholars. I remain an Emeritus Professor with UCL and am confident that the university will continue to play a leading role in the field of environmental law and the challenges yet to come. And it is equally clear that research and teaching in environmental law is flourishing in many other UK universities. The number and quality of articles from British academics being regularly published in the Journal on Environmental law – by both familiar names and an emerging cadre of younger scholars – is witness to just how far the discipline has matured in little over a generation.

---

[4] The Climate Change Act (2008) (2050 Target Amendment) Order SI 2019/1056 (26 June 2019) amended the 2050 target of 80% in the Climate Change Act, s 1 to 100%.

[5] Committee on Climate Change, *Net Zero – The UK Contribution to Stopping Global Warming* (London, Committee on Climate Change, 2019).

9

Swirling Worlds

The Royal Commission on Environmental Pollution

Science is fragmentary, incomplete; it progresses slowly and is never finished; life cannot wait.

Emile Durkheim

Some ten years before the creation of the current system of parliamentary select committees, the Royal Commission on Environmental Pollution (RCEP) had been established in 1970. The environment had been rising on the political agenda and two years later saw the 1972 UN Stockholm Conference on the Human Environment, the first major international conference on the environment in the contemporary era. The RCEP was an independent advisory body with extremely broad terms of reference and could largely choose its own subjects for investigation. It never felt inhibited by the term 'pollution' in its title and, rather like the early Friends of the Earth environmental campaigns, decided it should investigate the underlying causes of environmental problems rather than focus simply on 'end of pipe' pollution controls. Its chair was always a distinguished scientist as were the majority of its members. This clearly gave the body a distinctive authority, but membership also regularly included several non-scientists, included at various times journalists, economists and lawyers. As such, the RCEP was not a specialist scientific body and the members acted in their personal capacity rather than as representatives of any particular group or interests as happens in stakeholder groups. It would often describe itself as a committee of experts rather than an expert body.

As the in-house lawyer at Friends of the Earth and later in my early academic career, I followed the work of the RCEP assiduously and would regularly attend the press conferences when they launched their latest report. Before the growth of the work of parliamentary select commitees, it was, perhaps, the only official independent body that provided in-depth critiques of the way that environmental policy was working and their reports had immense authority. But, compared to the select committee inquiries, their investigations were normally much lengthier, taking a year or more and often involving intense discussions between members from their different disciplinary perspectives, something I had rarely seen amongst members of parliament. For almost ten years their sole legal member was Lord Nathan, who was chair of the House of Lords European Sub-committee on the Environment and later became the first president of the UK Environmental Law Association. He had retired from the Commission in 1990 and, for a time, the RCEP had no lawyer. I had never considered myself sufficiently eminent to be a member of such a distinguished body, but I realised I had made some impact when I attended one of the press conferences for the launch of their latest report. A journalist asked a question about the law and the chair of the Commission turned to me in the audience to see if I could provide an answer. Luckily, I was able to make some convincing-sounding reply and shortly afterwards received a letter from the Prime Minister's office asking whether I would consider joining the RCEP. This was before the Nolan principles established by the 1994 Committee on Standards on Public Life which now require all public appointments to be advertised and subject to lengthy application forms and interview processes. I entirely understand why the procedures were introduced for bodies having large executive functions and financial responsibilities. But I still have some concerns that where purely advisory roles are sought, demanding considerable time often on a voluntary basis (and Royal Commission members received no daily fees when I joined), the procedures favour the ambitious. Good candidates who would never think of themselves as potential members may well be deterred by the appointments process. To many, now, I suspect the way that I was appointed to the Royal Commission must be redolent of an old-fashioned system that lacked any transparency, but I wonder whether we should consider some new combination of procedures to allow for the best of appointments to such bodies.

I joined the RCEP when it was working on the last stages of its report on Freshwater Quality which was published in 1992. It was a lengthy analysis of around 300 pages with over 100 recommendations, but it also illustrated one of the challenges for the Commission and the way it went about its work. There was already considerable policy work on water being developed within government following water privatisation and, at EU level, new approaches to water policy were beginning to emerge which eventually resulted in the Water Directive 2000. The Commission seemed to work at a fairly leisurely pace and one day David Fisk, then chief scientist at the Department of the Environment, had a quiet word with me to say that he was worried that we were missing the boat, as it were, by taking so long to publish our report. Important policy decisions on the issue had already been taken.

Choosing a subject for a study was often not easy. It needed to have enough substance to justify an in-depth investigation, but also to be in an area where the RCEP could have real influence or introduce innovative thinking and where law and policy was susceptible to change. The next study tackled a discrete area, waste incineration. In this country, there was strong public opposition to new incinerators – quite different from other European countries such as the Netherlands where modern waste incineration was often favoured by local communities. The perception of waste incineration in this country had not been helped by the poor history of older incinerators, especially those operated by hospitals, which had generally enjoyed crown immunity from any prosecution for legal breaches. But my own views on incineration changed during the study and I became convinced that modern incinerators operated to the highest standards and preferably combined with energy recovery were a sensible component of waste management and, in many ways, preferable to landfill where there were still many unknowns as to what was really happening underground.

The Commission emphasised that incineration had to be seen in the context of a waste hierarchy where one should start by avoiding waste wherever possible and move onto recycling before considering disposal. The emission of dioxins from incinerators was then a particular cause for public concern, but we concluded that with modern emission standards incorporating large safety factors there should be negligible public health effects. But the subject also revealed some of the oddities in toxicology science, an issue that helped to stimulate the Commission's later study into environmental standards. Toxicology standards were normally derived from studies on exposure to small animals, yet the susceptibility of different species to dioxins was enormously variable. Rather bizarrely, experiments have shown guinea pigs to be some 5,000 times more vulnerable to dioxins than hamsters, but the reasons were unknown, let alone whether humans were more akin to guinea pigs or hamsters. In practice, because of the lack of certainly about effects on humans, a large safety factor was applied and human exposure standards were sometimes pitched at 100 times greater than those known to cause lethal effects to the most sensitive test animals. As a result, emissions standards could well be considerably higher than what was actually needed to protect human health, but the risk could not be taken.

The study recognised that the availability of cheap landfill was an economic deterrent to using other waste management options including incineration or promoting less waste and the Commission recommended a levy be introduced for waste deposited by landfill. Three years later, John Gummer, the Secretary of State for the Environment, introduced the landfill tax, the first environment tax in this country and one that remains in force today. The report was also distinctive in that it included a discussion of the so-called 'proximity principle' which was already reflected in EU waste legislation and provided that, generally, problems should be solved as close as possible to their source. But the Royal Commission's discussion brought out some of the potential contradictions when it came to incinerators. The proliferation of small incinerators for hospital waste could be said to be complying with the proximity principle but was environmentally damaging; the Commission felt it should be replaced by a lower number of large, properly staffed, plants.

It is difficult to judge the extent to which the report provided the basis for a new impetus in building waste incinerators. Seven years later, the government's new Waste Strategy noted that: 'If we are to achieve a sustainable waste management system, then incineration with energy recovery will need to play a full and integrated part in local and regional solutions developed over the next few years.' Pressure to reduce the amount of waste going to landfill as a result of the EU

Landfill Directive agreed in 1999 was clearly a key factor and both the RCEP and, to be fair, the government's own strategy had emphasised that waste incineration, even with energy recovery, had to be seen in the context of a waste hierarchy where waste reduction and recycling were the first preferred options. A recent report from the Green Party[1] has noted that the number of municipal waste incinerators tripled between 2010 and 2017, each with 30–40 lifespans and requiring massive amounts of waste to ensure full capacity and economic viability. At the same time, household recycling rates have stalled since 2013 and 2018/2019 predictions are that, for the first time, the amount of municipal waste incinerated will exceed that recycled. This was not, I think, a trend that the RCEP would either have predicted or welcomed.

The RCEP's next study concerned transport and its 1994 report, *Transport and the Environment* received enormous publicity. In its very first report published in 1971 the Commission had drawn attention to the problems for air quality that would follow from a predicted doubling of road vehicles in this country by 1995. In 1974, it again highlighted the impossibility of catering for the unrestricted use of motor vehicles. So, the new study was building on previous concerns of the Commission but was much broader and addressed nearly all aspects of transport, including their environmental effects, land-use planning, freight transport and cycling and pedestrian usage. The Commission recognised the enormous benefits that modern transport systems had brought to society, but government forecasts for road traffic in 1989 predicted a doubling of traffic by 2025. The Commission concluded in its report: 'Even allowing for technical improvements in vehicle design, the consequences of growth on such a scale would be unacceptable in terms of emissions, noise, resource depletion, declining physical fitness and disruption of community life.' In discussions with the Department of Transport, it became clear that a key driver for future policy direction with the Department was the use of targets for accident reduction – it then had a target to reduce deaths and injuries in 2000 by two-thirds from 1985 levels. The RCEP endorsed the use of longer-term targets in other areas of transport policy to help drive government action and proposed targets for increasing freight on rail, cycling and pedestrian use. The use of a long-term target as a policy instrument became a key recommendation for climate change in its subsequent report on energy.

In my early days at Friends of the Earth, I had been particularly involved in its bicycle campaign and was therefore delighted to see other members of the Commission take up the subject enthusiastically. On a visit to Delft in the Netherlands, members even took to riding cycles on the impressive, integrated network of cycle routes which completely separated cyclists from road vehicles. For a fairly modest outlay, a large proportion of the inhabitants now cycled to work in all weather conditions and there had been no fatal accidents or serious injuries in the last five years. The then chairman, Sir John Houghton, was so taken with

---

[1] *A Burning Problem – How Incineration is Stopping Recycling* (London, Green Party, July 2018).

the experience that on his return he decided to cycle from his home, five miles North of Oxford, to the city centre. The initial journey was straightforward and pleasant, riding on a dedicated cycleway beside the main road built in the 1930s. But once past the Oxford ring road and travelling towards the city centre, he found himself sharing the space with large buses in a bus lane and said he would never do it again. The failure to plan for complete systems of separated cycleways was all too familiar in many British towns and, with one or two exceptions, the picture remains depressingly the same today – cycling in many urban areas is not for children or the elderly.

There were then two economists on the RCEP and economic analysis featured fairly heavily in the Transport report. The Commission attempted to quantify the external economic costs of transport and whether road users paid their full costs in licence and fuel tax. But the exercise brought its own dangers. A table in the report attempted to estimate the costs for air pollution, climate change, noise and vibration and this was seized upon by road organisations to prove that car users easily repaid any environmental costs they imposed on society. But this ignored the fact that the tables referred only to 'quantified' costs and conveniently over-looked a rather smaller box stating that there were other costs such as loss of land, visual intrusion, loss of habitats and the separation of communities where the Commission could not estimate money values with any degree of certainty. Never-theless, even on the quantified costs alone, it was clear that drivers of heavy good vehicles were not paying for their full external costs – the Commission estimated they were paying at most 70 per cent of the costs imposed – and it was a fact that I seized upon in subsequent press and media interviews. I was later told by Richard Hawkins, an environmental lawyer and adviser to the Freight Transport Association, that at one of the Association meetings someone had said, 'What are we going to do about that bastard Macrory?'. I took that as a compliment that my arguments were having some impact. On fuel efficiency, we were struck by the largely conservative nature of the car industry and that, even using existing technologies, fuel efficiency could be increased dramatically. I argued the case for legally binding efficiency standards equivalent to those for emissions, but the economists' preference for economic instruments won the day. The Commission recommended a fuel tax escalator applied annually to fuel prices. It was not designed to drive people off the roads, but to send powerful signals to manufacturers to improve efficiency. The government had already introduced a fairly modest fuel tax escalator in 1993, but the Commission wanted to go further and recommended one that would lead to a doubling of the price of fuel in ten years 'in order to alter user's expectations it is important to make clear that the aim is a permanent and substantial increase in prices'. The incoming Labour government increased the annual escalator to 6 per cent but, a few years later, political protest at a time of rising oil prices led to its effective emasculation and the new coalition government in 2010 abandoned the concept. Some studies suggest that, before its suspension, the escalator was begin-ning to have an effect on improving fuel efficiency in cars and changing purchasing habits, but it illustrated to the lawyer in me that economic instruments are all too easily vulnerable to political change and misunderstandings as to their purpose. In retrospect, I still suspect that legally binding efficiency standards would have been a far more effective policy instrument.

The RCEP was never a stakeholder body as such and, in many ways, it was unashamedly elitist. But during the transport inquiry, we did try and engage more widely with more than just the experts or organisations who provided evidence. I chaired a public meeting of the Commission held in a fairly deprived part of Tyneside which brought home to me the fact that almost a third of households did not own a car at the time and were wholly dependent on public transport.[2] Bus privatisation within local authorities was being rolled out and many of those at the meeting complained that finding information on time-tabling had become incredibly difficult and complex with so many operators involved. Rail privatisation had also been proposed by the government and we had a meeting on the subject with the then Secretary of State John MacGregor. We explained we were not opposed to injection of new ideas and approaches that the private sector could bring to the industry, but thought the model being proposed, separating the track from the operators, was excessively complex. It would simply encourage internal friction and competition within the rail sector, when the railways should be directed at offering better services to compete with cars and short air flights. But he remained committed to the model they had proposed. My own preference has long been the approach used for buses in London where routes are operated by the private sector, but the consumer experiences what appears to be a seamless public service.

In one of our last study meetings before the report was published, Sir John Houghton noted that it now contained over 100 recommendations and invited us to go away and come back with what we each thought were the five most important. It was a good reminder of how experts from different disciplines, even when they have worked together on a subject for nearly three years, still perceive the world in quite distinct ways and there were quite remarkable differences in what were viewed as the most important recommendations. I considered our key proposal was that the Department of Transport should be restructured to reflect the fundamentally different approach which a sustainable transport policy would involve. But the engineers on the Commission considered some of the recommendations on technology far more significant, while the economists focused on the use of economic instruments.

When we published the report, Sir John Houghton decided that he and I should make the running on media and press interviews and he persuaded me to have media training beforehand. I was initially reluctant, but it proved invaluable. Our instructor reminded us that an interview on the radio would typically be only around 30 seconds and a maximum of three points could be made. Conciseness and focus were essential to get the message across, but I told him that this was not

---

[2] According to government figures, in 2018 the overall figures for households without access to a car had dropped to 20 per cent, but for those on the lowest income the figure was as high as 65 per cent.

easy for this report – we clearly could not go on as we were, but there was no single answer to the problem. He immediately said that those were the two key points to be made and indeed they stood me in good stead for the large number of radio interviews that followed on publication. I was able to add a further compelling fact that had emerged from our study. Out of nine selected European countries, Britain was sixth in terms of car ownership, but third in the average distance travelled by car every year. Even Germany, often seen as a country in love with the car, had a less car-intensive lifestyle. The only real challenge was my appearance on television's Newsnight on the evening of the launch. Rather preciously, perhaps, the Commission had insisted that I be interviewed on my own, as we did not want to become sucked into a debate with politicians, the car industry or environmental groups. The BBC agreed, but in the make-up room shortly before the live interview, Jeremy Paxman explained that the format would be slightly different as they had brought into the studio a large number of representative groups, a government minister and the opposition spokesman, as well as some ordinary members of the public. But he said he understood the Royal Commission was in a slightly different position and that he would just start with me, setting out our main conclusions and then, if time allowed, ask me for some concluding remarks. There was a new design to the Newsnight format; it was now a large studio with participants scattered around in seats surrounded by bits of old cars and Jeremy Paxman pacing around from one group to another. I gave a reasonably fluent opening statement and then relaxed a little, thinking how I should summarise at the end. In the background, I could just about catch the representative from the RAC saying the report would be disastrous for the economy and the next moment Jeremy Paxman was towering over me aggressively asking whether we had costed the report. I replied defensively we had done some costings, but he persisted. I adopted the lawyer's tactic of saying it all depended on what was meant by costs, but Paxman replied, 'You are ducking and weaving, Professor Macrory' and moved on to another participant. Nevertheless, the item was notable for the fact that Steven Norris, the Parliamentary Under-Secretary for Transport, acknowledged that building more roads created more traffic and would not, in itself, resolve the issue – environmental groups had long thought this to be the case, but it was the first time that a government spokesman on television had endorsed that view.

The Transport report attracted enormous publicity and provided an authoritative analysis of reconsidering approaches to transport. But it had less immediate impact on government, with the Chancellor of the Exchequer apparently saying that it was a 'nightmare report'.

Four years later, with a new Labour government in power, the Commission decided to revisit the subject as it was concerned that the full extent of the challenges posed by the future of transport had become even more evident and that progress on change was all too slow. I personally had some doubts whether it was wise to return to a subject so soon, but the report, *Transport and the Environment – Developments Since 1994*, was well received by government, though the environmental challenges of dealing with transport still largely remain.

The next study concerned soil and the environment. Given that the RCEP had already conducted studies on air and water, there was a logic to examining the other key environmental medium. Soil has always been somewhat of a Cinderella in policy and legal terms and has been largely taken for granted. But what emerged from the study was quite how vital this vulnerable asset was to life-support systems and, in many ways, how little was really known about soil and its resilience from a scientific perspective. The Commission called for far more explicit policies to protect soil in this country and its report, published in 1996, made a large number of detailed recommendations. Compared to the Transport report, the Soil study attracted far less publicity at the time; some considered it over-technical and detailed. But it was innovative and, as sometimes happened with Royal Commission reports, somewhat of a slow burner. Six years later, the RCEP commissioned an independent study to evaluate the impact of the report. Gratifyingly, the evaluation concluded that, although the report had not been a best seller or received mass media attention, 'in its own quiet way it seems to have been something of a "mould-breaker"'. A draft Soil Strategy was published by the government in 2001 and, although it was not as powerful as the Commission would have wanted, it would not have happened without the RCEP report. The evaluation concluded that the report's main achievement was not so much in securing agreement to all its recommendations but in raising awareness of soil issues within government and various agencies and bringing soil further up the environmental agenda. There were some good lessons to be learned for future reports. The report was lengthy at over 200 pages and could have done with an accompanying summary to get the key messages across to a wider audience.[3] The blanket list of 89 recommendations failed to bring out the key issues requiring a response.

The RCEP then embarked on a study of environmental standards. The issue had been touched upon in many of its previous reports, but this was the first time the Commission had looked comprehensively at the issue of standards, the forms they should take and how they should be set. As often happened with its inquiries, what started out as appearing to be a fairly narrowly bounded issue turned out to reveal far more complex and underlying questions and touching upon basic fundamentals as to how society thought about the environment. We began by adopting a broad definition of standards moving beyond those simply contained in legal requirements but encompassing any official judgment about the acceptability of environmental modifications from human activities that were intended to have some general application and expected to influence activities affecting the environment. As well as law, standards could be contained in general guidelines, codes of practice or even the criteria for deciding individual cases such as an environmental licence application.

The study acknowledged the key role of scientific assessment in the development of many environmental standards. But while the function of such assessment

---

[3] Subsequently, short summary reports were published to accompany the main reports.

was to provide evidence of impacts and the degree of uncertainly that still existed about the knowledge of the impacts in question, it was not the role of the scientist or a scientific committee to determine at what point the standard should be set on the dose-effect curve. That was essentially a political judgement and reflected the public value that was placed on whatever was being protected – humans, animals or, say, trees. It may seem an obvious distinction to have made, but we had evidence of confusion within some of the government scientific advisory committees as to their role and the point had not been made so forcefully before by an official body such as the Commission. Legal standards that are expressed in numerical terms may appear to have scientific authority but often disguise the fact that, in reality, other issues were at play. To take one example, one of my MSc students at Imperial College had recently conducted a detailed study on the origin of European Community standards for pesticides in drinking water, then set at 0.1 mg/litre for individual pesticides and 0.5 mg/l for total combined pesticides. The 0.1 mg figure had been chosen as the then level of detection, but when he asked the relevant Commission official about the origin of the 0.5 figure, he simply pointed to the number of fingers on his hand.

During the study we were conscious of the work of the British sociologist, Anthony Giddens, then director of the London School of Economics, who had been writing on how contemporary society handled environmental risks against a background of increasing scientific uncertainty and a growing lack of common societal values. He described this as a 'swirling world' and one he felt was, in many ways, immensely exciting in that it provided new opportunities for debate and discussion.[4] A key concern then for the RCEP was how the decision maker, be it a government department, an environmental regulator or a supra-national body such as the European Union, could better seek authoritative information of the relevant values held by the public to assist them in their conclusion. The Commission had two new members, John Flemming, an economist from Oxford University and the Reverend Professor Michael Banner, a moral philosopher from Edinburgh University. Both were extremely bright and became heavily engaged in the issue but revealed utterly different philosophical approaches. Professor Flemming argued that economists had developed the technique of cost–benefit analysis to provide just this type of information to the decision maker on the weight people give to different choices. Usually expressed in monetary terms, he argued this did not reflect real money and could be expressed in any currency, even bread or wine, but it was designed to indicate the relative importance the public gave to the issue in question. Professor Banner fundamentally disagreed, arguing that cost–benefit analysis was concerned with preferences while we were concerned here with values which were quite different. Individuals often did not know their values until exposed to argument and debate and they could not be gleaned from the

---

[4] The cover to the Standards report contained a reproduction of a quilt by Jennifer Hollindale entitled 'Swirling Worlds' though I suspect few picked up on the reference.

questionnaire surveys normally conducted in cost–benefit analysis. Furthermore, a society might endorse a value which was simply non-negotiable in any trade-offs – he gave the example of a policy of not bombing women or children in time of war – even if military strategists said this would shorten a conflict and save lives overall. The two of them conducted the debate at high level, with both producing paper and counter-paper at successive meetings. The arguments were watched with intense interest but somewhat bemused confusion by other members. At one meeting, I asked John Flemming whether he thought that values in the way Michael Banner had described them were, in reality, simply strong preferences and he agreed. In private, the chairman asked me whether there could not be a compromise between the two as with one exception (by economists in the Third report of the Royal Commission) there had never been a minority report. But I felt there it was not possible as these were two utterly different and irreconcilable approaches as to how the human mind thought about the world.

For my part, I remained fairly sceptical of some the claims being made for cost–benefit analysis, though I could not articulate my doubts with the same compelling logic as Professor Banner. But during the discussions, a real-life example occurred which demonstrated the pitfalls involved in using cost–benefit to justify the answer one wanted in the first place. The Environment Agency had wished to reduce levels of water abstraction by Thames Water from the River Kennet in Hampshire, which it claimed was damaging the river's ecology. At a public inquiry, Thames Water claimed the cost of finding alternative sources was £6.2 million, but the Agency argued the financial benefits of lowering abstraction would be far greater. The benefits to users such as the fishing community, based on charges for fishing licensing, could be estimated with reasonable precision but only came to £0.4 million. The Agency then used figures as to the value held by the public in the river which had been estimated from previous surveys at a suspiciously precise figure of an annual 32 pence per household. It was then a question of how many households were interested in the River Kennet and the Agency applied the figure to every household in the Thames Region – some 3 million, producing a figure of just over £13.2 million and well above the costs to Thames Water of finding new abstraction sources. But the inquiry inspector decided that the multiplier was too generous and applied the 32 pence figure only to the much lower population living near the River Kennet, producing a benefit of only £0.3 million. Nevertheless, the economists on the Commission argued this was simply a case of poor practice in cost–benefit analysis and did not undermine the underlying robustness of the technique. But other members found the real-life example persuasive. A lawyer is meant to be skilled at drafting and, with the help of the secretariat, I constructed a sentence tucked away towards the end of the chapter devoted to cost–benefit and economic analysis which provided a critical fulcrum for the report: 'To the extent that people's values (as expression of fundamental commitments to the environment or to equity, whether within society or between present and future generations) are regarded as not answerable to economic appraisal, the question then arises whether there is any other approach that could provide additional assistance to decision-making in that respect.' John Flemming was satisfied with this sentence as it did not say that we had concluded that cost–benefit analysis was wholly defective, but the passage allowed the Commission, in a later chapter, to explore different ways of exploring public values such as new forms of citizens' juries and other emerging techniques.

The report was also noticeable for its discussion of the precautionary principle which, in broad terms, implied that it was sometimes justifiable for government to take action in the absence of full scientific knowledge about the issue in hand. The principle is written into the EU Treaty as one of the core EU environmental principles underlining its environmental policies and had been applied by the European Court of Justice in several well-known cases. There remains ambiguity as to quite what the principle implies and to some decision-makers and politicians it still reeks of an approach which is antipathetic to scientific and rational analysis. The Royal Commission disagreed with this characterisation and regarded the principle 'as a rational response to uncertainties in the scientific evidence relevant to environmental issues and uncertainties about the consequences of action or inaction'. Uncertainty, in its view, was an inherent feature of science, but what was important for the decision maker to know was the degree of uncertainty and the prospect and time needed to reduce it. Under the Brexit proposals for national environmental law, the precautionary principle will be incorporated into our legal system[5] and the Commission's observations on the principle in the Standards report remain as relevant today. Indeed, much of the report is concerned with core issues that lie at the heart of the challenges for developing contemporary environmental policies but have rarely been explored in such detail by an official body.

The following study of the RCEP, under a new chair, Sir Tom Blundell, a distinguished bio-chemist from Cambridge University, was concerned with energy and its report *Energy – The Changing Climate,* published in 2000, proved to be one of the influential studies by the Commission during that period. We focused on the United Kingdom's response to the challenge of climate change and decided to look ahead to the year 2050, asking where we should be at that stage and then working backwards as to the sorts of policies and decisions that would need to be taken to reach that goal. Fifty years ahead provided a reasonable time frame. It was not so long as to be meaningless for present-day policies and we were conscious that decisions that were already being made such as the construction and location of housing which would have an impact over that timescale. At the time, the international commitment to reducing greenhouse gases, contained in the Kyoto Protocol, was only ten years ahead but we were clear that longer-term commitments and more substantial reductions would be needed. We reviewed the scientific understanding of climate change and concluded the evidence of human contribution was compelling and that a global figure of 500 parts per million by

---

[5] See further ch 13.

volume of carbon dioxide in 2050 was an upper limit that should not be exceeded to prevent intolerable and dangerous climate change. The question then was what contribution the UK should make. We concluded that, in the long term, the most promising basis for an international action was one based on the allocation of an equal right to nations on a per capita basis 'enshrining the idea that every human being is entitled to release into the atmosphere the same quantity of greenhouse gases'. Because the emissions produced by developed and less developed countries were currently unequal, there would have to be a period of adjustment over several decades before the quotas for all countries converged.

The approach, known as contraction and convergence, was one the RCEP supported and, on that basis, we estimated that the UK would need to reduce emissions by 60 per cent by 2050 and possibly 80 per cent by 2100. The 60 per cent target became our starting point for analysing the adequacy of current policies and it proved a depressing experience. There was a particularly uninspiring session with a young civil servant responsible for new building standards. We had evidence that a house built to the existing British regulations would consume four times as much energy as an identically sized house built to Swedish standards and almost double that in Denmark, but the civil servant responded that the British building industry was a very conservative and powerful body. More importantly, it became increasingly clear that few in government were looking beyond the Kyoto target date of 2020 and they did not possess longer-term energy scenarios of any detail.[6] The Commission therefore felt it had to construct own scenarios as to what mixes might be feasible if our 2050 goal was to be reached and produced four examples designed to illustrate the types of choices that would have to made. These ranged from a scenario involving no overall energy reduction but requiring both a large-scale use of renewables and some base-load power stations to one involving a substantial reduction in energy demand (66%), less renewables to reduce their environmental impacts but no base-load stations. All could, in theory, be achieved though the last scenario would be extremely challenging and probably involve a reduction or redefinition of current living standards.

The Commission deliberately did not advocate any particular route, though it became apparent that, realistically, some carbon-neutral base-load stations would probably be required to reach the 2050 target. At this point, there was a sharp division of views amongst the Commission's scientific members. Some argued that the only option for such base-load stations would be nuclear, while others felt this was environmentally unsound, especially as the disposal of nuclear waste still largely remained unresolved. There seemed to be no reconciliation between the opposing views, but we then learnt that carbon capture and storage was beginning to emerge as a technology which could neutralise carbon emissions from fossil fuel power stations. The Commission therefore presented this as an alternative to nuclear

---

[6] At the time, almost the only organisation producing detailed, long-term energy scenarios was Shell UK.

power if baseload generating stations were to be employed. I had never heard of carbon capture before and the subject stirred my interest, later developing into a major research programme on its legal aspects at UCL.[7] But it was revealing that in subsequent discussions by the UK government, carbon capture was never presented as an alternative to nuclear power – simply as part of a possible future energy mix that would include both technologies.

From a national policy perspective, one of the most challenging features of greenhouse gases as a pollutant is that the emissions have no direct local impact but contribute to a global load with major impacts, with the possibility of the most severe being first felt in other parts of the world. Clearly, an international response is needed, but with the UK's contribution of greenhouses gases being around only 2 per cent, to what extent should this country act in advance of other countries? I was asked to write a passage in the report explaining why it would be in the UK's national interest to do so. Similar arguments existed over the decision to ban slavery in the British Empire in 1833 – if we banned slavery, other countries would simply carry on with the practice and Britain would suffer economic loss. But I argued that leadership by example can be compelling and we could not hope to persuade countries such as India or China to adopt ambitious climate change policies if we were not taking robust action ourselves. In any event, we could show that many of the policies we were advocating would have other more immediate environmental and economic benefits for the United Kingdom.

The RCEP report received enormous publicity with the key recommendation of the 60 per cent reduction by 2050 becoming the headline in many national newspapers. Within a few days, the then prime minister, Tony Blair, had endorsed the 60 per cent figure and, in later speeches, described the report as being seminal. The concept of a long-term UK 2050 target finally made its way into the Climate Change Act 2008, a world leader in climate change legislation, though with increasing scientific evidence about climate change, the figure was raised to 80 per cent.[8] The report contained many detailed recommendations, some of which are gaining traction, though others, such as a carbon tax, have yet to gain acceptance. The Climate Change Act introduced the concept of regular carbon budgets designed to ensure a degree of certainty in the trajectory towards 2050, coupled with mechanisms involving an independent Climate Change Committee to review their progress. The Royal Commission had not gone into this level of detail, but the provisions were entirely consistent with its views of the real need in this area to inject longer-term thinking into government policy. Nevertheless, the scale of the challenge remains immense. As the report concluded: 'A sustainable energy policy for the UK should protect the interest of generations to come, but it must also achieve social justice, a higher quality of life and industrial competitiveness today. Achieving the right balance is formidably difficult.'

[7] See further ch 8.
[8] On 29 July 2019, the figure was raised to 100% – The Climate Change Act 2008 (2050 Target Amendment) Order 2019 SI 2019/1056.

In 2003, the Commission decided to study environmental planning. The role of town and country planning controls and how they related to environmental protection was an issue that had cropped up in many of its previous reports, but this was the first time it was to investigate the issue in depth. It was a highly complex subject and, compared to the time when the RCEP first started working on environmental issues, there was now a detailed body of environmental laws and new specialised regulators, sitting alongside the existing framework of town and country planning controls. Planning controls were regarded by some as unhelpful and over-bureaucratic and government's priorities for the planning system has repeatedly changed over the years, often aimed largely at speeding up the process in the interests of development. But as we delved into the issue, it became increasingly apparent that, despite all the aspirations, good intentions and density of controls, there was often little real sense of integration or an agreed understanding of the overall goals of the systems in place. Plan making had become a key tool for many bodies, but when we examined in more detail just one region, Cambridgeshire, we found in excess of 30 different plans being prepared by different governmental bodies, including regional economic strategies, biodiversity plans and air quality plans – often on different time-scales and different data sets – 'a plethora of plans' as the Commission described it. The legislation for town and country planning had never expressly stated its purpose. Some argued this was a strength, allowing it to adapt and change but, all too often, it was subject to the changing priorities of different governments. We felt the time had come to include a statutory purpose to provide rather more stability and coherence. Using the term 'sustainable development' would open up too many ambiguities and the Commission looked for a form of wording that did not merely restate potentially conflicting interests but gave a clearer sense of relationships. Our proposal was that the statutory purpose of town and country planning should be 'to facilitate the achievement of legitimate economic and social goals whilst ensuring that the quality of the environment is safeguarded and wherever appropriate enhanced'.

The Commission wanted to see a much closer relationship between land use planning and other aspects of environmental policy and recommended a new form of spatial strategy to help clarify the economic, social and environmental issues. At the same time, we argued that the government must produce a much clearer and definitive statement of overall environment priorities which would be reviewed and updated from time to time. The report was detailed and comprehensive, but its impact was less than it might have been because the Labour government had already proposed changes to the planning system towards the end of the inquiry and announced this in a Green Paper. We had concerns about some aspects of the proposals, notably the continued use of the vague concept of sustainable development and the fact that it was solely concerned with the planning system rather than linking it properly within the broader aspects of environmental policy and regulation. It illustrated one of the structural weaknesses of government department arrangements in that planning then fell within the responsibility of the then Department for Transport, Local Government and the Regions while environmental concerns largely rested with the Department of the Environment, Food and Rural Affairs (DEFRA). The Green Paper was very much a product of its own department rather than a more integrated cross-departmental response. The government's proposals for planning reform had largely been completed by the time the RCEP published its report and its recommendations did not have immediate impact. Yet re-reading the report 15 years later, it is once again clear that many of the insights and proposals remain of relevance. In 2018, the Department of the Environment proposed 15-year Environmental Improvement Plans which, in many ways, reflect the Commission's ideas for a statement of environmental priorities. Securing those goals will not be easy not helped by the fact that departmental arrangements in England have become even more disaggregated in the meantime, with separate government departments covering energy, environmental protection, transport and land-use planning.

The final study I was involved in before retiring from the Royal Commission concerned chemicals and the environment. Once again, this proved a scientifically complex issue but it also illustrated the challenges facing a national body such as the Royal Commission where control regimes were being developed at European Union level. A few months after the study was announced, the European Commission had published a White Paper outlining a new approach to regulating the placing of chemicals on the market. Legislation was being developed, eventually resulting in 2006 in the enormously important EU Regulation on the Registration, Evaluation, Authorisation and Restriction of Chemicals known as REACH. The Royal Commission was fully supportive of the general goals of REACH but felt that many aspects of the proposals emerging needed improvement. The testing requirements being proposed by the European Commission seemed rather old fashioned and we were convinced more modern methods of computational risk assessment, already widely used in the pharmaceutical industry, could provide far more rapid results. And we looked to an overall goal of using a range of policy instruments, including information and taxation, to encourage the greater substitution of chemicals with less hazardous substances. The proposed REACH legislation did not, it seemed to us, make enough of these linkages. Nevertheless, discussions on REACH were now well under way with Member States at EU level and the RCEP was reduced to urging the government to take on board our points in its negotiations.

The Royal Commission continued to produce a series of major reports covering such areas as fishing, the urban environment, adapting institutions to climate change and demographics. But as one of the early announcements of spending cuts by the new coalition government, the Secretary of State for Environment, Food and Rural Affairs decided to wind up the Commission on 1 April 2011, making a saving of around £1 million a year. Many saw this as simply a crude exercise in financial cut-backs, but, at a valedictory meeting involving both present and past members, I was a little surprised to hear the Secretary of State's chief scientist saying this was not the case and that he had personally advised that the Royal Commission was no longer needed. He said that, if needed, he could readily set up a committee involving different disciplines to advise the department on any particular issue. I recalled my early days at Imperial College where we delved into the distinction between multi-disciplinary and truly inter-disciplinary work,[9] and argued that one of the Royal Commission's strengths was its continuity and the willingness of members to explore in-depth with each other the different perspectives their own expertise brought to a subject – this was unlikely to be replicated by a one-off advisory committee. The fact that the RCEP had been a standing body lasting so many years had allowed it to develop certain core principles and insights which spanned its different inquiries, despite a changing membership, and all this would now be lost. But it may be that the Commission had indeed run its course. Compared to its early days, there were now many other independent bodies, including parliamentary select committees, providing authoritative reports and assessments on environmental issues and many of its initial insights had become the accepted language of government and policy. But its working methods and its ability to take longer environmental perspectives on the direction of current administrative and policy arrangements remained unique.

[9] See ch 4.

10

Environmental Courts and Tribunals

Between the strong and the weak it is the law which makes free and freedom which oppresses

Le Rochefoucauld

During the first decade of the new millennium, two major questions dominated much of my thinking and research about the future of environmental law in this country. First, was there now a need for some form of specialised environmental court or tribunal?[1] Second, what sort of sanctions should be employed by those bodies responsible for the enforcement of environmental law? Initially these were quite separate issues, but unexpectedly the solution that eventually emerged came about due to a strong connection between the two themes. The debate in the United Kingdom about the need for an environment court or tribunal proved to be a rather Byzantine affair lasting over ten years and it revealed many distinct visions of the future of environmental law, as well as the political challenges of securing institutional reforms. It was only in 2010 that a specialised environmental tribunal with fairly limited jurisdiction was established in England and Wales. This came about almost by chance because of the need for a new appeal body in the context of developments of new forms of environmental sanctions.[2] The story of developing a specialist environmental judicial body is by no means over, but understanding how we reached the current arrangements may provide pointers for thinking about the future.

For most of my career as an environmental lawyer, environmental cases were heard in the ordinary courts depending on the type of legal action being brought. Most criminal prosecutions for environmental offences came before the magistrates' courts with more serious cases going to the Crown Court. Disputes between private parties concerning environmental issues such as noise nuisance or other forms of pollution were heard by the ordinary civil courts. Actions in judicial review, challenging the legality of decisions taken by government or other public bodies such as the Environment Agency, were taken before

---

[1] Courts and tribunals are both forms of independent judicial bodies. Tribunals, though, tend to be more informal and cheaper for the user than courts. Decisions are usually taken by a combination of legal and non-legal members with relevant expertise.
[2] See ch 11.

the Administrative Court of the High Court. But in other jurisdictions, notably New South Wales, New Zealand and Sweden, various forms of environmental courts had been established since the 1980s, recognising that environmental law often requires specialised knowledge and distinctive approaches. The trend continued in other countries and US academics published a report published in 2009[3] which identified some 354 specialised environmental courts and tribunals established in 41 countries, with the numbers having doubled in the previous two years.

It is perhaps not too surprising that, in this country, the first proposal for some form of environmental court emerged during discussions on improving land-use planning controls. The comprehensive land-use planning system, introduced in this country in 1947, was well before the development of modern specialised environmental laws and, while planning controls have never been exclusively concerned with environmental protection, they have long played a critical role in the area. Appeals against refusals of planning permission by local planning authorities are made to the central government but conducted by an independent planning inspectorate who can be seen as an early example of a specialised quasi-tribunal operating in this field. In 1989, Robert Carnwath (then a planning law QC and now a Supreme Court judge) had been asked by government to review the enforcement of planning controls. He was mainly concerned with details of planning law but tucked away in the report was fairly cautious recommendation for the need for some new specialised environmental court or tribunal: '... there may be a case for reviewing the jurisdiction of the various courts and tribunals which at present deal with different aspects of what might be called "environmental protection" (including planning) and seeking to combine them in a single jurisdiction'.

No action was taken on the idea, but seeds were sown. Three years later the then Lord Chief Justice, Lord Woolf, gave a public lecture under the eye-catching title, 'Are the Judiciary Environmentally Myopic?' The lecture was organised by the UK Environmental Law Association, then just three years old and was probably the first time a British judge of such seniority had talked so extensively about environmental law. He argued that one of the challenges for environmental law was that real-life environmental problems, such as a major pollution incident, did not fall neatly into the familiar structures of law, such as public and private law, or criminal and civil law. He felt that there could be great benefits in having a new form of Environment Tribunal with general responsibility for overseeing and enforcing environmental law safeguards and handling all the legal issues arising from an environmental incident. It was clear that his vision went beyond that of a conventional court and he proposed that the new tribunal should be 'a multi-faceted, multi-skilled body which would combine the services provided by the existing courts, tribunals and inspectors in the environmental field. It would

---

[3] George (Rock) Pring and Catherine (Kitty) Pring, *Greening Justice: Creating and Improving Environmental Courts and Tribunals* (Washington DC, The Access Initiative, 2009).

be a "one-stop" shop which should lead to faster, cheaper and more effective resolution of disputes in the environmental area'.

The lecture created considerable public interest, but there was no immediate political response. But a few years later, the Department of the Environment, Transport and the Regions commissioned Malcolm Grant, then head of the Department of Land Economy at the University of Cambridge, to conduct a major study of environmental courts, including an examination of a number of specialist environmental courts in other jurisdictions. He was a little stymied in that his terms of reference required an analysis of possible options in this country rather than making a single recommendation and his report outlined six possible models, ranging from developing the planning inspectorate into a planning tribunal to a full-blown new Environmental Court as part of the High Court. The Grant Report provided much in the way detailed information and analysis but, because of the restricted terms of reference, lacked a single message which could engage the political machinery. It was debated in the House of Lords but there was fairly lukewarm response from the government minister: 'The government welcomes the opportunity to debate this issue. We are not persuaded of the need for an environmental court, certainly not on its possible shape.'

It seemed there was little appetite for change. However, the Minister of State for the Environment between 1997 and 2003 was Michael Meacher. He was not a lawyer and was not particularly liked by the then Prime Minister, Tony Blair, but in many ways, he was one of the unsung heroes of environmental law at this time. He was intellectually engaged in his brief and had a habit of arranging informal meetings with individuals outside government to find out what was really going on without the filter of his civil servants. They were uncomfortable with this practice, especially as no official records of these meetings were taken. I had met Michael Meacher at one of the board meetings of the Environmental Agency and he asked to meet me privately to talk about environmental law issues. At that time, I had never had a one-to-one meeting with a government minister and I sought advice from my long-standing environmental mentor, Tom Burke, as to the best approach to take. Tom, by then, had moved on from the environmental group world and had been a special adviser to three Secretaries of State giving him an insider feel for the workings of Whitehall. Tom's advice was to tell Michael Meacher something about the subject that he did not already know. We duly met in his offices with civil servants looking anxiously through the glass doors, but unable to hear what was being said. We started by discussing some of problems with enforcement on environmental law, but I then told him that, from a legal perspective, there was currently an opportunity which I had never seen before in my career to date. Three of the most senior judicial figures in the country were deeply interested in environmental law – Lord Woolf, the Lord Chief Justice, Lord Slynn, a senior Law Lord and the then President of the UK Environmental Law Association and Robert Carnwath, then a High Court judge but at the time the chair of the Law Commission, an independent body established in 1965 to review the state of the law in England and Wales. I felt that some advantage should be taken of this unusual judicial interest, though I was not sure in my own mind how best to do this. It was news to Michael Meacher and he duly noted down the names of the judges.[4]

My own feeling at the time was that the creation of a separate environmental court within the High Court was politically unachievable. I was also uncomfortable with the idea of having environmental crimes handled by a specialist court since this might suggest they were not crimes in the ordinary sense. To my mind, someone who deliberately fly-tipped waste should be considered as much of a criminal as a shoplifter and should appear before the ordinary criminal courts. What was needed was a much tougher sentencing practice rather than a transfer to a new, specialised court. Similarly, the civil courts handling environmental claims such as those in nuisance were working reasonably well and while the expense and costs rules of judicial review needed reforming, the judges handling environmental judicial review claims could hardly be described as lacking competence. But a particular problem had emerged during the Royal Commission on Environmental Pollution's 2002 study on Environmental Planning in which I had participated. Planning appeals were all handled by the planning inspectorate, but it appeared that appeals concerning decisions by local authorities or bodies such as the Environment Agency under specialised environmental laws (such as the refusal of waste management licences) went to a whole range of different bodies. Time did not permit the RCEP to study the issue in any depth, but it suggested that there was a case for combining these environmental regulatory appeals before a specialist tribunal.

As a result of the Royal Commission's recommendation, I was able to persuade Michael Meacher to fund a one-year study at UCL looking at environmental regulatory appeals[5] in much more detail and to test the arguments for a single tribunal. I had reckoned that the Ministry of Justice would probably be crucial in any decision making on the issue and was acutely aware of the less-than-enthusiastic response to Malcolm Grant's report. So, I arranged to meet a reasonably senior civil servant within the ministry before starting the research and asked him how I could ensure my report carried some bite within the government circles. His response was to make sure that I answered just three basic questions: What exactly was the problem? Could it be met by adapting existing systems? If not, what was needed and what would it cost? Studies produced for government often failed to address these basic questions explicitly. But he then said that the key was to ensure that there was a crisp executive summary to the report since no minister or senior civil servant would read a summary of more than two pages. Academics are not normally trained in the art of writing executive summaries, which need to contain

---

[4] Some weeks later, Lord Woolf told me that he had been invited to meet Michael Meacher and had had a fruitful discussion.

[5] In these sorts of appeals, the person making the appeal is entitled to question the merits of the original decision, and, in effect, have a complete rehearing. In contrast, judicial review claims are concerned only with the legality of the original decision in question.

a clear and convincing logic and argument and are quite different from abstracts of articles that appear in academic journals. It was invaluable advice and for this report – and for subsequent reports I have written – I devoted considerable time in ensuring there was a compelling, readable and succinct summary.

I hired a solicitor, Michael Woods, to assist in the research and our study of the appeal mechanisms for environmental regulation revealed an even more incoherent system than I had originally imagined. We examined over 50 different sets of regulations and found that appeals went to a range of different bodies including the planning inspectorate, the county court, the magistrates' court, the High Court and the Secretary of State. In some cases, there was no right of appeal at all other than by way of judicial review. There was no underlying principle in the choice of appeal route and the current picture seemed to be due to historical accident as much as anything else. The rights of appeal under the various laws were restricted to those directly affected by the decision in question – for instance, the operator who had been refused an environmental permit or wished to question the conditions imposed in the permit. Third parties such as neighbours or local environmental organisations have no equivalent right of appeal but were instead restricted to applications for judicial review challenging the legality of the decision rather than its merits, a much tougher hurdle and one involving considerable expense. As part of the study, I was given access to files in the Administrative Court to examine judicial reviews relating to environmental issues. Over a three-year period, we identified 55 judicial review applications of relevance with a slight majority being brought by companies and most of the rest brought by individuals or environmental organisations. Only four cases were successful and what was striking was the extent to which the failed cases were essentially concerned with the merits of the decision rather than its legality and dismissed by the courts as such. One could have simply concluded that the Administrative Court was being misused by claimants who disguised a challenge as one concerning legality when their real concern was with the merits of the decision in question. But my view was that this represented a real need for accommodating in some way merits appeals by third parties, not within judicial review, but within the regulatory appeals procedure. Our report suggested this issue should be at least seriously considered. Whenever the subject of third-party rights of appeal has been raised, governments of all persuasions have been uneasy with the idea mainly on the grounds that it could cause excessive delays to decision-making. Strangely, though, there was a precedent of some sort in the Control of Pollution Act 1974 concerning applications for water discharge consents. If minded to grant, a water authority first had to publish a draft consent and third parties were given a set period in which to persuade the Secretary of State to take over the application and decide himself. Nevertheless, even leaving aside the issue of third-party rights, we considered there was a strong case for channelling existing appeals rights to a single new Environment Tribunal. Normally, establishing a new tribunal would require new primary legislation, but the timing of our report was fortunate because recent reforms that were being developed in the tribunal system which had been brought about by the 2001

Leggatt Review on Tribunals would soon make it much easier to establish new tribunals as and when needed.[6] The attraction of a tribunal over a normal court was that it could combine both legal members and other experts such as environmental scientists, and tribunals tended to have far more flexible procedural rules than found in the courts.

As the research developed, I had considerable discussions with industry, legal practitioners, members of the judiciary, the environmental regulators and key government officials to win them over to the idea of a single environmental tribunal. We launched the report in 2003 at a conference held at the offices of Freshfields Bruckhuis Deringer in London to a wide audience and there was a positive reception. I was well aware that the proposal was, in many ways, more modest than that of a full-blown environmental division of the High Court, but it seemed to meet a clear need, was feasible, would be seen to be more efficient in regulatory terms than current arrangements (thus appealing to policy makers concerned solely with regulatory reform) and could act as a stalking horse for future developments. As Lord Carnwath noted in the introduction to the report: 'The authors show how (if we concentrate for a moment on the regulatory and civil aspects of public environmental law) we can devise a structure which would be manageable and economical and would build on the best features of existing practice.' But I made a fatal political mistake. In my efforts to win over the establishment, as it were, I had ignored the environmental group community. I had not realised that, at the same time as commissioning my report, Michael Meacher had also asked several groups to examine the issue of access to environmental justice. Their study was published shortly after the UCL report and was more focused on the perspective of environmental litigants in ordinary cases, often faced with an unsympathetic judiciary and heavy cost exposure. They dismissed my recommendation for a specialised appeals tribunal as being far too modest and failing to address the issue of environmental justice which required far more dramatic reform: 'We do not, however, believe that a tribunal of such limited scope as identified in the UCL report is, in itself, sufficient to achieve access to environmental justice. Moreover, we are concerned that the establishment of a tribunal limited to regulatory appeals could fill the "window of opportunity" to improve access to environmental justice at a time when more fundamental reform is clearly necessary.' They recommended a new specialist environmental division of the High Court which would handle judicial reviews and environmental civil claims such as nuisance and the impairment of human rights. There was some truth in their observation in that the UCL report was not directly concerned with access to environmental justice in the wider sense, though I felt that its proposals would assist third parties in that they would be permitted to participate in environmental appeals and, if our suggestions were taken up, they might even acquire some rights to appeal before the new tribunal.

---

[6] Part I of the Tribunal Courts and Enforcement Act 2007, implementing the Leggatt Review, created a basic legal framework for the tribunal system based on a First-tier Tribunal and an Upper Tribunal. The establishment and jurisdiction of individual tribunals within that structure is determined by administrative decision.

But I had neither persuaded them of the case, nor that, politically, their more radical proposal was unlikely to be achievable. The government was then faced with competing visions even within the specialised environmental law community and, unsurprisingly there was no further progress.

At the time, I thought the issue had probably died for some years. One of the problems with securing reform in this area was that while there was a general disquiet with aspects of the existing arrangements there was no particular scandal or event which was evidence of substantive failings demanding immediate change. But quite unexpectedly, the question of court reform became bound up with the issue of civil sanctions. Three years later I was asked by the Cabinet Office to review the system of regulatory sanctions.[7] One core recommendation was that, in addition to the use of criminal prosecutions, regulators should be able to impose a range of civil sanctions in appropriate cases. The advantage of civil sanctions was they could be imposed without the prior involvement of the courts, but those faced with a sanction had to have the right to appeal if they disputed that they had breached the relevant regulations or questioned the amount of the penalty imposed. I recommended that these appeals should not go the ordinary courts but to the tribunal system. By the time the legislation implementing my recommendations was passed under the Regulatory Enforcement and Sanctions 2008, the tribunal system had been reformed with the creation of a new First-Tier Tribunal[8] and the Act duly provided for appeals to be made to that body.

The first regulatory bodies to acquire the new powers to impose civil sanctions were the Environment Agency and Natural England in 2010. Officials within the tribunal system clearly anticipated there might be a large number of appeals and, in 2010, established an environment tribunal sitting with the General Regulatory Chamber of the First-tier Tribunal. After all the discussion about environmental courts and tribunals over the past ten years or so a specialist tribunal had been created, without any fanfare or fuss, but by a simple act of internal administrative reorganisation and all due to the fact that environmental regulators had been first off the mark to acquire the new civil sanctioning powers. As it turned out, the tribunal had little work to do in the first few years. In the limited areas of environmental law where civil sanctions had been first made available, the Environment Agency found that the use of enforcements undertakings voluntarily offered by the industry concerned was far more productive than the imposition of financial civil sanctions.[9] Enforcement undertakings are negotiated agreements and the environment tribunal had no role in the process, unless there is eventually a dispute as to whether the company has satisfied the undertaking.

Robert Carnwath was then Senior President of Tribunals and, towards the end of 2010, we discussed whether the new environmental tribunal, now that

---

[7] See further ch 11.

[8] Tribunals, Courts and Enforcement Act 2007.

[9] Enforcement Undertakings were one of the new forms of civil sanction introduced as a result of the 2006 Cabinet Office Review of Regulatory Sanctions. See further ch 11.

it was established but apparently with little to do, could be given other roles. We met with Ministry of Justice (MoJ) officials and Sir Robert proposed it might be timely to revisit and update the initial UCL report on regulatory appeals to see whether the tribunal should handle these sorts of appeals as well as those concerning civil sanctions. There was some unease on the part of the MoJ until I offered to do the research for free as part of my academic work. The report, *Consistency and Effectiveness – Strengthening the New Environment Tribunal,* was published by UCL in early 2011 and showed that, if anything, the appeals procedures and routes had become even more complex and incoherent since the original report. This was in part due to the creation of two new departments, Energy and Climate Change (DECC) and Business Innovation and Skills (BIS) who had taken lead responsibility for significant areas of environmental law and had developed their own appeals procedures in the areas of law concerned. DECC, for example, had appointed a senior barrister to act as an Appeals Officer in emissions trading. In one area of law, chemical regulation, I found a schedule containing four different appeals routes (the Secretary of State, magistrates' courts, the Employment Tribunal and the High Court) where clearly the choice of appeal route had been largely chosen according to the body making the initial decision (such as the Environment Agency or a local authority) rather than the underlying nature of the regulations themselves. Once again, I suggested that appeals could be usefully consolidated towards the environment tribunal. This time there was a more positive reception and the underlying policy since the publication of the report has been to ensure that appeals in any new environmental regulations are generally handled by the Environment Tribunal. Currently, it handles appeals in some 44 areas of environmental and energy regulation from emissions trading, single-use bags charges to marine licensing. There is one salaried judge, around six judges with environmental tickets and, at the time of writing, six more were being recruited. In addition, the tribunal members include half a dozen non-legal experts all, at present, hydrologists to handle nitrate zone designation appeals.

However, there were other important areas of existing environmental regulation, including environmental permitting and water discharge and abstraction consents, where appeals were still handled by the planning inspectorate and where I felt that the environment tribunal would be a more suitable forum. Both DEFRA and the (MoJ) were initially positive to the idea and the MoJ sought my advice about the type of non-legal expertise that might be needed within the tribunal if such a transfer took place. I was able to study all the appeals in these areas conducted by the planning inspectorate over the past three years to identify the types of issues involved and advised accordingly. But any further moves were then stalled by a quirk of obscure internal departmental arrangements of which I had been totally unaware until that point. In accordance with Treasury guidance, the MoJ, which was responsible for the tribunal system, imposed internal charges on other departments wishing to make use of 'their' tribunals. The charging scheme had fairly high sign-on costs for each new regulation to be handled by a tribunal and was clearly designed for areas of law with a large number of appeals. In contrast, in environmental law, there were numerous appeals provisions in different laws but each giving rise to a relatively small number of appeals; the departmental charging system was not really designed for this sort of structure. DEFRA, already cash strapped, felt it could not justify the costs involved and we were faced with the familiar problem that there was no crisis in the system demanding immediate action. The existing appeals were being conducted competently by the planning inspectorate and in around 50 environmental appeals, I found only one case where the Inspector, an engineer, felt the legal issues being raised were too complex for him to handle and that the parties should go to court – clearly the environment tribunal could have dealt with that case. The MoJ were equally resource stretched and seemed unwilling to make any exceptions to their charging scheme. I subsequently wrote lengthy letters to the MoJ on the issue, but there was no resolution and appeals concerning environmental permitting, water discharges and water abstraction remain within the planning inspectorate today.

As to civil sanctions, there have been several appeals before the tribunal concerning administrative notices, but not yet variable penalties. In 2017, for the first time, the Upper Tribunal, which determines appeals on points of law from the First-tier Tribunal, considered the legality of a stop notice served by Natural England. The case concerned the activities of a small company foraging sea kale on a beach near Dungeness. Natural England considered the company was damaging a protected site and had issued a stop notice under the 2010 Environmental Civil Sanctions Regulations. The company disputed the scientific assessment, but my main concern was with the legality of the stop notice in that it simply banned the activity without specifying any remedial steps that the offender could take, a clear requirement in the legislation. David Hart QC represented the company for free on the appeal and I offered to support him. I had never appeared in front of the Upper Tribunal and compared to the more formal and somewhat ponderous atmosphere of the High Court the proceedings were somewhat of a revelation. Barristers simply wore suits with no wigs and gowns and made their representations sitting down. Altogether it seemed a far more modern and effective way of discussing quite complex legal issues and reinforced my positive views of the tribunal system. At the start of the hearing, Nature England conceded that remedial steps should have been specified in the notice and, essentially, the Upper Tribunal referred the issue back to the First-tier Tribunal as determining these steps involved complex facts and the need for specialised expertise.

The work of the environment tribunal[10] continues, yet it is a judicial body that is little known in the wider community, including many environmental non-governmental organisations. In recent discussions on the creation of a new Office of Environmental Protection post-Brexit,[11] I advocated that the environmental tribunal could play a role in the OEP's final enforcement

---

[10] Strictly entitled the First-tier Tribunal (General Regulatory Chamber) (Environment)).
[11] See ch 13.

procedures.[12] Appearing in front of the House of Commons Select Committee on Environment, Food and Rural Affairs in early 2019, it was clear to me that members of the committee had never heard of the body and were impressed by its work and ethos. Its profile has not been helped by the development of the gov. uk public information website established in 2012 which increasingly holds all the information from government departments. Initially, the environment tribunal had its own dedicated website containing details of its legal and non-legal expert members and references to the cases it heard, but now a search of 'environment tribunal' directs the user straight to the gov.uk website which simply contains a bland description of its functions. Nevertheless, I remain convinced that the tribunal system will have an important and distinctive role to play in the future development of environmental law in this country and will continue to advocate its merits.

The development of the environmental tribunal, though, did not address the other significant issue of environmental law emerging during the 1990s – namely access to environmental justice by individuals or environmental organisations. Many such cases are brought by judicial review in the High Court challenging the legality of decisions taken by public bodies. Lawyers generally have to be involved, an expensive process in itself, but one exacerbated by the fact that the courts traditionally applied the standard costs principles, meaning that the party bringing the case would have to pay the costs of the other side if they lost. Litigation is often an unpredictable exercise and the potential risk of an adverse costs order which might run to tens of thousands of pounds was a chilling effect and deterrent for many. Individuals making a claim might be able to obtain legal aid, but this is not available to organisations and, while environmental groupss have sometimes found a willing individual eligible for legal aid who would front the case, this often is not possible.

The United Kingdom, along with the EU and other Member States ratified the 1998 Aarhus Convention on Access to Information, Public Participation in Decision-Making and Access to Justice in Environmental Matters. Most of the provisions in the convention concern access to information and rights of participation that were already largely being met in the UK. As to access to justice, Aarhus requires liberal rules of standing before the courts where individuals and environmental groups wish to challenge the legality of decisions made by government or public bodies. This was challenging for some countries such as Germany where standing rules were restrictive (essentially a claimant had to have some private right that was affected) but, in the United Kingdom, the courts had already adopted a liberal approach in judicial review cases and the provision was not difficult for the UK to meet. But Article 9(4) of Aarhus then contains a requirement that these court procedures must not to be 'prohibitively expensive'. It seems that the UK was comfortable in agreeing to this because officials assumed this provision referred

---

[12] For reasons discussed in ch13, I now consider that the Upper Tribunal might be more suitable for the sorts of serious cases the Office for Environmental Protection is likely to bring. In the enforcement positions in the Environment Bill 2019, published Oct. 2019, the government has accepted this argument. See further ch 13.

simply to the court fees that had to be paid on making an application and these were fairly modest.[13] Many disagreed with this interpretation of the provision and argued that it must also include the legal costs involved, including the possibility of adverse costs orders should the case be lost. This interpretation was later confirmed by the European Court of Justice in 2014.

Nevertheless, the government did nothing to address the issue. It was left to the courts themselves to try to develop some procedures that would reduce exposure to excessive costs risks. They had discretionary powers to impose what were known as Protective Costs Orders which had that effect, but the principles were not really suitable for mainstream environmental litigation and, in the event, a claimant had no idea whether such an order would be granted by the court until litigation had commenced. Relying wholesale on court discretion and the uncertainties of Protective Costs Orders did not seem to a satisfactory way of meeting the Aarhus requirements. Lord Justice Carnwath (as he then was) was clearly somewhat frustrated at the lack of government action and, in 2007, he promoted the idea of setting up a small expert group to examine the issue in more depth. He persuaded Jeremy Sullivan, then a High Court judge and someone who had already shown considerable interest in environmental law, to chair the working party. I was invited to join and the other members included the head of funding policy at the Legal Services Commission (responsible for legal aid), the head of legal services at the Environmental Agency, the lawyer for a leading environmental group and some practising lawyers who have been involved in environmental judicial reviews. It was, in some ways, a strange exercise and, as Mr Justice Sullivan admitted at the first meeting, he was not quite about the status of the group or to whom we were reporting. Nevertheless, we carried on and explored in detail existing cost procedures, concluding that current principles and practice were not in compliance with the Aarhus requirements on access to environmental justice. The final report, published in May 2008, *Ensuring Access to Environmental Justice*, had considerable impact, though substantial changes took several years to effect. In 2013, the government introduced new rules concerning Protective Costs Orders to include a special category of Aarhus environmental claims. In such claims, individual claimants would, in future, have a risk of cost exposure limited to £5,000, while organisations were capped at £10,000. This had the advantage of providing far greater certainly for all parties involved, though variations in the rules were introduced in 2017 which give greater discretion to judges to vary the cost involved depending on the individual financial circumstances of the parties involved, a change that caused considerable concern in many quarters.

I still had doubts as to whether tinkering with the cost rules for judicial review in the High Court would really meet the vision of Aarhus. I was well aware of the extent to which, in countries such as the Netherlands, equivalent cases are handled faster, often all in writing without oral hearings and with little cost for the claimant. Judicial reviews in the Administrative Court may offer a gold standard

---

[13] For example, the current fee for making the initial application for permission to apply for judicial review is £154.

of court review but, at the end of the day, may not deal satisfactorily with the broader concepts on environmental justice implicit in Aarhus. Environmental organisations and others with access to professional expertise can handle judicial review, but the procedures are rather less suitable for ordinary members of the public concerned with the legality of a local decision. In the tribunal system, the Upper Tribunal has the status of the High Court and the power of determine judicial reviews in categories of cases assigned to it. In many ways, the Upper Tribunal, which can combine both legal members (which could be a High Court judge) and other expert members, seemed a more appropriate forum for handling environmental judicial reviews. Its flexible procedural rules begin with the overriding objective of the rules stated to be to allow the Upper Tribunal to handle cases fairly and justly. This is elaborated to include '(a) dealing with the case in ways which are proportionate to the importance of the case, the complexity of the issues, the anticipated costs and the resources of the parties; (b) avoiding unnecessary formality and seeking flexibility in the proceedings; (c) ensuring, so far as practicable, that the parties are able to participate fully in the proceedings ...' The rules go on to oblige the court to encourage and facilitate alternative dispute resolution procedures such as mediation where the parties ask for this. It seems to me that the underlying ethos to these procedures is far more consistent with Aarhus than conventional judicial review in the Administrative Court.

Some categories of judicial review, such as education and immigration, have already been transferred to the Upper Tribunal, but not yet environmental judicial reviews. In 2013, though, the government consulted on the possibility of transferring planning and environmental judicial reviews from the High Court to the Upper Tribunal. Its main motivation was nothing to do with access to justice issues, but out of a concern that judicial reviews brought by third parties in the High Court were taking too long to hear and were holding up development. It felt the Upper Tribunal could act more speedily and more efficiently in this context. My own submission to the consultation supported the idea as, at least in relation to environmental cases, the Upper Tribunal seemed a far more suitable forum and was better aligned to Aarhus. But not all judges favour greater involvement of tribunals and High Court judges in the Administrative Court argued that they could speed up cases by establishing a separate planning court with judges specialising in the relevant law and introducing strong case management. This is indeed what happened in April 2014[14] and, from the point of view of speed of decision making, the new court has been effective. But I felt at the time it was a lost opportunity for developing more innovative methods of handling environmental judicial reviews and one which might not reoccur for many years. But as it turned out, only five years later and in the discussions on the implications of Brexit for environmental law, the whole issue of judicial review and the role of the tribunal system would be one that was, once again, very much alive.[15]

---

[14] The Planning Court currently handles judicial reviews concerning planning and related matters and EU environmental legislation.

[15] See ch 13.

11

Reforming Regulatory Sanctions

Parliament intended the 1950 [Shops] Act to be enforced and therefore cannot, I believe, be attributed to it the intention, by restricting the statutory penalties to figures which are derisory when compared to the prohibited activity, of turning a nation of shop-keepers into a nation of commercial recidivists.

Lord Justice Oliver, *Stoke Trent City Council v B & Q* (1983)

I had long been aware that, in most areas of environmental regulation, the core legal sanction in this country that was available to environmental bodies such as the Environment Agency was a criminal prosecution. From the early nineteenth century, legislation had developed what were known as strict liability offences, implying that, unlike most ordinary criminal offences such as theft or assault, it was not necessary to prove intention or recklessness on the part of the offender to secure a conviction – simply the act of the offence was sufficient to be guilty of the offence. This made it much easier to enforce the law, especially where companies were involved.[1] In practice, in this country, regulatory bodies have exercised considerable discretion in determining whether or not to bring a prosecution and where a case was brought before the court, the level of sentence imposed would reflect the level of intention or otherwise that had been involved. But the notion of strict liability criminal offences was an odd system in many ways, unknown in countries such as Germany or Austria where intention or recklessness is considered an essential ingredient of criminality, and strict liability was memorably described in a recent major study as 'the last vestiges of medieval morality'.[2] I had been impressed in my early days as a lawyer by a study written in 1981 by David Tench, the lawyer for the Consumers Association, entitled '*Towards a Middle System of Law*'. He had argued the case for forms of sanction that lay somewhere between criminal and ordinary civil law. My contacts with the Environmental Protection Agency in the United State made clear that the Agency had long used powerful administrative financial sanctions against companies that were in breach of environmental law, saving criminal prosecutions for the truly egregious.

---

[1] Where a company is prosecuted for an offence requiring intention or recklessness, a court must be satisfied that some senior officer (described as part of the 'directing mind' of the company) was involved.

[2] A Simester (ed) *Appraising Strict Liability* (Oxford, OUP 2005).

German colleagues also told me that regulators in that country made extensive use of administrative penalties that were imposed directly by the regulator on the offender. In contrast, in the United Kingdom, the criminal law was being made to do a great deal of work covering both the truly criminal as well as companies or individuals who were careless at the most.

The Environment Minister, Michael Meacher, had commissioned me to produce a report on the possible role of an environmental tribunal which was published in 2003. Shortly after completion of that report, I persuaded him to fund another study on the possible use of civil penalties in this country in the field of environmental law. The report, published at the end of 2003,[3] examined practices in other jurisdictions and noted examples that already existed in the UK in fields such as taxation law. We advocated the introduction of civil penalties in environmental law[4] – the current system was over-reliant on criminal prosecutions as the ultimate sanction and as we concluded did not provide 'the flexibility, fairness or moral accuracy to achieve optimal compliance and therefore adequate protect and conservation of the environment'. Our report contained detailed analysis on some major legal issues with civil sanctions. A key element is that the regulator is empowered to impose the sanction directly on the offender without going to court, but there was then an important question as to whether this was compatible with provisions in the European Convention on Human Rights which had been implemented within the UK under the Human Rights Act 1998. Article 6 (1) states that in the determination of civil rights and obligations or of any criminal charge against him, everyone is entitled to a 'fair and public hearing within a reasonable time by an independent and impartial tribunal established by law'. The European Court of Human Rights has held that, in the context of the Convention, what is or is not a criminal charge is not determined solely by the way a national law categorises the offence or sanction but has an independent meaning to be decided by the European Court. Critical factors were the nature of the offence and the character and degree of the penalty involved. I was pretty clear in my own mind that while a minor fixed penalty for, say, a parking offence might not be criminal under the European Convention, the type of large civil penalties we were proposing for environmental offences would be considered criminal. At first reading, the provisions in Article 6, requiring a hearing before an independent court or tribunal, would appear to be incompatible with such a system – the whole value of civil penalties was that a court was not involved unless an appeal was made. In an important case in 1984, *Ozturk v Germany*,[5] the European Court of Human Rights

---

[3] R Macrory and M Woods, *Environmental Civil Penalties – A More Proportionate Response to Regulatory Breach* (London, UCL Centre for Law and the Environment, 2003).

[4] The terms 'administrative' and 'civil' penalties are essentially the same in this country. The key feature is that a regulator is given power to impose a penalty without the need to first go to court. Those receiving notice of a penalty always have the right to appeal to an independent court or tribunal but, if they accept they were in breach, matters can be resolved quickly without lengthy judicial procedures.

[5] (1984) 6 EHRR 409.

held that the German system for civil penalties for road traffic offences was indeed to be considered criminal under Article 6 but if there was a right of appeal to an independent court or tribunal, this would satisfy the Convention requirements. We, therefore, concluded that the European Convention did not present major barriers in introducing civil penalties for environmental offences, provided there were appeal rights.

As with the report on an environmental tribunal, our study was well received but there was little political incentive for taking it forward. It seemed to me the case was pretty compelling, but the difficulties facing a government wishing to introduce them was brought home to me in the conference we organised to launch the report. The head of legal services at the Department of Environment, Food and Rural Affairs (DEFRA) chaired the closing discussion and summarised at the end: 'I see, you are proposing a system that will give regulators the power to impose financial sanctions on the regulated community, with a lower standard of proof than criminal law, without all the protections to defendants in criminal law and with the prospect of much larger penalties. Now that's going to be an easy sell in industry.'

Tom Burke has made a useful distinction between 'policy' and 'politics' – often the same word in other languages. He has described policy as the detailed map describing a route to be taken to achieve a specific goal, an exercise that requires, as with map making, careful, delicate and detailed analysis. Politics, however, is the experience of actually making that journey and reaching the destination and, as with any journey, requires different and sometimes rougher skills. We had done the map making, but there was no appetite to start the political journey. Lord Ashby, the first chairman of the Royal Commission of Environmental Pollution, had a similar analysis. In his view, any serious advances in environmental law or policy required a detailed analysis of the problem and what was needed to deal with it, but then some 'ignition' event, such as a major pollution event, to drive the politics. There were good examples of this dual process at work in our history of environmental law. In the late 1960s, a government committee had identified that the then legal controls on waste disposal (essentially a mixture of land use plan-ning controls to ensure a suitable disposal site and statutory nuisance procedures coming into play after problems occurred) were inadequate for modern waste management regulation. The committee recommended that a dedicated licensing system was required to ensure that day-to-day operations were properly regulated. The review gathered dust, but there was then was a well-publicised environmental scandal – the discovery on 24 February 1972 of the illegal disposal of 36 drums of dangerous sodium cyanide ash near a school in the Midlands. The government took immediate action, initially introducing the Deposit of Poisonous Wastes Act 1973, drafted in ten days and passed in Parliament within a month, to be followed later by the bespoke licensing system as recommended by the committee and contained in Part I of the Control of Pollution Act 1974. But the prior analysis is an important element if new law is to be effective – an ignition event without proper prior analysis can simply lead to knee-jerk legislation which may be ill drafted and not properly thought through.[6]

Ashby's analysis was compelling, but my own experience in dealing with the question of both environmental courts and the environmental sanctions suggested that ignition events are not always a necessary ingredient to secure substantive progress. Sometimes one finds that concerns with problems in environmental law happens to coincide with other, quite unconnected, developments taking place in policy thinking in other areas of government – it is what have I described as an 'unexpected alignment'. The trick and the challenge for the environmental specialist is to become aware of these parallel agendas taking place and to take advantage of them. When our report on environmental civil sanctions was published, I was on the board of the Environment Agency. Agency officers were clearly interested in the idea, but recognised there was unlikely to be any movement from their sponsoring department, DEFRA. But the chief executive tipped me off that there was currently a Treasury Review taking place on the general relationship between regulators and the regulated community and it was here, if anywhere, that any initiatives on sanctions might take place. This was the first time I had heard of the Hampton Review. It arose out of a decision by the Chancellor of the Exchequer, Gordon Brown, in 2004 to appoint a businessman, Philip Hampton, to conduct a review of regulatory inspections and enforcement across an enormous range areas including health and safety, food standards and environment protection. The primary aim was to reduce administrative burdens without compromising regulatory standards or outcomes. I duly arranged to meet Sir Philip and his secretariat and explained that I felt, as part of the review, he needed to explore the types of sanctions available to regulators and in particular whether there was more scope for using civil sanctions than just the criminal law. His final report was largely concerned with the attitude of some regulators who had a tendency to adopt a 'tick box' mentality towards enforcement and recommended a much greater emphasis on risk-based approaches where regulators focused their resources on securing the most effective outcomes. He took the point on the need for a richer range of sanctions. His report noted that there were far too many examples of criminal fines being imposed by the courts which failed to reflect the economic gains being made by illegal operators. He felt that civil penalties should be introduced as an extra sanctioning tool for regulators. But he also recognised this involved complex legal issues and recommended that the Better Regulation Executive, then within the Cabinet Office, should undertake a separate and comprehensive review of regulators' penalty regimes.

---

[6] The Dangerous Dogs Act 1991, which focused on breeds rather than individual behaviour, is often cited as an example of such 'knee-jerk' legislation and did not lead to a reduction of fatalities from dog attacks. In 2018, the House of Commons Select Committee on Environment Food and Rural Affairs concluded that 'changing the law on Breed Specific Legislation is desirable, achievable and would better protect the public'.

Shortly after his report was published, I was contacted by the Cabinet Office and invited to be the 'Reviewer' for this proposed study on regulatory sanctions. Five civil servants from the Cabinet Office were assigned to assist me in the exercise but, before starting, I visited a senior official to find out the exact status of a 'Reviewer'. It was not a term I had come across before – was I truly independent of the government or was this part of a Cabinet Office exercise? Or were they, so to speak, trying to have their cake and eat it? He told me that it was Gordon Brown, who had introduced the idea of 'Reviewers' and it was essentially a mechanism to push more radical policy agendas across other government departments. And yes, it probably was the case that the Reviewer was both independent and part of a government exercise – apparently, I was the first appointed Reviewer (there had been around five before me) to have asked this question. This probably betrayed the lawyer in me.

The scope of the review was enormous, covering some 50 national regulators as well as local authorities and dealing with nearly every field of regulation aside from the financial sector. We were dealing with areas of law well outside my expertise, but when it came to the question of sanctions there were remarkably common patterns. In nearly every area of regulation the ultimate sanction was a criminal prosecution and there was broad dissatisfaction with the level of fines imposed in the magistrates' courts. Many of the offences were drafted in strict liability terms, but some allowed a defence of acting with all due care or similar wording. It was unclear whether there was any principle at work in the way that these offences were drafted, even within the same field of law – at the time, for example, waste offences permitted a defence of acting with due care while water offences did not. As part of the Review, I therefore commissioned a leading criminal law academic Andrew Semester, to review the way offences were drafted across a range of regulations and why a due diligence defence was included in some but not others. He concluded, as I had suspected, that there was no principle at work; it was simply due to historical accident and the inclination of the particular draftsman. Some regulators had access to various sorts of administrative notices such as improvement or stop orders[7] but, again, there was little consistency across the board. Financial regulators and taxation authorities had access to civil penalties in many areas but this was very unusual in other areas of regulation.

In December 2005, we launched an initial paper which outlined some of the key issues raised in the Hampton Report and included a discussion of sanctions systems in Germany where there was extensive use of civil penalties in preference to the criminal law and Australia where both the criminal law and a wide range of civil penalties and other forms of sanctions were used in many areas of regulation. The paper invited evidence based on a set of core questions. Over the next three months we were faced with an enormous amount of submissions, as well as the results of our research in both the academic and practitioner literature.

---

[7] Even then, the only formal sanction for failing to comply with an administrative notice was a criminal prosecution.

Meetings were held that involved a range of different regulators, including those in the financial sector, to discuss the enforcement challenges they faced – a valuable exercise in itself since regulators often operate within their own silos and had few opportunities to exchange experience and views with those in other fields of law. One clear finding emerged. In almost every area of law we looked at, be it environment, health and safety at work, or food hygiene, there were, at one end of the scale, true criminals at work who knew precisely what they doing and who were often making considerable money from non-compliance. At the other end of the scale there were operators or companies who had committed a strict liability offence but with no intention of doing so and with a complete absence of negligence, such as a wholly unexpected breakdown of equipment. In the middle were operators who might be careless at most, but could hardly be described as being truly criminal. As for sanctions, I was astonished to find how little rigorous research had been conducted in this country and elsewhere on the actual effect of different types of sanctions. One of the problems was that, often, one was not comparing like for like or there were so many other factors that might encourage compliance that it was often difficult to single out the type of sanction being employed as a critical factor.

We could easily have been overwhelmed by the amount of evidence being submitted to the review and I decided that the best way forward was to come up with a set of principles which should underlie an effective sanctioning system, ask whether the existing systems met these and what needed to be done to ensure they did. These principles did not come out of thin air and I read an enormous amount of literature on the subject, until eventually, we felt able to consolidate the issue into six core principles.[8] Initially, these had been developed simply as an internal aid to the review to help interrogate the existing systems and to test any proposals we were making. But it became clear that this formulation of a set of sanction principles had not been expressed in this way before and they became a cornerstone of the eventual report.

We recognised that the criminal law would remain an important element of any sanctioning system and the report contained many recommendations for improving current practice. To deal with the problem of low fines in the criminal courts, we wanted to see new sentencing guidance for regulatory offences from the Sentencing Council.[9] But we were also aware that, in dealing with these sorts

---

[8] These stated: (a) sanctions should aim to change behaviour – punishment, per se, was not the objective although sometimes this would be needed; (b) sanctions should aim to eliminate financial gain made from non-compliance; (c) a sanctions system should be responsive to the different circumstances in which breaches occurred and the regulators should have discretion as to how to respond in the most effective way; (d) sanctions should be proportionate in that they should be sufficiently flexible to reflect the broad spectrum of circumstances in which regulatory breaches occur; (e) sanctions should help restore harm done by the regulatory breach; and (f) sanctions should act as a deterrent to others. Slightly to my embarrassment, these have since become known as the 'Macrory principles'.

[9] The Sentencing Council, established in 2010, produces sentencing guidelines for the courts. Under the Coroners and Justice Act 2009, courts must follow the relevant guidelines unless it would be contrary to the interests of justice to do so.

of offences, especially where companies were involved, courts essentially had only two options – a fine on the company and/or imprisonment of the directors or those directly responsible.[10] We felt that there should be a much richer range of sanctions available to the criminal courts such as publicity orders requiring the offender, at their own expense, to take out advertisements in the media to acknowledge their offence to the wider community. Drivers convicted of speeding offences now often have the opportunity to take a speed awareness course as an alternative to paying a fine and research indicates this has a long-term positive effect on driving habits. We felt that similar initiatives might be developed for regulatory offences so that offenders truly understood the rationale for, say, food hygiene requirements or health and safety regulations. Criminal prosecutions before magistrates are generally heard before the nearest court to where the offence was committed, but we recommended that prosecutions for different classes of regulatory offences be designated to particular courts within regions. This would allow the magistrates and court officials in these courts to develop expertise in the regulatory area concerned. We also felt that the time had come to rationalise strict liability offences and generally incorporate a due care defence but where the burden of proving this defence was up to the individual or company being prosecuted.[11] Finally, we wanted to see the greater use of restorative justice for regulatory offences where the offender or the chief executive of a company is required to meet those that have harmed by their action – again, research suggested this could have a dramatic effect.

The underlying aim of these proposals was to ensure that criminal prosecutions for regulatory offences were reserved for the most serious offenders who could be described as truly criminal. But it was also clear that the availability of civil sanctions for regulators would be an important and valuable tool, mainly to deal with the sort of case where there was no evidence of intention or recklessness, but where, equally, a caution or warning was not a sufficient response. We advocated a system of smaller fixed penalties for minor breaches but potentially far larger 'variable' penalties to be used in more serious cases but where a criminal prosecution was still not considered appropriate. In line with the European Convention on Human Rights, there had to be an appeal system against the imposition of civil sanctions and I recommended that the appropriate judicial forum was not the ordinary courts but the tribunal system. Coupled with the idea of civil sanctions was the concept of enforcement undertakings, an idea already well developed in Australian regulatory law. Instead of having a sanction imposed by the regulator, the offender could offer an undertaking to the regulator specifying the steps that would be taken (such as retraining of staff or investment in new

---

[10] Confiscation of assets involved in the crime is also possible.

[11] In line with general principles on statutory defences, the defence would be proved on the balance of probabilities rather than the criminal standard of beyond all reasonable doubt.

equipment) to avoid non-compliance in the future. This would be coupled with payments to a charity or similar body that reflected any economic gains made by non-compliance or compensation for any damage done – even if unintentionally. It would remain up to the regulator's discretion whether to accept the offer of an undertaking, but here there was some compelling research which suggested that where a company suggests its own sanction rather than having one imposed externally this can have a stronger, long-term, impact on the organisation.

Various forms of civil sanction have already been used in this country, but it was clear from the evidence that there was considerable distrust by some in industry that these powers might be abused and simply be used as a source of revenue by authorities. As one of the submissions from a trade body noted, civil penalties 'could become a nice little earner' for the regulator and could be used 'as a quick and easy means of boosting "paperwork" compliance and making their figures look good.' I understood the concerns and was very conscious at the time of a succession of stories in the press about privatised rail companies imposing substantial penalty fares on passengers who had innocently bought the wrong ticket and, in some companies, it appeared that there was even a policy of incentivizing enforcement by allowing the revenue collectors to keep a proportion of the penalties they imposed. It was clear that if civil sanctions were to be introduced it would be equally important to address these issues to prevent abuse of the powers by introducing principles of what I described as 'regulatory governance'. This became another key component of the report.

Under the new system, regulators would have more options in how they responded to a breach – whether to issue warnings, initiate a prosecution, impose civil sanctions or accept an enforcement undertaking. It was important that this choice was determined by the correct response to any breach in light of the general sanction principles rather than extraneous factors such as pressure to meet internal targets that can inevitably creep into any bureaucracy. I was clear that any revenue from civil sanctions should not go directly to the regulator – even if ring-fenced for enforcement purposes – otherwise many would suspect that the real reason for choosing a civil sanction was to secure extra income for the regulator, especially during a period of public finance squeeze. Equally, the choice of sanction should be based on factors contained in a published enforcement policy – a document that could help ensure consistency of approach by the regulator and in itself give valuable signals to the regulated community to encourage good behaviour. I was aware that the Environment Agency had long published an enforcement policy in relation to its existing powers and rather naively assumed this was universal practice. But we conducted research on the issue and found that only 17 of the 50 or so national regulators within the scope of the review had a published policy – one even saying that they kept their policy confidential as they 'did not want to give the game away'. The importance of having such a published policy was brought home to me when we visited the United States. The Environmental Protection Agency had the power to impose administrative penalties while the Department of Justice could bring criminal prosecutions for environmental offences and another division with it could seek financial penalties from a civil court.[12] But there seemed little in the way of published enforcement policies clarifying which route was appropriate in which cases; one official admitted to me that it could often depend on which branch of the administration happened to get first notice of the breach in question. I recommended that there must always be a published enforcement policy and that regulators should be required to publish regular data on their outputs, meaning the number and types of different enforcement actions being taken. But it was equally, if not more, important that regulators produce reports on outcomes (ie what was actually being achieved in terms of environmental quality, reduction of accidents or whatever substantive area of law was involved). I had no problem in seeing, say, a reduction of criminal prosecutions in favour of civil sanctions, provided the overall outcome was not diminished. Again, the importance of this became apparent during our visit to the United States at a meeting with the head of criminal environmental prosecutions at the Department of Justice, the head of environmental civil penalties within the same department and the head of administrative penalties at the Environmental Protection Agency. They each described the powers they had and the amount of activity they had been engaged in over the past year. But when I asked what environmental outcomes this had all achieved since surely this should be driving their decision making, there was a rather embarrassed silence. The head of civil penalties admitted that his key driver was the need to meet internal targets for the amount of penalties secured and the head of prosecutions later wrote to me that it was a question he had never properly considered before. In discussing the issue of outcomes with UK regulators I received conflicting advice – some said it was extraordinarily difficult to come up with robust outcome measures, others said it was much more straightforward. It is not an easy issue, but it was one of my disappointments that this was the only recommendation on regulatory governance that was not included in the legislation that followed the review.

About three-quarters of the way through the review, I was pretty clear of the analysis and reforms that were needed and we published a consultation report. Generally, there was a favourable response. I continued to have many discussions with industry, trade bodies, regulators and various non-governmental organisations to explain my thinking. As we approached the deadline for publishing the final report, my Cabinet Office staff kept taking me to meetings with various officials within the Home Office, the Ministry of Justice and other departments. I now realise that it was an exercise in squaring-off other departmental interests to ensure there was cross-departmental support and was an aspect of internal governmental

[12] In the US, the term 'administrative penalties' refers to financial penalties imposed directly by the regulator such as the Environment Protection Agency, while 'civil penalties' refer to higher financial penalties imposed by a civil judge. These powers are reserved for more serious cases, but where a criminal prosecution is still not considered appropriate. In the UK, the legislation that followed my report used the term 'civil penalties' to described penalties imposed by the regulator, though I have never been sure why the choice of terminology was made.

machinery I could not have addressed without the expert support of the officials attached to the review. The meetings paid off and, within a few days of publication of the report in 2006, the government announced it was accepting all of its recommendations and would be promoting primary legislation to give effect to the ideas contained within it. The Labour Party was still in power, but I felt that my recommendations were essentially non-party political and asked if I could talk to the Conservative Party about the report. The Cabinet Office were uncomfortable with the idea but said if I did so in my private capacity that was up to me. I duly met Oliver Heald, then the shadow Attorney General, and found that he had already commissioned a leading city law firm to review my report. Gratifyingly, they had concluded that it all seemed eminently sensible.

One of the oddities and weaknesses of this type of exercise is that as soon as the final report is published, the review, as such, ceases to exist and the civil service team supporting it is immediately assigned to other tasks. The Reviewer is left in limbo, becoming a private citizen again with no special access to government. I asked the Cabinet Office if I could remain an informal adviser to the departmental team responsible for drafting the legislation to implement the recommendations as this might assist its process and they readily agreed. My recommendations clearly cut across the interests of many different government departments and I would have preferred to see the Cabinet Office retaining responsibility for promoting the new legislation. But, at the time, the Department of Business, Enterprise and Regulatory Reform (BERR)[13] was trying to resist pressure that it was no longer needed and, as part of their regulatory reform agenda, they offered to take on the promotion of the new legislation. However, when I first met the team within BERR, I was informed that they had no real jurisdiction in criminal matters (which fell largely within the Home Office and the Ministry of Justice) and would therefore focus on my proposals for civil sanctions and regulatory governance. I felt this was a major set-back, as the review had much to say on improving the way we handled criminal offences in the regulatory sphere and undermined the idea of viewing sanctions as a complete and coherent response system that cut across criminal and civil matters. I no longer had any official status and, despite my best efforts, it proved far more difficult to press for the reforms I had suggested on the criminal side.[14]

Nevertheless, my attendance in the Bill team meetings did prove to be of value as I could explain in more detail my thinking when particular issues, not directly addressed in the report, came up. But I had a rather frosty relationship with the team's departmental lawyer who may have felt somewhat threatened by my presence. When we discussed appeal procedures against civil sanctions, I argued that the legislation should state clearly that if the offender argued that no offence had

---

[13] Newly created in 2007 out of the older Department of Trade and Industry.
[14] For example, the review recommended that the Sentencing Council produce guidance for regulatory offences, but it was not until 2014 that the Council produced sentencing guidelines for environmental offences.

been committed, the burden of proving the offence in the appeal procedure should be on the regulator. This reflected the presumption of innocence in the European Convention on Human Rights, but also seemed only fair. The last thing I wanted to see was civil sanctions being viewed as an easy option for the regulator, but rather as the correct response in light of the sanction principles in any particular case. The departmental lawyer firmly rejected my proposal saying it was inappropriate to include such a provision in the legislation and that it would be a matter for the appeal tribunal to determine. As I describe later in this chapter, it later turned out that this omission had considerable and damaging political consequences as the system of civil sanctions was later rolled out.

The Regulatory Enforcement and Sanctions Bill started its legislative process before the House of Lords. I was asked by BERR to make a general presentation in a parliamentary committee room on the report and there seemed to be general cross-party support. However, a former Conservative Attorney General, Sir Nicholas Lyell, mounted a strong opposition, claiming the proposals for civil penalties were in breach of Magna Carta and were giving far too much power to regulators. I arranged to meet him to discuss my report. His first question was to ask me whether I had actually read all the evidence submitted to the review and the considerable amount of published literature referenced in it. I was told later this was a tactic he often used with heads of similar reviews to undermine their position since, in practice, most had simply relied on filleted summaries provided by their civil servant team and had to admit they had not read the full material. Fortunately, I was able to reply that as an academic wanting to fully understand the issues I had read, in full, everything submitted to the review as well as all the literature referenced in the final report, including a 200-page report by the Australian Law Commission on civil sanctions. We were then able to move on to a more constructive dialogue, where I was able to explain that I fully understood his concerns about giving too much power to regulators and this was why I had given so much attention to issues of regulatory governance in the report. Sir Nicholas admitted that he had nothing against my report, as such, but remained concerned about the way the government had gone about the legislation. He continued to oppose the Bill in the Lords, but it was passed and Part 3, which concerned civil sanctions, came into force on 8 September 2008.

About halfway through the review, I had been invited to address a meeting of a body called the 'Regulators Group'. I had not heard of it before but, far from being some sinister organisation, it was a six-monthly meeting of key regulators held in the Treasury, mainly to discuss recent case law and similar items of common interest. I outlined my key thinking and the need to move away from such a dependence on criminal sanctions and strict liability offences, but my remarks were met with stony silence and no questions were asked. A few weeks later, someone leaked to me the minutes of the meeting, which, on my item, simply said 'Professor Macrory challenged the way we have done things for a hundred years. But he is just an academic'. I felt this betrayed a rather distorted view of academia, but it should have warned me of the conservatism that often exists with bodies used to familiar ways of doing things. I had assumed that all regulators would welcome access to these new forms of sanctions and, in the final report, did not recommend that they be imposed on regulators. Instead, individual regulators and their sponsoring departments could acquire them as and when they saw fit through orders made under the Regulatory Enforcement and Sanctions Act. In retrospect, allowing such discretion was probably mistaken. Several key regulators, including the Health and Safety Executive, seemed perfectly satisfied with their existing powers of notices and criminal sanctions and were simply not interested in acquiring civil sanction powers.

The first movers turned out to be DEFRA who produced regulations in 2010 giving civil sanction powers to Natural England and the Environment Agency though, initially, in a very limited number of areas such as packaging regulations. For this first tranche, the Agency did not press to have the powers extended to the much broader and more significant area of environmental permitting because they were in the process of revising these regulations and planned to come back in a year. But by the time they did so, the Conservative/Liberal Democrat coalition government had come into power and this delay, based on perfectly pragmatic reasons, turned out to have considerable impact on the coherence of the system I had proposed. Oliver Letwin had been appointed Minister of State for Government Policy within the Cabinet Office and insisted that all proposed regulations from any department passed across his desk. The new DEFRA draft regulations extending civil sanctions to environmental permitting caught his eye and he began to raise concerns about the proposals. He was particularly anxious that regulators might use these powers to bully small businesses who would not necessarily have access to legal advice or the resources to exercise their rights of appeal and would simply pay up to avoid further trouble. On 8 November 2012, a new policy was announced in relation to civil sanctions orders made by ministers under the Regulatory Enforcement and Sanctions Act. From now on, any new powers to impose financial civil penalties would generally only be granted in respect of companies with more than 250 employees.[15] The timing of the announcement was designed to coincide with a conference UKELA had organised in London the same day to explore sanctions generally and where Oliver Letwin had agreed to be the keynote speaker. He explained his thinking, which mainly concerned the potentially unfair relationship with regulators and small businesses. I argued that it seemed odd because now the only formal sanction for small businesses would be a criminal prosecution and, during my review, it was often these very businesses, including farmers, who had welcomed the idea of civil penalties as an alternative to criminal proceedings. I later explained to him that I understood his concerns and that all

---

[15] Voluntarily agreed enforcement undertakings were excluded from the restriction. It is unclear whether this policy is still operative. Regulations, for example, made in 2018 by the Department for Business Energy and Industrial Strategy introducing civil sanctions for offshore environmental offences apply to all sizes of company.

my recommendations on regulatory governance were designed to prevent abuse of power by regulators. I also mentioned that I had tried, though unsuccessfully, to have a provision included in the new legislation that in any appeal the burden of proof would be on the regulator to prove the offence in question if that was in issue.[16] He replied that if this had been in the Act itself he would not have had the concerns he did. I now wonder if, had I been more forceful in discussions with the departmental Bill team and resisted the opposition of the in-house lawyer to a burden of proof provision whether Oliver Letwin's policy might never have come into being. As such, the policy restricting civil penalties to larger companies undermined the coherence of the system I had proposed in the review and continues to do so. When the Environment Agency and DEFRA eventually decided in 2015 to extend civil sanctions to environmental permitting, they decided it was not worth including the complications about business size for civil financial penalties, and these were excluded altogether, whatever the size of company involved. Enforcement undertakings were still available but now against the background of a possible criminal prosecution.

As recommended in the Sanctions Report, the Regulatory Enforcement and Sanctions Act 2008 provided for appeals against civil sanctions to go to the newly established First-tier Tribunal. The great advantage of the new tribunal system established the year before was the administrative flexibility it provided to organise the tribunal into different specialised tribunals and chambers as and when needed and without the need for new legislation each time. As I described in the previous chapter, the 2010 order granting civil sanction powers to the Environment Agency and Natural England led to the immediate establishment of an environment tribunal as part of the First-tier Tribunal to handle the appeals against the new sanctions. Under the Act itself, the amount of the variable penalty as a civil sanction was essentially uncapped, but DEFRA was aware of the political sensitivities involved in creating these new powers and the 2010 order provided a maximum limit of £250,000.[17] In line with my recommendations on regulatory governance, the Act required a published statement on how variable penalties should be calculated to provide transparency and consistency. Again, probably due to the sensitivity surrounding the new powers, DEFRA was unwilling to delegate this task to the environmental regulators and developed the guidance themselves. It was largely written by an economist and there were passages in the document that I found hardly comprehensible. I thought perhaps I was being naïve, but the then-head of legal services at the Environmental Agency told me that he, too, could not

---

[16] When DEFRA was proposing the 2010 regulations for civil sanctions in the environmental field, I was at least able to persuade them to include a provision that the burden of proving an offence in any appeal rested on the regulator. But there was no guarantee that such a provision would always be included in subsequent implementing regulations and it would have been preferable that it was contained in the governing Act.

[17] Strangely in the equivalent regulations applying to Wales there is no upper limit. In Scotland, where civil sanctions were introduced for environmental offences in 2015, the upper limit is £40,000.

understand much of it. It was perhaps another reason why, in practice, variable penalties have rarely been used.

As the civil sanctions regime for environmental offences began to be rolled out from 2010, the most striking aspect was the extensive use of enforcement undertakings. Initially they were largely used in the context of packaging regulations introduced in 2007 which required companies producing a large quantity of packaging material to register with the Environment Agency and fulfil certain recycling requirements. Failure to comply with the regulations was a criminal offence and, before 2010, the Agency had prosecuted companies in the criminal courts even where failures were due to an oversight. Now companies could offer an enforcement undertaking specifying the steps they would take to get back into compliance and paying a sum of money to an environmental charity representing any savings they had made by non-compliance, together with an uplift of around 25 per cent because the law had been breached. In around half the cases, the companies themselves voluntarily disclosed the breach to the Agency and offered an undertaking. I had not expected enforcement undertakings to prove so effective and provided they were applied in appropriate cases it seemed that all parties benefited – the company concerned was committed to take steps to prevent reoccurrence but, without the stigma of a criminal conviction, they could be seen not to have made any economic advantage from the breach and the environmental sector received extra resources. The only body losing out was the Treasury who would otherwise have received the income from criminal fines or imposed civil penalties and I am not sure they were fully aware of what was going on. In line with one of the recommendations in the Sanctions Review, summaries of enforcement undertakings are made publicly available and a recent example involving a water utility gives a good idea of why they can be such a constructive mechanism. The offence related to water discharges. In its undertaking, Yorkshire Water agreed to take a number of actions: remediate and restore the site affected, carry out improvement and infrastructure works, implement an improved monitoring and response procedure, conduct a CCTV survey and cover the Environment Agency's costs. In addition, the company would contribute £200,000 to Yorkshire Wildlife Trust. For the right case, this response is surely preferable than a prosecution and imposition of a fine.

To date, over 400 enforcement undertakings have been accepted by the Environment Agency resulting in around £14 million being paid by companies to environmental charities or towards funding environmental improvements. When I originally was considering the idea of undertakings during the Sanctions Review, I had thought of them in the context of the civil not the criminal sanctioning process. Essentially, they were to be offered as an alternative to a civil financial penalty being imposed by the regulator. By the time it came to the final report, we decided they could also be offered as an alternative to a criminal prosecution and the Act provided for this. But I now have some doubts whether this was wise. Ideally, in my view, once a regulator decides that the breach in question is sufficiently serious to warrant a criminal prosecution, that is the route to be followed rather than allowing the alleged offender to then try to negotiate a different option.

Otherwise, the public could view this simply as an opportunity for offenders to buy themselves out of trouble. This aspect is especially important as the use of enforcement undertakings has moved from the fairly technical world of packaging regulation to more mainstream pollution offences. A recent list of enforcement undertakings accepted by the Environment Agency for the period June to October 2018 lists 13 enforcement undertakings, many involving water utility companies for pollution offences and now containing fairly large sums (over £500K in some cases). The Agency still has discretion as to whether it accepts an undertaking and its enforcement policy states that enforcement undertakings will not normally be accepted for serious pollution incidents unless there is evidence of low culpa- bility or, at the most, negligence. The 2014 Sentencing Guidelines produced by the Sentencing Council had a dramatic effect in the criminal courts, particularly for more serious offences and where larger companies such as water utilities, are involved. Fines approaching £1 million or more are now regularly imposed and this means that the pressure on the Environment Agency to accept an enforcement undertaking as an alternative to prosecution in such cases will have increased substantially. To ensure public confidence in the system, the Agency must continue to exercise its discretion carefully and be prepared to explain the rationale for its decisions, particularly in the larger cases.

The introduction of civil sanctions in this country as a new form of sanc- tioning response in the environmental field has largely been a positive process. However, in the original Sanctions Review, I presented a personal vision for an effective sanctioning system and, despite the government's acceptance of all the review's recommendations, the story shows that turning that vision into political reality has not proved easy. The Regulatory Enforcement and Sanctions Act 2008 that followed the review was largely focused on civil sanctions and issues of regulatory governance and, apart from the action by the Sentencing Council, there has been little progress on the large number of recommendations I made to improve the handling of regulatory offences by the criminal courts. The diffi- culties raised by the 2012 Cabinet Office policy on restricting civil sanctions to larger companies has meant that the power to impose civil financial penalties has now been excluded from key areas of environmental regulation whatever the size of the company involved. Some regulators in other fields of law apart from the environment have taken the opportunity to acquire civil sanctioning powers, but the take-up – largely, I suspect, due to a degree of conservatism within depart- ments and regulators – has not been as extensive as I had originally expected. RESA was intended to provide a common and robust framework for all civil sanc- tion powers, but more recently some government departments, including DEFRA, have introduced civil sanctions for specific areas of environment law without using it and to replace existing criminal offences rather than providing an alternative to prosecution. Wholesale decriminalisation may suit a regulatory reform agenda but was never implicit in the Sanctions Review. Devolution has produced substan- tive differences in approach. The maximum limits for variable civil penalties in environmental offences now differ considerably in England, Wales, and Scotland.

In England and Wales, regulators must be satisfied beyond reasonable doubt that the offence has been committed (the criminal standard of proof) even where they are imposing civil penalties, while in Scotland the civil standard of proof, the balance of probabilities, applies. The Scottish Environment Protection Agency is now using enforcement undertakings not simply to prevent reoccurrence of the regulatory breach in question, but to require companies to demonstrate commitments to longer-term environmental or community benefits including more sustainable business practices. In Northern Ireland, to date, no civil penalties are available and regulators must still rely on prosecutions or cautions. Companies operating throughout the United Kingdom, therefore, face distinct sanctioning systems and it is undoubtedly a messy picture. While the Sanctions Review strictly covered England and Wales only, I did not predict the extent of the differences that now exist across the country. But, far from being a source of despair, it could be seen as something that can offer invaluable opportunities for some serious comparative research into the effectiveness of different regimes and approaches being applied and in the context of largely similar environmental laws. As I found out to my surprise in the Sanctions Review, robust research on the issue of sanctions and their actual impact on improving compliance and securing better environmental outcomes has been all too sparse. But there is now a rich source of material which I hope will be pursued before the question of regulatory sanctions is reviewed again in the future.

12

The European Dimension

Almost everything is wrong about the European Community except that it is exists as a community of law which united democracies in Europe

Sir Ralf Dahrendorf, 1991

The environment dies in silence

Ludwig Kramer

European environmental law has long been a focus of my work, both as an academic and a practitioner. The first piece of research I was engaged in at Imperial College in the early 1980s was a comparative study of planning public inquiries in Britain and France and in the context of the newly agreed EU Directive on Environmental Assessment. A little later the opportunity arose to become involved in a project on a much wider European stage. During the Cold War, governments and politicians across the East–West divide would often meet to negotiate treaties and there were opportunities for cooperation within the mainstream scientific research community. But it was less easy for legal academics, geographers and other social scientists to collaborate and the Vienna Centre[1] had been established in 1963 to help foster research in these fields. In 1984, the Centre initiated a comparative programme examining how environmental law was being implemented in practice across a range of European countries, both East and West, the first such project of its kind. Nigel Haigh of the Institute for European Environmental Policy had been involved at its early stages and I was invited to contribute as an environmental lawyer, funded by the Economic and Social Research Council. Participants took turns in hosting meetings every six months, alternating between Eastern and Western Europe. The first meeting I attended took place in Moscow, soon after President Gorbachev had come to power. It was an extraordinary period of European history to be engaged in such an exercise and, looking back, I feel immensely privileged to have been a part of the enterprise. The final meeting was held three years later in East Berlin shortly before the collapse of the Berlin Wall and our twice-yearly discussions became a sort of microcosm of the enormous political developments taking place outside our meeting rooms.

Early meetings were somewhat guarded and stilted. Some of those from Eastern European countries were clearly communist party members and their

---

[1] Technically known as the European Coordination Centre for Research and Documentation in Social Science.

presentations would start with an obligatory opening stating that industrial pollution was a problem caused by the capitalist system and that Marx had been a true environmentalist. I told them that, in Britain, the worst polluters at the time were not, as they were clearly thought, private industries but the large public sector state bodies such as the Central Electricity Generating Body or the public water companies. It was not easy to enforce laws against them and they often had sponsoring government departments who would protect them. But as we began to know each other better, discussions became more open and relaxed and our only real problem was with East Germany. Their first representative was clearly not a party member and was, perhaps, a little too revealing about environmental problems in that country. She was suddenly removed and replaced by someone else from the same research body, the Institute for Sociology and Social Science in Berlin. We complained, only to be told that they could see no problem with the change – 'We are from the same Institute and we all think the same.'

Over the next three years we produced some valuable comparative reports on areas such as waste management and air pollution and, finally, what was the first comprehensive comparative study on environmental policy and law across Eastern and Western Europe.[2] But it was not always easy. It became clear that many of the researchers from Eastern European countries, with the notable exception of the Hungarians, were not used to the free-flowing discussion familiar in Western academic circles. We held sessions to formulate the issues and questions to be addressed in national papers to be prepared for the next meeting and it was often uncomfortable to see the extent to which the Western academics dominated these discussions. At one point I turned to my environmental law colleagues from Eastern Europe to ask what they thought should be included, only to be told by the Russian delegate: 'Just tell us what we should write on and we will do it.' But I developed a good relationship with my Czech legal counterpart and was able to find out a lot more about the application of environmental laws to state enterprises in that country. In both Czechoslovakia and the United Kingdom, air pollution from sulphur dioxide was then a major issue and the proportion of SO_2 that came from their state enterprises and the public sector bodies such as the Central Electricity Generating Board was of a similar order.[3] In both countries, the national air pollution legislation formally applied to such bodies but it was clear that, in practice, the fact that they were part of the state brought its own tensions and challenges in ensuring compliance with the law. I was able to develop a detailed comparative analysis[4] which concluded: 'In Czechoslovakia and the United Kingdom, state enterprises in the energy production field give rise to a major proportion of SO_2 emissions in each country, yet in both countries such enterprises are bound by

---

[2] Gyorgy Enyedi, August Gijswijt and Barbara Rhode (eds) *Environmental Policies in East and West* (Taylor Graham, London 1987).
[3] 65% in the UK and 53% in Czechoslovakia.
[4] Richard Macrory 'Air Pollution and the Regulation of State Enterprises' in William Butler (ed) *Yearbook on Socialist Legal Systems 1989* (New York, Transnational Juris Publications, 1989).

legislation regulating air pollution. When it comes to the practical application of these laws, it is clear that the institutional position of such enterprises and their relationships with various agencies of the State, result in complex nuances and cross-currents of interest which may not be reflected in an analysis of the formal and technical substance of specialist pollution law.' In the United Kingdom, electricity production was about to be privatised under the Electricity Act 1989 and most of what I had written now gives an impression of a bygone age. But some of the issues raised in the paper could yet become pertinent again.[5] The benefits and disadvantages of renationalisation of key sectors of industry clearly remains a matter of debate in this country, but the firmer and more equal enforcement of environmental law that has proved possible against privatised industries such as water companies has been one of the unexpected advantages.

We held one of the Vienna Centre meetings at Imperial College, London. Our hosts in other countries had laid on impressive cultural excursions and I duly arranged two distinctive events. The first was a dinner in a London club, hosted by Richard Hawkins, a long-standing friend and fairly eccentric environmental lawyer. We dined in a private room in the Carlton Club where Disraeli had planned the carve up of the Balkans following the Russo-Turkish War in the 1870s. In an age where the iron curtain still existed, many of those from the Eastern European countries had not visited London before and I tried to explain that the club was hardly a true representation of modern Britain but a sort of extravagant theatre – as we moved to our dining room, we passed club members in the library in dinner jackets fast asleep, snoring and with their faces covered by newspapers. But I had not appreciated the extent to which historical images of London were so deeply embedded in the minds of our colleagues from the East. The Polish representative stood up to give a toast of thanks and, in tears, said that he had read Sherlock Holmes stories since his childhood and had never dreamt that one day he would be actually dining in a London club. The next evening, we visited the Players Theatre under the arches at Charing Cross which laid on traditional music hall evenings. I had warned them in advance of our visit and the extrovert Master of Ceremonies welcomed, in turn, the visitors from so many European countries – 'Stand up, Bulgaria; Stand up West Germany and East Germany' and so on. As each participant duly stood, the rest of the packed house cheered and applauded and I took some pride in seeing this display of the best of British warmth and openness.

By the mid-1980s, European Community environmental legislation was rapidly developing and making an impact within the United Kingdom. The European Court of Justice was beginning to make important rulings in the area and it was clear that it was a legal dimension that could not be ignored. In my academic work I then took a conscious decision that I could no longer handle all areas of

---

[5] The 2019 Labour Party Manifesto contained extensive renationalisation proposals including a commitment to 'bringing our energy and water systems into democratic public ownership.'

environmental law and decided that, in future, I would largely concentrate on national and European Community law, leaving international environmental law, despite its importance, to others. Beyond the formal institutional arrangements for policy and law making, one of the less-visible aspects of the membership of the European Union was the extent to which informal networks of policy makers and expert bodies began to develop to share common interests. In 1992, for example, national regulators and authorities concerned with the implementation of pollution laws formed an informal network to compare their experiences and promote best practice. The European Union Network for the Implementation and Enforcement of Environmental Law (IMPEL) now has over 50 member organisations, from some 36 countries, including all EU Member States and many other European countries. I was then a member of the Royal Commission on Environmental Pollution (RCEP) and, increasingly, we found ourselves having to visit the European Commission in Brussels as the EU legal and policy framework was often critical to our studies. The RCEP was an independent expert advisory body on environmental matters and similar bodies were then being established in other European countries. During the 1994 Transport Study, we heard that our German equivalent, the German Council of Environmental Advisors, were also studying transport issues and invited them over to London. We had an immensely productive discussion where it was clear that both countries were facing similar challenges on transport. As with the Royal Commission, the German Council was dominated by heavyweight scientists, but each body had one legal member. Over dinner, I rather tentatively asked my counterpart, Eckard Rehbinder, a distinguished German professor of environmental law, whether members of his Council were paid and he replied that they each received a large monthly stipend, together with individual research and administrative assistance. When I told him that members of the RCEP received no fee[6] but were simply given a briefcase with the royal crest on it, together with a filing cabinet that had to be returned on retirement, he looked at me rather sadly and simply remarked, 'It's extraordinary what the British will do for their Queen'.

This initial meeting led to more interaction with other European advisory bodies, until eventually an informal network was established – the European Environment and Sustainable Development Advisory Councils (EEAC). I chaired the body between 2001 and 2003 and it still exists, with some 14 advisory organisations from 11 European countries – though, sadly, with the demise of the Royal Commission and the Sustainable Development Commission in 2011, there is now no longer any UK participation. Other important informal environmental law networks have since developed. The European Network of Prosecutors for the Environment (ENPE) was established in 2012, greatly encouraged by the British Environment Agency, bringing together 17 prosecuting bodies across

[6] The then chairman refused fees because it might have been seen to jeopardise the RCEP's independence, though a modest daily attendance allowance was later introduced on the RCEP in general, see further chap. 9.

Europe to share best practice and common challenges. The Environment Agency is distinctive because it is both a regulator and a prosecuting body and, in most other European countries, the work of prosecution is handled by the public prosecutor's offices. The network has been especially valuable because environmental prosecutors clearly often felt fairly isolated within their organisation and have welcomed the contact with their counterparts in the rest of Europe. Similarly, in 2004, an informal network of European judges engaged in environmental law was established again with a strong UK input and encouragement from Lord Carnwath, then a Court of Appeal judge. Annual conferences have been held on such matters as climate change and the judiciary, the protection of the environment and the criminal law, access to environmental justice and human rights and the enforcement of environmental law.

Academic environmental lawyers within the EU also began to develop informal networks. Anyone researching EU law at the time had ready access to the decisions of the European Court of Justice, but it was extraordinarily difficult to find out about decisions on issues of EU environmental law being taken by national courts in other member countries. Ludwig Kramer, then head of the legal unit at DG Environment in the European Commission, wanted to encourage greater interaction within the European academic community and, with funding from the Commission, I organised a seminar in 1984 at Imperial College involving a small group of leading environmental law academics in a number of Member States. European directives require Member States to introduce legislation transposing their obligations into national law. But where no such transposition had taken effect, the European Court of Justice had already developed in the 1980s the so-called 'direct effect' doctrine under which provisions of directives considered 'sufficiently precise and clear' could, in effect, leap-frog into the national system and be invoked before a national court. The purpose of the seminar was to explore and compare the extent to which national courts were applying this doctrine in environmental cases. There was wide variation in practice and it proved an illuminating exercise, producing insights which could not have been discovered in any other way. This led to a further series of annual seminars examining on a comparative basis how particular aspects of EU environmental law were being handled in the courts at national level. After a gap of some years, the academics involved decided to revive the exercise in 2001 with a meeting in Bremen under the title of the 'Avosetta' group. It was named after the protected bird which was at the centre of the major environmental decision of the European Court of Justice in 1991 involving Germany and the European Commission, though unbeknownst to the other academics, that case has a particular and rather uncomfortable resonance with me for reasons that will become apparent later in the chapter.

The Avosetta group remains an informal gathering of leading academics lawyers that now covers most EU countries and meets annually on subjects such as emissions trading, environmental liability and access to environmental information. The focus of discussion continues to be very much on how, in practice,

EU environmental law issues are treated in different Member States and though I have now attended almost 20 such meetings, each time I find myself learning something new about the different legal cultures and ways of handling things within Member States. A particularly interesting session was held in 2003 on how the core environmental principles written in the EU Treaty were being handled by different national courts. The principles had been written into Belgian national law and it was somewhat of a revelation to hear how there had been over 20 court cases on the 'polluter pays principle' – and, somewhat counterintuitively, that these cases had been brought not by environmental organisations but by industries challenging the legality of eco-taxes and similar measures on the grounds that they were not the polluter.[7] Fifteen years later, this comparative research has become all the more relevant as the question of how these environmental principles should be handled in the UK legal system is now high on the political agenda in the light of Brexit.

But it was the European Commission's work on the enforcement of environmental law obligations against Member States that now became a particular area of my interest and research. In 1989 I had attended a conference of environmental groups in London where the Ludwig Kramer gave the lead presentation. He explained that, under the EU Treaty, the European Commission had a duty to ensure that Member States fully implemented their EU legal obligations. If it suspected a breach of obligations, it had the power to send a formal infringement notice to the Member State concerned. If they were dissatisfied with the response, this could be followed by a more formal 'Reasoned Opinion' but, if the Commission felt there was still no satisfactory resolution, it could refer the case to the European Court of Justice. Ludwig Kramer explained that the Environment Directorate within the Commission had no powers to carry out inspections within Member States and they were, therefore, largely dependent on members of the public or national environmental groups to notify them of cases where they suspected government or other public bodies were not complying with their EU legal obligations. The Commission had a simple complaints procedure for members of the public to provide them with such information – no costs were involved, it did not require the use of lawyers and, he said, they would investigate all complaints received. The presentations of these powers of the European Commission and the opportunity they afforded to the public were something of a revelation to many of those present, including myself. In fact, they had long been available in all areas of EU law but had been not be used to any great extent by other directorates within the Commission. Ludwig Kramer was clearly determined to expand infringement proceedings in the environmental field and wished to bring these powers to the attention of the wider environmental community across Europe. He explained why it was so important for environmental law with a pithy phrase, 'The environment dies in silence'. From a legal

---

[7] See Richard Macrory (ed) *Principles of European Environmental Law: Proceedings of the Avosetta Group of European Environmental Lawyers* (Groningen, Europa Law Publishing, 2004).

perspective this reflected the fact that in many areas of EU law such as intellectual property, competition law, or employment rights, the law gave companies, trade unions or individuals clear interests which would help to ensure that EU obligations were met in their countries. In contrast, the environment often had no such legal interest and, while public bodies such as local authorities or environmental regulators were often given legal responsibilities to protect the environment, it was precisely these bodies who often failed to comply with their EU environmental obligations – whether through conflicting interests, resource constraints or simple oversight. Hence the need for the European Commission to pay special attention to this area of law.

A few months later I took a six-month sabbatical. At the time, an academic in my position interested in EU law would often seek a placement at the European Court of Justice but I decided it would be far more interesting to work in Ludwig Kramer's infringement unit. It was developing rapidly and beginning to have a real impact on Member States and I was delighted when he accepted my request to join his team. The unit then contained around 12 lawyers, highly motivated and from many nationalities; most of the work was concerned with infringements and dealing with complaints. Ludwig Kramer was – and remains – a charismatic and inspirational character. A former German judge, he believed passionately in the rule of law and the need to ensure that Member States fully complied with the legal obligations to which they had agreed in EU environmental legislation. He was deeply distrustful of the willingness of politicians and policymakers to compromise on their legal commitments or simply ignore those that were inconvenient. The power to bring infringement proceedings was the most potent legal remedy available to the European Commission and proceedings often reflected the form of EU law being used. There are two main types. The first, EU Regulations, have immediate legal force within Member States and override any conflicting national legal provisions. They have been used fairly rarely in the environmental field and mainly in areas where the provision is totally new to Member States or where commonly applied legal standards are essential – vehicle emissions standards, for example, where there are products being traded or the trans-frontier movements of waste. Most EU environmental law has, however, taken the form of EU directives, a distinctive form of legal instrument, unique to the European legal system. They essentially contained a set of obligations on Member States, but then deliberately give a considerable amount of discretion to each country as to how to fit these within their national legal and administrative systems. It was the extent of this discretion that gave rise to most problems of implementation.

It took some time for many Member States to realise that directives created real legal obligations. I had organised a conference at Imperial College in 1987 to discuss EU environmental law and one of the speakers was Derrick Wyatt, a leading academic in EU law and a practising barrister who often advised and represented the UK government on EU environmental law issues. As he explained, in the early days, the UK had a 'tendency towards regarding EEC directives as helpful if eccentric recommendations to be gently eased into the United Kingdom scheme of doing things, ideally by government circular rather than legislation and ideally without cost'.[8] But whatever the strict definition of directives in the underlying EU Treaty, their legal effect within Member States, even where no national transposing measures had been implemented, began to change through a number of important principles developed by the European Court in the 1980s. The direct effect doctrine had already been the subject of the comparative research seminar I had organised at Imperial College. But the court had also held that, if possible, any national law should be interpreted by the courts in a way that was consistent with relevant EU directives. In a further series of cases, the Court ruled that provisions of directives, especially where they could be said to create some sort of individual rights, could not be transposed merely by means of an informal administrative circular (a practice particularly favoured in some areas of environmental law by Germany, the Netherlands and the UK) but had to be contained in national legislation which was clearly legally binding.

Infringement proceedings were categorised by the European Commission into three types. The first and simplest, covered a failure by a Member State to submit national transposing legislation within the time limit specified in the directive in question, normally two or three years. Six months before the deadline, the Commission would remind all Member States that it expected to see the text of transposing legislation submitted on time and proceedings in the form of the initial formal infringement letter would be commenced immediately if they failed to do so. In a series of cases the European Court had given little sympathy to various defences raised by Member States to justify delays, such as internal constitutional difficulties with devolved administrations or lack of parliamentary time, but it was still surprising how often the deadlines were missed.[9]

The second type of infringement was where the text of national legislation had been sent on time, but the Commission considered it did not properly reflect the provisions of the directive in question. This was not often an easy exercise. Drafting of national laws reflects distinct national legal traditions and the amount of legislation needed was often considerable (for example, over 20 different sets of regulations from the UK implementing the 1985 directive on environmental assessment were sent to the Commission). I wanted Member States to accompany their submissions with a clear compliance table matching the provisions of the directive to the relevant transposing provisions in the national law, but this has never been a legal obligation and practice varies. Not surprisingly, Member States were unlikely to alert the European Commission to any possible deficiencies tucked away in the detail of the national legislation – that, they felt, was for Commission lawyers to discover. I remember at the time seeing the Commission's infringement

[8] Derrick Wyatt, 'Litigating Community Environmental Law – Thoughts on the Direct Effect Doctrine' (1998) 10(1) *Journal of Environmental Law* 9, 10.
[9] Since 2009, the Court of Justice has been empowered to impose financial penalties on Member States who fail to transpose in time. This has led to significant improvements in meeting deadlines.

officer dealing with the UK staring glassy-eyed at a copy of the Environment Protection Act 1990 which had been submitted without any detailed guidance as to how it transposed the EU law in question. To be fair, though, the UK government now has a better record of providing accompanying tables explaining how the provisions of the national legislation were intended to reflect each obligation contained in the directive in question. But I still feel it should be a clear legal obligation on all Member States to send this sort of compliance table. Ludwig Kramer strongly believed in the literal text of the directives and infringement proceedings for failure to transpose correctly were increasingly launched against many Member States. If they eventually reached the European Court, the Commission normally was successful in its arguments and the impact of these infringement cases was such that some Member States began copying out directives word for word into their national law to avoid any accusation of non-transposition. This may have been a good defensive tactic, but rather undermined the key characteristics of a directive in that it is a form of EU law deliberately designed to allow a Member State to reflect its provisions within their own national legal traditions and style of drafting. In this country, more recently, the Environment Agency and the Department of Food, Environment and Rural Affairs have met the problem by increasingly using a drafting technique known as 'transposition by reference'. The national legislation in question simply cross-refers to the relevant directive rather than actually transposing provisions into national law. The European Commission has been uncomfortable with this development and I, too, am uneasy as it can lead to extraordinarily complex national provisions which are not easy for lawyers and non-lawyers to understand and requires constant cross-checking with the directive in question.[10]

I also questioned another aspect of the process. By the time Member States sent their transposing legislation, it has been agreed at national level and there was an understandable resistance to suggestions from the infringement unit that it failed to properly reflect the obligations within the directive concerned. Having to change legislation, even secondary regulations, is a cumbersome business and would involve some loss of face. It seemed to me it would have been more productive for draft texts to be first sent since this could have led to more constructive discussion and less confrontational attitudes between the Commission and national governments. Occasionally, that did indeed happen. One example was when water privatisation was proposed for England and Wales and there were concerns that provisions in the draft legislation (later to become the Water Act 1989) concerning discretionary enforcement mechanisms might not be compatible

---

[10] An example from Schedule 7, para 5 of the 2016 Environmental Permitting Regulations illustrates my point: 'The regulator must exercise its relevant functions so as to ensure compliance with the following provisions of the Industrial Emissions Directive – (a) Article 5(1) and (3); (b) Article 7; (c) Article 8(2); (d) Article 9; (e) Article 11; (f) Article 13(7); (g) Article 14; (h) Article 15 (excluding the penultimate sub-paragraph of Article 15(4)); (i) Article 16; (j) Article 17; (k) Article 18; (l) Article 20(1) and (2); (m) Article 22 (excluding the last sub-paragraph of Article 22(2)); (n) Article 26(4).'

with duties to enforce EU water law. Officials from the UK did come over to the Commission to discuss the draft provisions in question, even at one time bringing over the parliamentary draftsman responsible for the legislation. But this was very much the exception and notification of draft national laws has never been a requirement in EU directives.

But it was the third category of non-implementation that caused the most controversy within Member States. Non-communication and non-transposition are focused on the black letter of the law, but the European Commission began to bring infringement proceedings where the national law transposing a directive might be fully in place, but obligations under EU law had not been implemented in practice. Germany once tried to challenge this before the European Court of Justice, arguing that non-implementation, in practice, was a matter for national courts not the European Commission but the court held that failure to implement in practice was indeed a breach of the Member State's EU obligations, and could be the subject of infringement proceedings. Although such infringement proceedings were formally directed at the national government, they could be respect of any failure by any public body within the country, including a local authority, a body such as the Environment Agency, or even a privatised company such as a water authority when it was exercising what were considered to be public functions. Examples could include a decision to grant a permit for an individual power station on the grounds that the permit did not comply with EU requirements for environmental assessment or where a road scheme had threatened protected habitats under EU law. These proceedings sometimes caused enormous resentment amongst national governments – the decision of the Commission to bring infringement proceedings in respect of the Newbury bypass, already something of a national environmental cause-célèbre and in 1996 leading to some of the biggest anti-road protests ever seen in this country, apparently reached John Major, the then Prime Minister. He was reportedly apoplectic at what he saw as unwarranted European interference with an important national road scheme. Within the Commission's implementation unit, we sometimes had intense arguments as to whether a particular alleged infringement was really one of failure to transpose correctly rather than non-implementation in practice. There was, for example, a case where no environmental assessment procedures had been followed for a large development, but it turned out the national legislation contained no provisions for this class of project. Was this really a failure to transpose the directive or to apply EU law in practice? In truth, the Commission often preferred cases of failure to implement in practice because it brought home to Member States that their obligations under EU law were not mere legal formalities and could not be ignored, whatever the cost. The ordinary citizen has little interest in the technical aspects of formal transposition of directives and is far more likely to be far more worried by the environmental implications of a specific local development. By bringing infringement proceedings in such cases, the European Commission was able to demonstrate that it was not some remote bureaucracy but could have a real connection with the concerns of local individuals and environmental groups.

As Ludwig Kramer has described in his 1989 London talk, the European Commission had no powers of inspection within Member States and was almost wholly reliant on complaints being sent to them by members of the public and environmental groups to alert it about problem areas. The complaints procedure was not contained in Treaty provisions but had been developed by the Commission, was very informal and no costs were involved. There was a model complaint form and all complaints received were numbered and registered. On one occasion, an Irish environmental group had sent their complaint in the form of video describing illegal landfills and there was one of those slightly bizarre bureaucratic discussions as to whether it was an acceptable form of complaint. We decided it was and the video was duly logged and registered. As knowledge of the Commission's interest in environmental complaints began to spread, national groups made more and more use of the procedure. Ludwig Kramer boldly announced that his unit would investigate any complaint received and later, in giving legal advice on environmental matters in my practice as a barrister, I often told clients they should first make a complaint to the Commission rather than initiating potentially expensive national legal proceedings. Such was his growing reputation as a tough and incorruptible lawyer that even a letter to government or a public body including the words, 'cc Ludwig Kramer, European Commission' would sometimes have the desired effect. But the policy of investigating all complaints began to overwhelm the small unit at times. The French infringement officer often complained to me that he was spending most of his time dealing with complaints about the hunting of birds and he doubted whether this was the most serious of environmental issues affecting the country. The UK then had the largest number of complaints, though this probably said as much about the extent of highly active environmental organisations in the country, coupled with the expense of taking legal action before the national courts, as it did about the state of the environment compared to other Member States. Friends of the Earth had mounted a campaign concerning the levels of pesticide residues in drinking water and sent a complaint to the Commission which was duly registered. But in classic campaigning style, they also encouraged all their local groups and members of the public to send complaints about their local supplies and soon thousands were arriving. Each had to be numbered and registered and soon the Secretary General of the European Commission[11] became alarmed at this enormous spike in complaints in the environmental field compared to other areas of EU law. There was concern that DG Environment was being a little too enthusiastic. I went over to London to explain to Friends of the Earth that the point had been made and that, unlike a national political campaign, the number of complaints received would make no difference and, indeed, there was a danger that their campaign would overload the Commission's internal procedures, ultimately damaging the system.

---

[11] The Secretary General is the most senior civil servant in the European Commission, reporting to the President of the European Commission and having overall responsibility for the various directorates within the Commission.

The complaint procedure was extraordinary in many ways in that it allowed individuals living in the remotest parts of Europe or the smallest local environmental group to have direct contact with a supra-national institution and help kick-start legal proceedings between the Commission and Member States. The first environmental infringement case against the United Kingdom to reach the European Court concerned the quality of bathing waters. Under the 1976 Bathing Water Directive, Member States were first required to send the Commission lists of designated bathing waters defined in the directive as water where bathing was authorised or 'traditionally practiced by a large number of bathers'. They were then obliged to ensure these waters met the standards contained in the directive. The United Kingdom had adopted a minimalist approach and sent an initial list of just 29 waters – far fewer than the number submitted by Spain and France (with more than a 1,000 each) and even smaller than the 41 submitted by land-locked Luxembourg. The UK's resistance to designate more bathing waters was no doubt influenced by concerns of the financial impact this might have in the build-up to water privatization at the time. The Commission then received a postcard from a British individual headed 'Save our Shorelines' which referred to Blackpool which had not been included on the UK list. It was on that basis the Commission began investigations, leading to formal infringement proceedings in 1986. The UK government continued to resist further designation and, when the case eventually reached the European Court in 1993,[12] the Court held that designation was not simply a matter for discretion by Member States but that the presence of facilities such as changing huts, toilets and lifeguards meant that Blackpool should have been designated. As a result of the judgment, the number of bathing waters designated by the UK rapidly increased and, by 2018, some 420 had been designated in England – really the result of the impact of a single postcard sent by an individual citizen.

When I started my work in the infringement unit there was no public information about the number of complaints or the number and type of infringement proceedings. The Blackpool decision had caused considerable resentment in some circles in the UK and we received a visit from members of the House of Commons Environment Select Committee to find out more about infringement proceedings. One of the members of the committee complained about the state of Spanish beaches he had visited on a recent holiday and aggressively asked why nothing was being done about them compared to the action that been taken against the UK. I explained that he was entitled to send a complaint in respect of the Spanish beaches he had visited since there was no requirement to be a citizen of the country concerned or a local resident of the area affected – this all came as something of a revelation to the committee. But the enforcement activity of the Commission was then essentially treated as a form of diplomacy subject to traditional principles of inter-governmental confidentiality. During my spell with the infringement unit,

---

[12] *Commission v United Kingdom* C-59/90 [1993] ECR 1-1409.

I was taken to lunch by senior UK government representatives in Brussels who were desperate to understand more about the internal policy of the Commission in bringing infringement proceedings. The UK was then acquiring the reputation of the 'dirty old man of Europe' and there was a feeling that the country was being unfairly picked upon by the Commission. It was a frustrating meeting in many ways because I had, in my briefcase, a table of the current infringement proceedings, country by country, which clearly showed this was not the case. The number of cases being brought against the UK was about the same as in Germany and France. Demark and the Netherlands had the fewest number, while more were being taken against Southern European countries. But it was a confidential paper which I could not show to the British officials and could only give very generalised hints. A few weeks later, the Environment Commissioner, Carlo Ripa de Meana, a flamboyant former Italian politician and strong environmentalist, decided that it was time to go public as to what was happening, whatever the sensitivities of national governments. DG Environment organised a press conference where, for the first time, they published country-by-country tables for current environmental infringement proceedings. At the time it caused some unease amongst Member States, but the practice has continued, with annual reports on implementation and infringement being published.[13]

From time to time, I suggested to Ludwig Kramer that perhaps we should have a clearer enforcement strategy, prioritising the types of complaints and infringement proceedings we should initiate. But he always resisted, arguing that it would be invidious to distinguish between, say, urban air pollution in Greece and the loss of a protected habitat in Spain. But, some ten years later, the Secretary General of the Commission did indeed publish a Communication[14] indicating that there would now be greater prioritisation of infringements. Member States would be encouraged to resolve issues without the intervention of the Commission and there would be more emphasis on ensuring that the communication of transposing laws was made on time and truly reflected the obligations in directives. The most recent formal communication from the Secretary General of the Commission emphasises that, while it still welcomes complaints from the public, individual cases of non-implementation will not normally be dealt with unless they raised issues of wider principle, a problem of compliance of national legislation with EU law, or some systematic failure to comply with EU law.[15] The reference to a systematic failure came as a result of one of the most important infringement cases which had been initiated by the Commission in 1998 and concerned illegal landfill sites in Ireland. The normal practice then would have been to initiate infringement proceedings in relation to each illegal landfill but there was then a danger that

---

[13] In recent years, though, these reports have become rather less detailed and country-by-country comparisons have diminished.

[14] European Commission, *A Europe of Results* (2007 COM (207)).

[15] Communication from the European Commission *EU Law: Better Results through Better Application* 2017 C 18/02), para 3.

individual sites might be authorised before the case came to court, rendering the legal action defunct. Instead, the Irish enforcement officer within the unit argued imaginatively in the pleadings before the Court that the extent and number of the illegal sites represented a systematic failure in the government's administrative system and it was this overall failure, rather than the problems at each site, that represented the breach of EU obligations. It was the first time this argument had been made before the Court and the judges accepted the idea: 'Ireland had not yet met its obligation, by which it had been bound since 1977, to ensure that all municipal landfills hold the requisite permit. The failure to fulfil obligations, which is the result, all at once, of extremely belated transposition of Article 9 of the Directive, of systematically refraining from requiring existing unauthorised activities to cease while the licensing procedure took place and of a lack of appropriate measures for ensuring that facilities were promptly made subject to the domestic system finally set up, was as at that date both general and persistent in nature.'[16]

The move away from a commitment to investigate all complaints to one of greater prioritisation was, I think, inevitable, though it was not welcomed by some national environmental groups. The focus on ensuring that national law properly reflected the EU legal obligations was logical, but would be worthless if either national citizens or environmental organisations did not then have adequate access to national courts or other judicial bodies to enforce those laws. It is a sensitive area for the European Commission which might be seen as interfering too much in the national legal ways of doing things, but the shift in emphasis on infringement proceedings has meant that the Commission now needed to pay greater attention to ensuring that individuals and groups had greater access to national legal remedies. The EU was a party to the 1998 Aarhus Convention, which contained provisions of access to environmental justice. These requirements have been included in several EU environmental directives such as environmental assessment giving the Commission a clear justification for reviewing such issues at national level.

Within DG Environment, the small legal unit kept itself somewhat detached and, while I was there, it was largely preoccupied with handling complaints and bringing infringement proceedings. I had concerns that the legal unit was not sufficiently engaged with other policy units within the DG, particularly those responsible for drafting new EU legislation and where the experience the unit had had with previous infringements might be extremely useful in improving the text and enforceability of new proposals. An opportunity then arose with a proposed Landfill Directive.[17] The Spanish official in the waste unit responsible for the draft sent round a memo, saying he was having one last internal meeting for any comments before circulating the draft to other Commission directorates

---

[16] *Commission v Ireland* Case C-494/01 [2005] ECR I-3331.
[17] See ch 6 on the political problems that arose when a UK Parliamentary Committee wished to investigate the draft Landfill Directive.

and eventual publication. Ludwig Kramer knew of my feelings about the lawyers engaging with policy units and asked me and the French desk officer to look at the draft. We both agreed that we would independently examine the text and then share our views before I attended the meeting. I assumed that because we came from such different legal traditions our analysis would differ considerably, but it turned out that nearly all our concerns with the text from a legal perspective – the official in question was an engineer rather than a lawyer – were the same and we came up with a series of suggestions to improve the draft including more precise definitions. I turned up to the meeting to find myself the sole attendee and I had a long, informal discussion with the official on his draft but, coming from a different discipline, he still resisted some of our proposed amendments as being unduly legalistic.

One of my other suggestions was that the Commission might do more in giving guidance on the meaning and implications of new EU environmental legislation to forestall problems and differing interpretations within Member States. Other than in the field of chemical policy there was then no general practice of providing such advice. Ludwig Kramer was uncomfortable with the idea on the grounds that it was not for the European Commission but the European Court to provide definitive legal interpretations. I explained that, in the United Kingdom, at any rate, it was regular practice for government to issue advisory circulars and guidance on new laws and regulations but containing an explicit proviso that it would be for the courts to provide any final interpretation of the legislation in question. An opportunity then arose to provide such guidance, though it was one that ended up with my name being castigated in front of the European Court. I had been contacted by the Royal Society for the Protection of Birds (RSPB) who had been participating in a private bill procedure in the House of Lords. There had been arguments over the interpretation of the 1979 Birds Directive and the extent to which it permitted Member States to promote development in sites which had already been designated for conservation. According to the RSPB, the UK government lawyers were arguing before the House of Lords committee that while Article 2 imposed a general obligation on Member States to maintain bird populations covered by the directive, this duty was then qualified with the phrase, 'while taking account of economic and recreational requirements'. This, they said, was a balancing test and gave a large degree of discretion to allow national economic interests to outweigh bird conservation in any particular case. There had been no decision of the European Court on the point to date, but RSPB were sure that the European Commission might have another interpretation and told me would be very useful if this could be submitted to the House of Lords committee to demonstrate there were differing official views on the meaning of the directive. I examined the Commission's internal files on the directive, and found that officials had considered the meaning of Article 2, but their interpretation, while appearing to allow for exceptional cases where economic and recreational interests might prevail, placed far more emphasis on the general duty of member States under Article 4 of the directive to avoid the deterioration of habitats affecting protected birds. Their view was certainly a much tougher hurdle than the simple balancing test being promoted by the UK government. I sought advice from Ludwig Kramer who agreed that a letter could be sent, explaining this interpretation, but he then suggested that I could sign the letter in my own name. I was flattered to do so as this would be the first official communication from the Commission carrying my name, and my letter concluded: 'The Commission is prepared to accept that economic and recreational interests may in specific instances prevail over the protection provided for in Article 4 but only where they are of such paramount importance that their realisation should outweigh the significant disturbance to the area in question; the Commission does not accept, given the objectives and wording of the directive, that in such cases it is simply a question of equal balancing.' I do not think my letter had the impact that I hoped with the House of Lords committee, but sometime after I left the Commission and had returned to London, I met a senior lawyer in the Department of the Environment who told me that I was in a lot of legal trouble and my name had come up in proceedings before the European Court. The Commission had brought a case before the European Court against Germany in respect of coastal protection works improvement works which threatened protected birds under the directive. It was now taking a much stricter interpretation of the Birds Directive and was arguing that economic considerations could never be a legal justification for damaging a protected site – only if there was a threat to human life and the works were restricted to the minimum necessary might they be acceptable. The UK government had intervened in the case to support Germany and produced the letter I had sent to the RSPB some months previously to illustrate that the European Commission was being wholly inconsistent in its legal interpretation. The lawyer from the Commission Legal Services representing the Commission before the court had had no prior knowledge of the letter and was apparently furious. He explained it away as the work of a visiting academic on an unauthorised frolic of his own. The decision of the court[18] largely followed the Commission's arguments and held that Member States could only reduce the extent of designated special protection area on exceptional grounds such as the protection of human life. The so-called German *Dykes* case was hailed by many environmental organisations as an environmentally progressive decision by the Court.[19] Back in London, though, Nigel Haigh of the Institute of European Environmental Policy was rather more sanguine and felt that the judges had not appreciated the policy consequences of their fairly absolutist interpretation of the directive. As a consequence, Member States would be now more reluctant to designate new sites and would probably seek changes in future legislation to give them more leeway to allow interventions on public policy grounds. His prediction

[18] *Commission v Germany* C-57/89 [1990] ECR I-4337.
[19] On the facts of the case, the Court held that the Commission had not proved the works in question, designed to reduce the risk of flooding, fell outside the restrictive criteria proposed by the Court and the case was dismissed.

on changes was all-too true. The 1992 Habitats Directive introduced provisions allowing for interference with protected sites for 'imperative reasons of public interest including those of an economic or social nature'.[20] As for my letter, I was a little annoyed to have had my actions characterised before the Court in the way they were, but accepted this was necessary for legal tactical reasons. Out of professional pride, though, I did write to Ludwig Kramer afterwards, confirming that my actions had been authorised and had been intended to reflect the then internal views of the Commission. As to the general question of the provision of advice, the Commission has since been far readier to issue guidance documents in many areas of EU environmental law to assist those applying the legislation in their countries. There are now, for example, over ten guidance documents on the 2014 environmental assessment directive, but with carefully drafted qualifications such as: 'This document represents the views of the Commission services and is not binding in nature. It is not meant to be definitive.'

My experience of working inside the Commission's infringement unit was short and intense but immensely rewarding and I learned much. At the time, I had, of course, little idea that some 30 years later, the Commission's powers of bring infringement proceedings in respect of governments and public bodies would prove one of the defining political issues in considering the environmental implications of Brexit. Post-Brexit, the Commission would have no such power in respect of the UK and government has been faced with the challenge of how to replicate its role. Much of the work of the UK Environmental Law Association on Brexit issues, discussed in the final chapter, was concerned with this very question.

---

[20] Although the provisions also contain several strict procedural requirements to ensure the overall coherence of European protected sites, they were clearly introduced to deal what Member States viewed as an over-restrictive interpretation of the Birds Directive by the European Court.

13

Brexit and Environmental Law

Two days before the Brexit referendum in June 2016, I was in Germany taking part in one of the annual meetings of the Avosetta group of European environmental lawyers. I was asked to give an update on the situation in the UK and explained that I thought the result would be much closer than had been originally predicted. The official remain campaign had seemed largely negative in tone, focusing on the adverse financial consequences of leaving the EU, while the leave campaign had adopted a powerful slogan, 'Take Back Control', which appealed to many who felt they had been largely excluded from any economic benefits that might have resulted from EU membership. Despite the best efforts of environmental groups, the value of EU environmental policy and law had featured little in the campaigns and the wider media. Listening to my presentation, my long-standing German environmental law colleague, Gerd Winter, responded that perhaps it would be better if the UK left the EU. We often appeared very negative and had never really subscribed to the wider political aspirations of the EU and though we should remain friends and in close contact, leaving might be preferable for both. I told him that he had almost persuaded me to vote leave, at which he replied, 'No, No, don't – we actually we need you, we need the UK'. It was a conflicting view that I suspect many in mainland Europe have often felt about the UK and its role in the EU.

Most of the British environmental groups had strongly advocated remaining in the EU and continued to do so after the referendum result. The UK Environmental Law Association (UKELA), though, remain neutral and wisely in my view. But it adopted a policy position that the UK's current environmental legislation should be preserved pending proper review and full and open consultation. It stated that the level of environmental protection and opportunities for public participation and environmental litigation before the courts must not be diminished by any futures changes in legislation. And it recognised that the development of a post-Brexit framework of environmental legislation could present a unique and critically important opportunity for the UK government and devolved administrations to explore ways of improving and strengthening environmental regulation. UKELA decided to set up a Brexit Task Force to develop its response and the then chairman, Stephen Sykes, told me that the trustees wanted me to chair this group. I had had little to do with UKELA in recent years and was initially reluctant to take on the task. But this was probably the most important period for

British environmental law for a generation and I felt it was not possible to duck the responsibility. I wanted a co-chair and recommended Andrew Bryce, a solicitor with long practical experience of environmental law and the second chairman of UKELA back in the 1980s. I was only too delighted when Andrew readily agreed to join me.

The first real implications of Brexit for national environmental law, as well as other areas of law, was a statement in parliament in October 2016 that the government intended to introduce a 'Great Repeal Bill' that would repeal the European Communities Act 1972. But far from repealing detailed EU legislation, it intended to preserve regulatory stability in the immediate period following Brexit by converting existing EU laws into national law as far as possible, a technique known as 'roll-over'. Shortly afterwards, the House of Lords EU sub-committee on Environment and Energy launched an inquiry on the implications of Brexit for the environment and climate change. It was the first parliamentary select committee to inquire into the issue, wholly fitting because the House of Lords had long taken an interest in EU and environmental matters. Together with my legal colleague at UCL, Professor Maria Lee, and Andy Jordan, an environmental policy specialist from the University of East Anglia, we gave evidence on the challenges of Brexit for environmental law. I made the point that in terms of the roll-over of existing EU environmental law, this should be reasonably straightforward in many cases. For example, some legislation transposing EU law into national law contained references to relevant EU directives but there was no reason why, in legal terms, these should not remain, even though a directive might have no distinct legal force post-Brexit. It would be equivalent to national regulations referring to an international guidance document or code of practice. Provisions in legislation requiring notification or referral to the European Commission would clearly require a substitution with a new reference to some national body. But there were some areas of EU environmental law such as emissions trading or chemical regulation where the legislation was so intimately integrated into an EU institutional framework that simple roll-over would simply not be possible. Furthermore, the exercise was essentially only concerned with the black letter of the law and, as Maria Lee pointed out, EU environmental law had to be seen as being 'embedded in an EU governance structure'. Many of these important features would not be captured by the roll-over requirements and would be lost unless replicated in some way. One key area of concern was the European Commission's role in monitoring how Member States comply with their EU legal obligations and their power to bring infringement proceedings where, as the previous chapter described, the Commission had been especially active in the environmental field. We suggested that, in future, we might need to replicate the Commission's role with some new form of independent environmental ombudsman or an equivalent body which could monitor how government and other public bodies complied with their legal duties. The committee agreed and in its report noted that the evidence strongly suggested that, 'an effective and independent domestic enforcement mechanism will be necessary, in order to fill the vacuum left by the European Commission in ensuring the compliance of the government and public authorities with environmental obligations'.[1] But it was clear that the government was, at the time, strongly against the idea. The then Secretary of State for Environment, Food and Rural Affairs, Andrea Leadsom, argued that government was politically accountable for any failings to parliament and was legally accountable through ordinary judicial review actions taken by non-governmental organisations and individuals. This was at a time when ClientEarth was engaged in a lengthy series of judicial review actions against government for failure to comply with NOx limits under EU legislation and the success it was having in the courts could be said to have proved her point.

Meanwhile Andrew Bryce and myself had to decide how best the UKELA Brexit Task Force could contribute to the debate. Fourteen of the major UK environmental organisations had already established a coalition called GreenerUK, but we felt that UKELA should remain a little detached and focus on producing a series of reports exploring legal issues in a number of key areas. The leading environmental policy expert, Tom Burke, was a patron of UKELA and we sought his views on our proposed strategy. He strongly supported the approach and felt that UKELA needed to establish a reputation for authoritative and independent analysis but should not become directly engaged in the politics. That should be left to others who could use our reports as they thought best. He also suggested that we hold a launch event for the press to announce our intentions but avoid a traditional legal venue such as the Law Society or an Inn of Court. Doing so could imply that our work was intended mainly for a legal audience with lawyers simply talking to lawyers, and Tom felt it was of critical importance to make clear that UKELA's legal insights were relevant to a much wider constituency. We took his advice and the launch event was held on 28 June 2017 at the South London offices of the environmental think tank E3G which Tom Burke chaired. To a packed audience of environmental and legal journalists, we announced that, over the next few months, UKELA would publish a tranche of reports under the overall title, 'Brexit and Environment Law', to be followed by a major conference in the Autumn. I concluded my opening remarks by noting that UKELA's 'goal all the time is to advance a real understanding of the legal issues involved, provide what we hope will be a robust analytical underpinning for the difficult decisions that will need addressing and to ensure that our environmental law is not jeopardised by what is to come'.

UKELA was able to provide funds to employ two researchers to assist in the exercise – Rosie Oliver, a former lawyer with the Department of Environment, Food and Rural Affairs (DEFRA) and Joe Newbigin, a young barrister who was subsequently to join government legal services – and my UCL Faculty generously provided free desk space for them. The reports that resulted covered a number of important areas. To the surprise of many, the decision to leave the EU included

---

[1] House of Lords European Union Committee *Brexit: Environment and Climate Change* 12th Report of Session 2016–2017 14 February 2017 HL Paper 109, para 84.

leaving Euratom, the parallel European treaty covering nuclear matters. We engaged two leading experts in nuclear law, Stephen Tromans QC and Paul Bowden, a partner at Freshfields, to write a report on the issue. Much of discussion at the time on the implications of leaving Euratom had been concerned with issues of security and safeguards for fissile material, but the UKELA report deliberately focused on environmental standards and the management of spent fuel and radioactive waste which had received far less attention to date. It highlighted the enormous amount of work needed to ensure smooth transitional arrangements.

Another report covered European cooperative bodies in the environmental field. We identified over 20 such bodies existing at the time. Some of these were official institutions set up under EU law such as the European Environment Agency or the European Chemical Agency. But others were informal networks that had developed bottom up as it were, such as the European Union Forum for Judges for the Environment and a recently established European Network of Prosecutors for the Environment. The report provided for the first time a systematic analysis of these bodies, asking first whether post-Brexit the UK could legally still remain a member of such bodies. This required analysis of the relevant EU legislation or the terms of association of the more informal bodies (eg the EU regulation establishing the European Environment Agency rather surprisingly did allow participation by non-Member States). We followed this with a more subjective ranking indicating which bodies we felt the UK should, as a matter of priority, aim to continue to be a member post-Brexit. Another report in our series considered how environmental standards were elaborated within EU institutional arrangements. Particularly important in this context was the procedure for developing EU-wide emissions standards and best practice for many industrial facilities – known as the Seville process after the city where meetings are held. It is a long, drawn-out and complex process but one that at least tried to engage with both industry and environmental organisations and was pretty transparent in its workings. We were anxious that, post-Brexit, some of the best features of the Seville process were not lost when the UK began to develop its own environmental standards.

The European Union (Withdrawal) Bill had now been published. As predicted, it contained provisions to 'roll-over' as far as possible existing EU law immediately upon Brexit, but it was clear that many amendments to national legislation would be needed to avoid meaningless references to EU law and institutions. The Bill, therefore, gave extensive powers to government ministers to amend or repeal existing laws to ensure the provisions remained legally operable post-Brexit and these included powers to amend or repeal provisions in primary Acts of Parliament by means of regulations. Generally, provisions in an Act of Parliament can only be amended a new Act, but there clearly would not be parliamentary time to use this route, hence the need for the new powers. Powers to amend primary legislation by regulations, so-called 'Henry VIII clauses,'[2] though politically and constitutionally

---

[2] Named after the Statute of Proclamations published by Henry VIII in 1539 giving him power to make statutory changes without going through Parliament.

troublesome, have featured before in legislation in this country, but never on such a broad scale. Not unexpectedly, these clauses gave rise to heated political debate in parliament but there was little in the way of hard data on the extent of changes in primary legislation that would be needed. Our report, 'Brexit, Henry VIII Clauses and Environmental Law', therefore analysed 29 Acts of Parliament concerning the environment, ranging from the Endangered (Species and Export) Act 1976 to the Climate Change Act 2008. We found that direct references to EU law in such Acts was fairly rare and that the need for Henry VIII powers would be far less extensive than some MPs had been asserting. Seventeen of the Acts we looked at contained no references to EU law and in the remaining 12 Acts of Parliament we concluded only six changes would be needed and a further 30 advisable, though perhaps not legally essential. As we suspected, the vast majority of amendments that would be needed would be in existing environmental regulations rather than Acts of Parliament. Amending regulations by new regulations is familiar practice, but we urged DEFRA to publish proposed amending regulations in a logical and intelligible manner, so that it was possible to have an overall picture of the changes needed. Ideally, we argued, all draft roll-over regulations for, say, waste or air pollution would be grouped and published together. But the size of the task and the time pressures on government has meant this has never proved possible and, to date, almost 100 amending regulations have been published in the environmental field in an apparently haphazard fashion – making it near impossible for all but the most dedicated to follow the scale of changes proposed.

The UK is bound by some 40 international conventions concerning the environment and the government stated that it would continue to be bound by these treaties post-Brexit. It was a sensible commitment, but there were legal uncertainties because the EU was often involved in such treaties. There were some examples, such as the International Whaling Convention, which the UK had ratified and where the EU had no legal competence – clearly, the UK would continue to be bound by such conventions post-Brexit. But there were other treaties in areas such as fishing where the EU had exclusive legal competence and had ratified treaties on its own, binding all the territory of the European Union. Post-Brexit, the UK would no longer be automatically bound by such agreements, unless it subsequently made a conscious decision to ratify. But the vast majority of international environmental treaties have been so-called 'mixed' agreements where the subject matter meant that both the EU and Member States had competence; such agreements were, therefore, ratified jointly by the EU and the Member States. There were legal uncertainties as to what would happen in such cases on Brexit. Would the UK automatically be bound by the full scope of the agreement because on Brexit it had acquired all the competences formerly belonging to the EU, or would more had to be done? UKELA published a substantive report on the subject and systematically analysed some 40 environmental treaties to determine whether they were EU-exclusive agreements, mixed agreements, or those that fell outside the competence of the EU. Such a comprehensive analysis had not been published before and the report became something of a bible for those dealing with the issue.

Post-Brexit, international environmental law is likely to be of increasing significance in this country as being effectively the only supra-national legal constraint on the country, aside from those that may be contained in any transitional agreement with the EU or any subsequent trade agreement. Quite how international environmental law will impinge on our national way of doing things post-Brexit is less predictable. Traditionally, this country has followed what is termed a 'dualist' system of international law, meaning that, unless international commitments have been transposed into national law, the domestic courts will give no direct legal effect to them.[3] Litigants must rely upon the national law and cannot invoke provisions of international treaties unless they have been transposed. Courts do, though, refer to international treaties as an aid to interpretation of national law and their readiness to do so may increase post-Brexit. But the UK dualist system of international law was reaffirmed by the Supreme Court in 2017 in the iconic *Miller* case, concerned with whether the consent of parliament was needed before government could trigger the process to withdraw from the European Union.[4] Interestingly, though, in a 2015 judgment of the Supreme Court[5] concerning a human rights treaty which the UK had ratified but not transposed into national law, one of the judges doubted whether the dualist doctrine should apply where it was the government that was being taken to court. He felt the national courts should be entitled to hold it to account for international obligations to which it had committed, whether or not they had been transposed. But it was a bold analysis and he was a sole dissenting judge. Maybe it will stay that way, but it could be a pointer to the future for a revaluation of the dualist system by the courts post-Brexit. A further complication is that many international environmental obligations have been implemented within this country by means of EU legislation which has sometimes elaborated and expanded on the international commitments. For example, the 1989 Basel Convention on the trans-frontier shipment of wastes applies only to hazardous waste, while the EU regulations giving effect to the convention within the EU extends to non-hazardous waste as well. Post-Brexit, the government could decide to strip back the legal obligations to only those contained in the relevant international treaty. In a number of judgments in the 1980s, the European Court of Justice insisted that obligations under EU environmental directives had to be transposed into national systems by means of explicit legislation rather than softer and informal forms of instruments such as circulars or policy statements which it described as mere administrative actions that could all too easily be changed. No such doctrine has been developed in respect of international conventions and, as a matter of law, governments are entitled to transpose

---

[3] In contrast, other countries such as the Netherlands, have adopted a 'monist' approach and provisions in international treaties are incorporated automatically into the national law. Other jurisdictions such as the United States adopt a mixed approach and the courts have held that some treaties do require national transposing legislation before they can be enforced by the courts.

[4] *R (Miller) v Secretary of State for Exiting the European Union* [2017] UKCS 5.

[5] *R (on the application of SG v Others) v Secretary of State for Works and Pensions* [2015] UKSC 16.

obligations in whatever form they wish. The problems this can raise was illustrated in a 2016 appeal decision before a planning inspector concerning the refusal of the Environment Agency to grant a water abstraction licence which could have affected a specially protected conservation site.[6] The inspector noted that the site was protected under the 1971 Ramsar Convention, which the UK had ratified, but had implemented by means of a policy statement circular rather than national legislation. The policy statement had, probably through an oversight, been recently withdrawn by the government in a general cleaning up and consolidation of planning policy guidance with the result that the inspector could give no legal weight to the Ramsar implications. Fortunately, in that case, the site was also protected under EU habitats legislation, which provided equal legal protection, but it shows the sorts of difficulties concerning the legal effect of international obligations that could arise in the future.

The UKELA Brexit report, 'Enforceability and Accountability Issues', proved to be one of the most challenging to write, but probably had the most immediate impact on government thinking. We developed the arguments initially raised in front of the House of Lords select committee for the need for a new independent body to replace the enforcement functions of the European Commission and to hold government and other public bodies to account for failures of environmental law duties. We knew that the then Secretary of State, Andrea Leadsom, was still adamantly opposed to such a body and therefore deliberately couched the report in what we hoped was an eminently reasonable tone which might yet win her over. We acknowledged that judicial review by non-governmental environmental organisations was valuable and would continue post-Brexit but felt this would not replicate the role of the Commission. Environmental groups have their own agendas and do not necessarily cover all areas of environmental law. As the report stated: 'Judicial review can provide a powerful, long-stop check, but we question whether the process can by itself replicate the more systematic enforcement role hitherto conducted by the European Commission.' Because of the political sensitivities, the report deliberately refrained from advocating any particular form of new body, but pointed to examples in other jurisdictions such as New Zealand or Hungary where the vulnerability of the environment and the need to hold public bodies to account had been recognised by establishing various forms of independent environmental ombudsmen or parliamentary commissioners.

It was a well-argued report and I was told later that it was positively received by officials within government. But I had doubts that the Secretary of State would change her opinion. Timing, however, is everything and, quite unexpectedly, a few weeks after the report was published, there was a cabinet reshuffle and Michael Gove was appointed Secretary of State for Environment Food and Rural Affairs. He immediately saw the logic of our argument and the attraction and advantages of a new body. He knew that in bringing infringement proceedings the European

---

[6] Appeal Refs APP/WAT/15/316 and 317 16 September 2016.

Commission has been able to resolve the vast majority of cases by discussion with government rather than going to court. Although settlement and negotiation in judicial review claims are possible, it rarely happens in practice unless one party wholly concedes the case in advance. Faced with the threat of legal action by an environmental group, a natural tendency for government will be to resist rather than lose face. But where the investigation and alarm bells are raised by an official independent body, a less defensive and more constructive response aimed at seeking solutions could be expected. Michael Gove began consultation on a new body to be known as the Office for Environmental Protection, modelled on the Equality and Humans Rights Commission established in 2007 under the Equality Act 2006. Draft clauses for the new body were published in December 2018 and, in early 2019, two House of Commons select committees carried out a pre-legislative scrutiny of the draft legislation. Pre-legislative scruntiny allows a parliamentary committee to take evidence on the actual text of a proposed law, and to make recommendations to government to improve the draft before it is finally put before parliament. Andrew Bryce and myself had now stepped down as co-chairs of the UKELA Brexit Task Force as we had completed the first phase of UKELA's work with the publication of the key Brexit and environmental law reports. We felt that UKELA's work would be now entering a new phase as we awaited the final outcome of Brexit and it was time to hand over the reins to a younger generation of practising environmental lawyers. But we made one last joint appearance before the House of Commons Environment, Food and Rural Affairs Committee in early 2019.

Our evidence was very much focused on the structure and legal powers of the proposed Office for Environmental Protection. In terms of enforcement, the proposed powers for OEP contained a three-stage procedure. First, the service of an initial notice requiring further information about the alleged breach of environmental law duties. Matters might be resolved at that stage but, if not, the OEP could follow up with a Decision Notice stating that it was satisfied the body concerned was in breach. If the body still resisted, the OEP could then refer the matter to the courts. In many ways, this reflected the European Commission's infringement procedures which began with a formal letter to the Member State, followed by a more formal 'Reasoned Opinion' and finally the power to refer the case to the European Court of Justice. A public complaints system would also be established, similar to that provided by the European Commission, allowing anyone to notify the Office for Environmental Protection of potential breaches of environmental law duties by public bodies. In general terms, I very much welcomed the initiative and argued that, even if the UK was eventually to remain within the EU, the OEP would be a valuable addition to the institutional structure of our environmental law. But there were areas where we felt the proposed powers of the new body could be improved.

One of the most innovative features of the OEP's proposed enforcement powers was that the Information and Decision Notice could specify not only the alleged breach of environmental law duties but also the steps that OEP thought the relevant public body should take to remedy the breach. In ordinary judicial review, judges are rarely engaged in the solutions needed and normally go no further than stating that the government or public body has acted illegally. The proposed powers were very much consistent with the view that one of the advantages of the new mechanism was its potential to resolve problems without the need to go to court. But the Office for Environmental Protection will need to tread a careful path of specifying steps required to come back into compliance but without impinging too much on the detailed policy prerogatives and expertise of the public body they are dealing with.

There are, though, bound to be cases which cannot be resolved at these early stages and would need to go to court and it was here that I had my greatest criticism of the draft clauses that the government had proposed. They provided that any court action would be by way of ordinary judicial review before the Administrative Court. I felt that this was unimaginative approach, simply reverting to the traditional way of dealing with such issues. I had always been conscious that, despite Michael Gove's enthusiasm for the OEP, other government departments who might be at the receiving end of its investigations would be rather more nervous. The draft Bill had clearly been discussed with these other departments and I suspected that they had insisted on judicial review as the final remedy – a procedure with which they were familiar and could handle without undue disruption. I argued that rather than a single judge in the Administrative Court, we should at least be thinking of using the tribunal system which employed very flexible procedures and where the members could be not just lawyers, but could also include experts such as scientists or economists as appropriate to the case in hand. Although it had been existence for over ten years, I was intrigued that the members of the select committee clearly had not heard about the First-tier Environment Tribunal which now handled many environmental appeals[7] and they appeared impressed as they learnt about its structure and approach. Given that OEP would probably only take cases to court that were particularly serious, I later felt that, in fact, the Upper Tribunal would probably be more appropriate than the First-tier level. The Upper Tribunal has similarly flexible rules of procedure and can employ legal and expert members. But unlike the First-tier Tribunal, the Upper Tribunal has power to determine judicial reviews in classes of cases referred to it and so could be readily incorporated into the proposed procedures if the government still insisted on judicial review. But I also questioned another aspect of the procedure. When the European Commission brings infringement procedures, it can be in respect of failings by any public body such as the Environment Agency or local government, but it is central government which is at the receiving end of the process and has the obligation to respond. It seemed to me that there could be examples of serious and systematic failings where, even though the formal legal responsibility fell to a body outside central government, it was justifiable that

---

[7] See further ch 10 for the development of the environment tribunal.

government should take on the obligation of dealing with the situation – perhaps by providing increased resources to the bodies concerned, better advice, or securing improvements to the law in question. It would be very difficult to incorporate this concept of what I termed 'extended responsibility' within traditional concepts of judicial review, but I urged that thought should be given to somehow involving central government in appropriate cases that eventually went to court. I suspect that the Department of the Environment, Food and Rural Affairs (DEFRA) found some of the criticism and recommendations of the two select committees concerning the draft clauses helpful in strengthening their own internal negotiations with other government departments concerning the body.

Many of the environmental non-governmental organisations were supportive of the idea of an Office for Environmental Protection, but felt its legal powers should be stronger. Here I disagreed with some of their views. Some argued that the notices served by the OEP should be legally binding on government departments and other public bodies with non-compliance sanctioned by a penalty. But I felt that if this happened, a body on the receiving end of a notice was likely to revert far too quickly to a defensive stance while one of the key attractions of new procedures was that it would encourage both sides to engage constructively to try to find a solution. The infringement notices and reasoned opinions served by the European Commission are not legally binding as such, but are treated seriously because member states know that they can be ratcheted up to formal court proceedings if they do not engage properly. Before the Select Committee, I quoted the African proverb, 'Talk softly but carry a big stick' which seemed to me to epitomize how the OEP should go about its work.

I was also uncomfortable with proposals from some organisations that the judicial body dealing with enforcement should have the power to impose financial penalties on those bodies in breach of their duties. It was said this would replicate the powers available to the European Court of Justice to impose financial penalties on member states, but the powers to impose such penalties come into play only where a member state fails to comply with a judgment of the court.[8] It seemed to me that, other than for totemic reasons, no added powers were needed in the national context since the powers of the European Court were really equivalent to a contempt of court which the national courts already possess strong sanctions – financial penalties, and even the power to imprison ministers or senior civil servants directly involved in failing to comply with a court order.

Part I of the Environment Bill, setting up the OEP, was laid before parliament in October 2019 and important changes were made to reflect some of the concerns raised during the committee hearings. The three-stage enforcement process remained, but in particular, the final court stage is no longer by way of ordinary judicial review before the Administrative Court but comes before the

---

[8] The European Court may also now impose penalties on member states that fail to send national transposing legislation to the European Commission within the time limits specified in directives. But this is not relevant here.

Upper Tribunal in an action termed an 'environmental review'. The provisions provide that in determining whether to an authority has failed to comply with an application, the tribunal must apply the principles of judicial review. I would, though, predict that, given that it can employ expert members such as economists or environmental scientists, and that it will be dealing with an action brought by an official public body rather than a third party individual or environmental group, the Upper Tribunal may prove to be somewhat less deferential to government and public bodies than sometimes happens in ordinary judicial review actions before the Administrative Court. I was also pleased to see a new provision that provides that when making an application for an environmental review against a public body other than a government department, the OEP must provide the relevant minister with a statement as to whether it considers the minister should participate in the review by, say, applying to be a party to the proceedings. As the Explanatory Notes[9] to the bill explain, "Delivery bodies may adopt an approach to implementation influenced by factors or messaging emanating from central government. To this extent, it may be helpful for Ministers to provide input to the proceedings". This provision is coming as close to the notion of 'extended responsibility' which I favoured as was probably politically possible.

The need for a new independent supervisory body in the environmental field arose out of a realisation that simply rolling over the black letter of European environmental law immediately post-Brexit would not replicate benefits of the wider European legal architecture that underpinned the legislation. There was a similar concern over the question of environmental principles. Introduced in 1987, the European Treaty provisions concerning the environment provide that European environmental policy must be based on several core principles including prevention, rectification at source, the 'polluter pays' principle and the precautionary principle. The Treaty also contained a general goal that EU policy on the environment must aim for high level of environmental protection. These principles, though they do not give direct legal rights to individuals as such, have on several occasions been invoked by the European Court of Justice to assist in the interpretation of EU environmental legislation. Home-grown UK environmental law has rarely contained such broad principles, though they have sometimes appeared in government policy documents. During the passage of the European Union (Withdrawal) Bill in 2017, many of the environmental organisations focused on the need to include such principles in our law post-Brexit, so much so that they were able to secure an amendment that the government would be obliged to include such principles in any future legislation on the environment. The draft legislation concerning the Office of Environmental Protection produced in 2018 included provisions concerning environmental principles, but many criticised the

---

[9] Explanatory Notes were first introduced in 1999 to assist parliamentarians to understand the purpose and meaning of proposed legislation. They are written by the government department promoting the legislation in question.

text of the Bill as being too weak in that it simply required the Secretary of State to 'have regard' to such principles.

We did not include the question of environmental principles in the UKELA programme of Brexit reports, partly because environmental groups had clearly taken a lead on the subject and it was an issue that had already become highly politicised. Personally, I also found it a difficult issue. I felt that some were exaggerating the potential impact of environmental principles, seeing them as some sort of magic bullet which would transform the effectiveness of future law. I was also wary of those who argued that public bodies should have an overarching legal duty to apply the principles in all their decision-making since this seemed to be a recipe for litigation in the courts. Giving the principles such legal force could lead to unexpected consequences that might not necessarily be favourable to the environmental community. As noted in Chapter 12, in 2003, the Avosetta environmental law group explored how EU environmental principles were then being handled in national courts. The EU environmental principles had been written into Belgian environmental law and there have been over 30 legal challenges before the national courts concerning the 'polluter pays' principle – not brought by environmental NGOs, but by industry arguing that environmental taxes and similar measures were contrary to the 'polluter pays' principle because they were not the polluter.[10] Those in the EU Treaty had developed at a particular point in time and it was arguable there were other more modern principles such as non-regression or substitution which might be more suited for the future.

Furthermore, the choice of which principles to include was not easy. Those in the EU Treaty had developed at a particular point of time, and it was arguable there were other more modern principles such as non-regression or substitution which might be more suited for the future. Many dismissed the duty in the draft legislation that government must 'have regard' to the principles as being far too weak, and essentially meaningless. But I felt it this was over-exaggeration, and where the 'have regard' duty has been used in other legal contexts, courts have held that the relevant minister must address the issue seriously, and in effect make a reasoned justification if they decide the principle is not applicable to the decision in hand. There was a great deal of discussion and disagreement on how these principles should be incorporated in the law but the final version contained in the Environment Bill 2019 laid before parliament in October continues to reject making them having direct legal impact. Instead they are to be reflected in a policy statement made by the secretary of state, followed by a duty on every minister when making policy to 'have due regard to the policy statement'.[11] Principles will

---

[10] See ch 12.

[11] 'due regard' is a slightly stronger legal test than simply 'regard'. The draft provisions are further qualified by providing that after having due regard, the minister is not obliged to do anything or refrain from doing anything that would not have a significant environmental benefit or would in any other be disproportionate to the environmental benefit.

undoubtedly play a more important role in the development of our environmental policy and law in the future. Certainly, from a political perspective, the experience at European level suggests that the fact that the Treaty contains the principles and the overall goal of a high level of environmental protection (which was not replicated in the Bill) has provided a justification for the Environment Directorate of the European Commission to be environmentally ambitious in its proposals. Their legal expression in some form at national level may equally encourage an environment secretary of state to be equally progressive, even when other departments within government are rather less enthusiastic. But the extent to which the British judiciary will in future feel empowered and encouraged to use the principles in the interpretation and development of environmental law is rather less predictable.

* * *

I restrained myself from completing this final chapter until 31 October 2019 because I thought on that date there would some certainty, one way or the other, on Brexit.[12] But it was not to be, and at the time of writing the story is by no means over. Nor is this the place for a detailed and systematic analysis of the impact of EU law on this country's environmental law and policy over the past forty years or so, and its strengths and weaknesses. At the very least the period following the Brexit referendum has forced myself and other environmental lawyers in this country to re-evaluate critically the significance of EU environmental law, and to think how best not to lose some its most effective aspects should the UK leave the EU. The European Union began developing environmental policies and law a few months before I qualified as a barrister in the 1970's, and since then much of my legal work, both as an academic and practitioner, has involved EU environmental law, and led to a great deal of fruitful and invigorating discussions with colleagues in other member states. I have no doubt these interactions will continue even after Brexit, and could indeed have more potency since one could begin to really compare and test the effects on national environmental law, both good and bad, between European countries that are both within and outside the European Union. Conversely, if we were to remain within the EU, I have argued that we should retain the idea of the Office for Environmental Protection as a valuable addition to our future environmental governance, even though it was born in the context of Brexit. But any further prediction on the final Brexit outcomes will be mere speculation, and at this stage it is probably wiser simply to repeat a sentence that appears in many places in the new Halsbury's Laws on Environmental Law published in April 2019: "At the date at which this title states the law, the United Kingdom is preparing to exit both the European Union and the European Atomic Energy Community, and the consequences of these actions (to the extent that they can be discerned) must be kept in mind whilst reading any relevant law …."

---

[12] Given the 2019 General Election result, it is clear the UK is due to leave the EU on January 31st 2020, but the nature of any subsequent trade arrangements between the EU and the UK, including provisions concerning environmental protection, will not be known for at least another year.

Environmental law is never static, and a new generation of environmental lawyers will need to engage critically in the debates on how law can best be developed and used to meet the existing challenges and those yet to become apparent. Law does not have all the answers but will continue to be one of the essential components of any effective policy response. The themes I have selected for this book by no means cover all areas of environmental law and policy, and very much reflect my personal involvement and experiences. I am conscious, for example, how little I have been engaged directly in the development of international environmental law – something I now somewhat regret but it was a deliberate choice made some years back to largely focus on national and EU law to avoid overspreading myself. Looking back, I have been struck how some of the subjects with which I was engaged now seem to be redolent of a world that truly no longer exists, but equally how many legal issues that were of concern a generation ago remain of relevance and indeed have become more so in the light of the current rethinking of our direction of environmental and policy. I find it somewhat dispiriting at times to see how the core campaigning issues during my early days at Friends of the Earth over forty years ago – transport, energy, wildlife protection, agriculture, and resources – remain as pressing today. But then I remind myself that I was fortunate to be involved in the early days of an organization that was not dealing with some transient concerns but addressing fundamental issues that have a degree of universality and permanence. I am also struck by just how long it took to secure significant changes in policy and law at national level – over ten years in the case of a specialized environmental tribunal and a similar period for improving the way we sanction regulatory offences. I hope what I have written will provide some insights of how we have reached the present position, and encourage the next generation of environmental lawyers to realise that individual input can have an influence. Whether my own contributions have been significant or have had any long-lasting value must be for others to judge. For my part, I would be content with the judgment made by the Sanskrit poet Kalidas on an ancient ruler whom he much admired: 'The initiation of his policies could only be determined by their results'.

PUBLISHED WORKS
BY RICHARD MACRORY

(2019) 'The Office for Environmental Protection – Environmental Fig-Leaf or Game Changer?', *Environmental Law and Management.*

(2019) 'Environmental Law in the United Kingdom post Brexit' ERA *Forum Journal of the Academy of European Law.*

(2019) 'Brexit and Environmental Law' in Biondi, Birkinshaw, and Kendrick (eds) *Brexit – The Legal Implications* (The Netherlands, Wolters Kluwer).

(2019) *Halsbury's Laws: Environmental Law* (Consulting Editor) (London, LexisNexis).

(2018) 'Strengthening the Judicial Handling of Environmental Law Post-Brexit' *Environmental Law and Management*

(2018) 'Environmental Courts and Tribunals – The British Experience' in Ureta and Pineiro (eds) *New Perspectives on Environmental Law in the 21st Century* (Madrid, Marcial Pons)

(2018) (with B Milligan) 'The History and Evolution of Legal Principles Concerning the Environment' in Orlando and Kramer (eds) *Principles of Environmental Law* (Cheltenham, Edward Elgar).

(2018) 'Brexit and International Environmental Law' in Fitzgerald and Lein (eds) *Complexity's Embrace – The International Law Implications of Brexit* (Waterloo, Canada, Centre for International Governance Innovation).

(2018) (with I Havercroft and R Stewart) (eds) *Carbon Capture and Storage: Emerging Legal and Regulatory Issue* (2nd edition) (Oxford, Hart Publishing).

(2017) 'Carbon Capture and Storage' in Brownsword, Scotford, and Yeung (eds) *Oxford Handbook on the Law and Regulation of Technology* (Oxford, OUP).

(2017) (with G Jones) 'Afterword: Aarhus and HS2' in Jones and Scotford (eds) *The Strategic Environmental Assessment Directive* (Oxford, Hart Publishing).

(2015) 'Environmental Sanctions – Challenges and Opportunities' *Environmental Policy and Law.*

(2015) 'The Enforcement of Environmental Law: Challenges and Opportunities' *Science for Environmental Policy: Environmental compliance assurance and combatting environmental crime* (Brussels, European Commission).

(2014) *Regulation, Enforcement and Governance of Environmental Law* 2nd edition (Oxford, Hart Publishing).

(2014) (with I Havercroft) *Legal Liability and Carbon Capture and Storage – A Comparative Perspective* (Canberra, Global Carbon Capture and Storage Institute).

(2014) 'Judges and the Government' *International Journal of Law in the Built Environment.*

(2014) 'European Moves on Environmental *Enforcement*' in *International Comparative Guide to Environment Law 2014* (London, Global Legal Group).

(2013) 'The Long and Winding Road – Towards an Environmental Court in England and Wales' *Journal of Environmental Law.*

(2013) 'Sanctions and Safeguards – the Brave New World of Regulatory Enforcement' *Current Legal Problems* (Oxford, Oxford University Press).

(2013) 'The United Kingdom' in R Macrory, J Jans, and A Moreno Molina (eds) *National Courts and EU Environmental Law* (Groningen, Europa Law Publishing).

(2013) (with V Madner and S Mayr) 'Consistent Interpretation of EU Environmental Law' in R Macrory J Jans and A Moreno Molina (eds) *National Courts and EU Environmental Law* (Groningen, Europa Law Publishing).

(2013) 'Environmental Enforcement and *Sanctions*' in *International Comparative Guide to Environment Law 2013* (London, Global Legal Group, London).

(2012) 'The Role of the First Tier Environment Tribunal *Judicial Review.*

(2012) 'The UK Climate Change Act – Towards a Brave New legal World?' in Backer, Fauchald and Voight (eds) *Pro Natura* (Oslo, University of Oslo).

(2012) 'Environmental Sanctions under Scrutiny' in *International Comparative Guide to Environment Law 2012* (London, Global Legal Group).

(2011) 'The Environment as an Instrument of Constitutional Change' in Jowell and Oliver (eds) *The Changing Constitution* (Oxford, Oxford University Press).

(2011) *Consistency and Effectiveness – Strengthening the New Environmental Tribunal* (London, UCL Centre for Law and the Environment).

(2011) 'Weighing up the Performance' *Journal of Environmental Law.*

(2011) (with R Stewart and I Havercroft) (eds) *Carbon Capture and Storage: Emerging Legal and Regulatory Issues* (Oxford, Hart Publishing).

(2010) 'Environmental Courts and Tribunals in England and Wales – A Tentative New Dawn' *Journal of Court Innovation.*

(2010) 'Reforming Regulatory Sanctions' in Oliver, Rawlings and Prosser (eds) *The Regulatory State* (Oxford, Oxford University Press).

(2010) *Regulation, Enforcement and Governance of Environmental Law* (Oxford, Hart Publishing).

(2009) '"Maturity and Methodology": A Personal Reflection' *Journal of Environmental Law.*

(2009) (with J Jans et al) 'Gold-Plating of European Environmental Measures?' *Journal of European Environmental and Planning Law.*

(2009) 'Reforming Regulatory Sanctions – A Personal Perspective' *Environmental Law Review.*

(2009) (with J Maurici) 'Rethinking Regulatory Sanctions – Regulatory Enforcement and Sanctions Act 2008 – An Exchange of Letters' *Environmental Law and Management.*

(2008) 'New Approaches to Regulatory Sanctions' *Environmental Law and Management.*

(2008) Environmental Public Law and Judicial Review *Judicial Review.*

(2008) (with J Jans, L Kramer and G Winter) 'Weighing Up the EC Environmental Liability Directive' *Journal of Environmental Law.*

(2008) 'Public Consultation and GMO Policy – A Very British Experiment' *Journal of European Environmental and Planning Law.*

(2008) 'Supra-national Enforcement of Environmental Law: Reevaluating Compliance Mechanisms in the EU' in *International Comparative Guide to Environment Law 2008* (London, Global Legal Group).

(2007) 'Is EU Enforcement an Endangered Species?' *ENDS Europe Report.*

(2007) (with K Dunseath) 'Time to Act? Should the UK be Taxing Aviation Fuel?' *New Law Journal.*

(2007) (with J O'Hara) 'Present Liabilities for Past Land Contamination' *Journal of the Law Society of Western Australia.*

(2007) 'Supra-National Enforcement of Environmental Law: Compliance Mechanisms in the European Union' in *International Comparative Legal Guide to Environment Law 2007* (London, Global Legal Group).

(2006) *Regulatory Justice: Making Sanctions Effective* Final Report, Macrory Review (London, Cabinet Office).

(2006) 'Compliance Mechanisms in the European Community – A Global Model' in *International Comparative Legal Guide to Environment Law 2005* (London, Global Legal Group).

(2005) 'Chemicals in Products: Safeguarding the Environment and Human Health' in Weill (ed) *European Proposals for Chemical Regulation: REACH and Beyond* (Paris, Institute du developpement durable et des relations internationals).

(2005) 'The Enforcement of EU Environmental Law: Some Proposals for Reform' in Macrory (ed) *Reflections on 30 years of EU Environmental Law – A High Level of Protection?* (Groningen, Europa Law Publishing).

(2005) (ed) *Reflections on 30 years of EU Environmental Law – A High Level of Protection?* (Groningen, Europa Law Publishing).

(2005) 'Law and the Environment: Lessons from the European Experience' in *International Comparative Guide to Environment Law 2005* (London, Global Legal Group).

(2004) *Trust and Transparency: Reshaping Environmental Governance in Northern Ireland* (London, Centre for Law and the Environment, University College London).

(2004) 'Principles of Judicial Review on Environmental Assessment' (Case Analysis) *Journal of Environmental Law.*

(2004) (with I Niestroy) 'Emerging Transnational Policy Networks: The European Environmental Advisory Councils' in N Vg and M Faure (eds) *Green Giants? Environmental Policies of the United States and the European Union* (Massachusetts, MIT Press).

(2004) (with R Purdy) *Geological Carbon Sequestration: Critical Legal Issues* (Norwich, Tyndall Centre, University of East Anglia).

(2004) 'Principles into Practice – Lessons from the European Experience' in International *Comparative Guide to Environment Law 2004* (London, Global Legal Group).

(2004) (with M Woods) *Environmental Civil Penalties – A More Proportionate Response to Regulatory Breach* (London, Centre for Law and the Environment, University College London).

(2003) (with M Woods) 'Modernizing Environmental Justice' *Town and Country Planning.*

(2003) (with S Turner) 'Cross-border Environmental Governance and EC Law in Anderson, O'Dowd and Wilson' (eds) *New Borders for a Changing Europe* (London, Frank Cass).

(2003) (with M Woods) (2003) *Modernizing Environmental Justice: Regulation and the Role of an Environmental Tribunal* (London, Centre for Law and the Environment, University College London).

(2003) (with R Purdy) 'Satellite Photographs: 21st Century Evidence?' *New Law Journal.*

(2003) 'Technology and Environmental Law Enforcement' in Winter (ed) *Recht und Um-Welt* (Groningen, European Law Publishers).

(2002) (with S Turner) 'Cross Border Environmental Governance and EC Law' *Regional and Federal Studies.*

(2002) (with A Kontoleon and T Swanson) 'Individual Preference-based Values and Environmental Decision Making: Should Valuation have its Day in Court?' in T Swanson (ed) *Introduction to the Law and Economics of Environmental Policy: Issues in Institutional Design* (Amsterdam, Elsevier).

(2002) (with S Turner) 'Participatory Rights, Transboundary Environmental Governance and the Law' *Common Market Law Review.*

(2002) 'Regulating in a Risky Environment' in M Freeman M (ed) *Current Legal Problems 2001* (Oxford, Oxford University Press).

(2001) 'Standards, Legitimacy and the Law – The New Environmental Agenda' *Australian Environmental and Planning Law Journal.*

(2001) (with R Purdy) 'Use of Satellite Images as Evidence' *Droit et Ville.*

(2001) 'The Legal Control of Pollution' in R Harrison (ed) *Pollution – Causes, Effect and Control* (London, Royal Society of Chemistry).

(1999) 'The Amsterdam Treaty: An Environmental Perspective' in D O'Keeffe and P Twomey (eds) *Legal Issues of the Amsterdam Treaty* (Oxford, Hart Publishing).

(1999) 'Environment Standards in the United Kingdom' in N Greco (ed) *Crisi del diritto, produzione normativa e democrazia degli interessi* (Rome, Edistudio Srl).

(1999) 'The Environment and Constitutional Change' in R Hazell (ed) *Constitutional Futures – A History of the Next Ten Years* (Oxford, Oxford University Press).

(1999) 'Integrated Prevention and Pollution Control: the UK Experience' in C Backes and G Betlem (eds) *Integrated Pollution Prevention and Control* (The Hague, Kluwer International).

(1999) (with R Purdy)) 'Regulation and Control of Releases of Non-Indigenous Species in Great Britain' in A Fisahn and G Winter G (eds) *Die Aussetzung gebietsfremder Organismen* (Berlin, UmweltBundesAmt).

(1999) 'Subsidiarity and European Community Environmental Law' *Law & European Affairs.*

(1999) 'Environmental Standards – New Procedures for New Paradigms' *Science in Parliament.*

(1999) 'Environmental Standards, Legitimacy, and Social Justice' *Acta Juridica* (University of Capetown).

(1998) 'Future Trends in Environmental Regulation' *Environmental Assessment.*

(1998) (with M Hession)) 'The Legal Duty of Environmental Integration: Commitment and Obligation or Enforceable Right?' in T O'Riordan and H Voisey (eds) *The European Union and Sustainable Development* (London, Frank Cass).

(1998) (with Turner T Smith J) 'Legal and Political Considerations' in Douben P (ed) *Pollution Risk Assessment and Management* (Chichester, Wiley and Sons).

(1998) (with R Purdy) 'Regulation and Control of the Release of Genetically Modified Organisms in the United Kingdom' in Winter G (ed) *Die Prüfung der Freisetzung von gentechnisch veränderten Organismen* (Berlin, Erich Schmidt Verlag).

(1997) (with R Purdy) 'Enforcement of EC Environmental Law against Member States' in Holder J (ed) *Impact of EC Environmental Law in the United Kingdom* (Chichester, Wiley & Sons).

(1996) 'Environmental Citizenship and the Law – Repairing the European Road' *Journal of Environmental Law.*

(1996) (with M Hession) 'High Noon for the Mad Cows', *The Guardian* 11 June.

(1996) 'Transport: Private Gain and Public Good' in W Sheate *Difficult Choices in Environmental Decision-Making* (London, Imperial College).

(1996) 'Sources and Categories of Legal Acts – Britain' in G Winter (ed) *Sources and Categories of European Union Law – A Comparative and Reform Perspective* (Baden-Baden, Nomos Verlagsgesellschaft).

(1996) 'Community Supervision in the Field of the Environment' in H Somsen (ed) *Protecting the European Environment: Enforcing EC Environmental Law* (London, Blackstone Press).

(1996) 'A Sustainable Transport Policy' in H Wiggering and A Sandhovel (eds) *Agenda 21 – Implementation Issues in the European Union.* (Amsterdam, European Environmental Advisory Councils).

(1996) 'The Legal Control of Pollution' in R Harrison (ed) *Pollution, Causes Effects and Control* 3rd edition (London, Royal Society of Chemistry).

(1996) 'The Scope of Environmental Law' in G Winter (ed) *European Environmental Law* (Aldershot, Dartmouth Press)

(1996) (with M Hession) 'Balancing Trade Freedom with the Requirements of Sustainable Development' in N Emilou and O'Keeffe (eds) *The European Union and World Trade Law: After the GATT Uruguay Round* (London, John Wiley & Sons).

(1995) (with S Hollins) *Bibliography of European Environmental Law* (Oxford, Oxford University Press).

(1995) 'Environmental Case Law: European Community and Legislation: Great Britain' in R Paehlke (ed.) *Conservation and Environmentalism – An Encyclopedia* (New York, Garland Publishing).

(1995) 'Community Environmental Policy and Law 1995' *Environmental Information Bulletin* (London, IRS).

(1995) (with N Emmott) 'The Contribution of IPC to Waste Minimisation' *Environmental Policy & Practice.*

(1995) 'The Road to Cleaner Air' *Legal Times Environment Supplement*, 16 October.

(1995) (with M Hession) 'The Indefinite Article – Nuclear Testing and Community Law' *The Guardian*, 25 October.

(1994) (with M Hession) 'The Legal Framework of European Community Participation in International Environmental Agreements' *New Europe Law Review.*

(1994) (with N Atkinson) 'Enigmatic Centralism, Government Policy and Environment in the UK' *Studi parlimentori e di politica costituzionale.*

(1993) 'Science, Law and Liability' *Science Progress.*

(1993) 'Principles of Civil Liability for Environmental Contamination' *Property Review.*

(1993) 'European Community Water Law' *Ecology Law Quarterly.*

(1993) 'Water Pollution in India' (Book Review) *International Comparative Law Quarterly.*

(1993) (with M Hession) 'Maastricht and the Environmental Policy of the Community: Legal Issues of a New Environment Policy' in D O'Keeffe and P Twomey (eds) *Legal Issues of the Maastricht Treaty* (London, Chancery Publications).

(1992) (with S Withers) 'United Kingdom Policy and Legal Framework' in *Waste Management Year Book* (London, Longman).

(1992) *Using EC Environmental Law* (London, Council for the Protection of Rural England).

(1992) *Universities and the Environment: Environmental Regulation – Opportunities and Obligations.* (London, Committee of Vice-Chancellors and Principals).

(1992) 'Environmental Assessment and EC Law' *Journal of Environmental Law.*

(1992) 'The Enforcement of Community Environmental Law: Some Critical Issues' *Common Market Law Review.*

(1991) 'Nuclear Installations and the Statutory Duty to Compensate for Loss' *Journal of Environmental Law.*

(1991) 'EEC Environmental Law and Corporate Liability' *Proceedings of 9th Annual International Conference on Anti-Trust Law* (Oxford, European Study Conferences).

(1991) 'Environmental Impact Assessment in the UK' *Quaderni della Rivista Giuridica Dell'Ambiente.*

(1991) 'The Implementation and Enforcement of EEC Environmental Policy – A New Form of Federalism' in M Clark, M Crommelin and C Saunders (eds) *The Constitution and the Environment.* (Melbourne, Centre for Comparative Constitutional Studies, University of Melbourne).

(1991) 'Environmental Law: Shifting Discretions and the New Formalism' in O Lomas (ed) *Frontiers of Environmental Law* (London, Chancery Law).

(1990) 'The Privatisation and Regulation of the Water Industry' *Modern Law Review.*

(1990) 'EEC Environmental Policy and the Direct Effect Doctrine' *ENDS Report.*

(1990) 'The Legal Control of Pollution' in R Harrison (ed) *Pollution, Causes, Effects and Control* 2nd edn (London, Royal Society of Chemistry).

(1990) 'Closing Responsibilities – Decommissioning and the Law' in M Pasqualetti (ed) *Nuclear Decommissioning and Society – Public Links to a New Technology* (London, Routledge).

(1990) 'Environmental Assessment – Critical Legal Issues in Implementation' in D Vaughan (ed) *Current EC Legal Developments – Environmental and Planning Law* (London, Butterworths).

(1990) 'The United Kingdom' in T Smith Jr and P Kromarek (eds) *Understanding US and European Environmental Law* (Amsterdam, Kluwer Academic).

(1990) 'UK Pollution Control – Legal Perspectives' in A Clark (ed) *Environmental Technology: Assessment and Policy* (Chichester, Ellis Horwood).

(1989) 'Air Pollution and the Regulation of European State Enterprises: A Comparative Legal Model' in W Butler (ed) *Yearbook of Socialist Legal Systems* (Washington DC, Transnational Publications).

(1989) 'British Environmental Law – Major Strands and Characteristics' *Connecticut Journal of International Law.*

(1989) 'Control of Hazardous Wastes: Enforcement in Practice' *Connecticut Journal of International Law.*

(1989) (with W Sheate) 'Agriculture and the EC Environmental Assessment Directive: Lessons for Community Policy Making' *Journal of Common Market Studies.*

(1989) (with S Withers) 'Waste Management in the United Kingdom' (Berlin, Science Centre Berlin).

(1989) (with D Gilbert) *Pesticide Related Law* (Farnham, British Crop Protection Council).

(1989) *The Water Act 1989* Current Law Statutes Annotated (London, Sweet & Maxwell).

(1988) 'Air Pollution and the United Kingdom' in B Rhode (ed) *Air Pollution in Europe* Volume 1, (Austria, Vienna Centre).

(1988) 'Industrial Air Pollution – Implementing the European Framework' *55th Annual Conference Proceedings* (Brighton, National Society for Clean Air).

(1988) 'Environmental Management and Agricultural Production' in J B Ojwang and J Kabeberi (eds) *Law and the Public Interest* (Nairobi, Institute for Development Studies and Faculty of Law, University of Nairobi).

(1988) 'Environmental Case-Law in the United Kingdom' in A Postiglione (ed) *La Giurisprudenza Ambientale Europea a la Banca Dati Enlex della CEE.* (Milan, Dott. A. Giuffrè).

(1988) 'Pravo okruzhaiushcei sredy v Velikobritanii' ('UK Environmental Law') in OS Kolbasov, M Slavin and A Timoshenko (ed) *Pravo Okruzhaiushcei v SSSR I Velikobritanii* (Environmental Law in the USSR and Great Britain) (Moscow, Akademiia nauk SSR).

(1987) 'Environmental Policy – The Challenge Ahead' in *European Environmental Yearbook* (London, Doctor International).

(1987) 'The United Kingdom of Great Britain and Northern Ireland' in G Enyedi et al (eds) *Environmental Policies in East and West* (London, Taylor Graham).

(1987) (with R Grove-White) 'Electricity: Change Must Entail More Care for the Environment' *The Independent*, 10 October 1987.

(1987) (with Z Madar and C Onz) 'Air Pollution Control in Britain, Middle Europe and Eastern Europe' *Environmental Policy and Law*.

(1986) *Environmental Policy in Britain: Reaffirmation or Reform?* Discussion paper (Berlin, International Institute for Environment and Society).

(1986) 'Science, Legislation and the Courts' in G Conway (ed) *The Assessment of Environmental Problems* (London, Centre for Environmental Technology, Imperial College).

(1986) 'Is Environmental Law Coming of Age?' *CEED Bulletin No 10* (London, UK Centre for Environmental Development).

(1985) *Water Law: Principles & Practice* (London, Longman).

(1985) 'The Role of Third Parties in the Regulatory Process' in J Bates (ed) *Industry and the Regulatory Agencies* (London, International Bar Association).

(1984) 'Street Noise – Problems of Control' *Journal of Planning and Environment Law*.

(1984) 'L'Environment Impact Assessment nel Regno Unito' in N Greco (ed) *La Valutazione di Impatto Ambientale* (Milan, Franco Angeli).

(1983) 'Caught in the Cross-Fire – Geologists and the Law' *British Geologist*.

(1983) (with J Peachey) 'Underlying Themes in the Policy Process' in *Britain Europe and the Environment* (London, Centre for Environmental Technology, Imperial College).

(1983) 'Environmentalism in the Courts' in T O'Riordan and K Turner (eds) *Progress in Resource Management* (London, Wiley and Sons).

(1983) (with M Hudson et al) *Bicycle Planning – Policy and Practice* (London, Architectural Press).

(1983) 'Laws for the Land' *Nature*.

(1982) (with M Lafontaine) *Public Inquiry & Enquête Publique – Forms of Public Participation in England & France* (London, Institute for European Environmental Policy).

(1982) *Nuisance Law* (London, Longman).

(1982) 'Problems of Law' in R Macrory (ed) *Commercial Nuclear Power: Legal and Constitutional Issues* (London, Centre for Environmental Technology, Imperial College).

(1981) 'Lead in Petrol' *Journal of Planning and Environmental Law*.

(1980) 'Planning Procedures in the Nuclear Age' *Journal of Planning and Environmental Law*.

(1980) 'Cross-examination and Natural Justice' *New Law Journal*.

(1979) 'Cycle Lore' *New Law Journal*.

(1974) (with B Zaba) *Polluters Pay: The Control of Pollution Act Explained* Friends of the Earth Publications, London.

INDEX